The encyclopedia of

Consoles, handhelds
& home computers 1972 - 2005

Winnie Forster

English edition by Rafael Dyll (translation) and David McCarthy (localisation).

Contents

Bandai Wonderswan
Tare Panda no Gunpey
Edition (Japan, 2001)

Preface and Acknowledgements
(revised and expanded edition)

This book is not a direct translation of `Spielkonsolen und Heimcomputer´ (GP1 on figure below), but a greatly expanded edition of Gameplan's first book, which hasn't been released anywhere before. While Gameplan initially just went for some small enhancements, adding one or two UK-related chapters, the momentum of research soon took over. The book grew and grew. The result was entitled **Game.Machines** and went to print early 2005.

Growing up in a country without a strong national games industry did have its advantages: You had to be at home in many countries. As there weren't many home-grown games, German punters were treated to software from all over the world, right from the beginning. Apart from the US, the UK was the major source of hard- and software during the '80s.

Since the author of **Game.Machines** happened to be a Spectrum owner in a C64-dominated scene, writing an improved UK edition was not only a logical but also a desired step. Before entering the industry in 1990, I had frequently travelled to London as a teen, spending hours at Forbidden Planet in Denmark Street, and dropping by at Shekhana Computer Services, which sold 8-Bit games for £7.95 a tape. While other kids swapped warez, I had to jump across the channel to get my regular dose of interactivity.

After 1990, I had the chance to compare the European scene to the Japanese and US industry, visiting individuals, conferences and game companys in Tokyo, L.A. and the Bay Area, speaking to developers, sales people and gamers. The similarities, but also the distinctions between games people all around the world keeps on thrilling me. Because this medium was forged by many, I tried to take a global, not a regional view on the history of games and hardware.

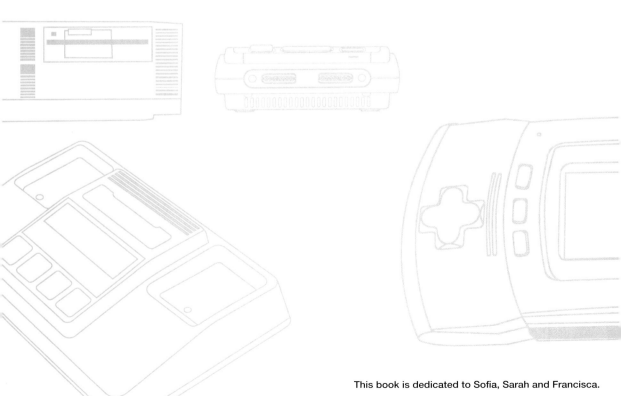

This book is dedicated to Sofia, Sarah and Francisca.

Compared to the German book of `Spielkonsolen und Heimcomputer´, lots of extra material went into **Game.Machines**, including 200 hardware pictures specifically shot for this edition by Christian Boehm, who worked for 'Playboy' before turning to Game Boy and PlayStation. Text and pictures were shaped by Wolfgang `Wonz´ Müller, former art director of OPM and a veteran of game magazine design. Rafael Dyll wrote the translation. Educated in South Africa, Rafael turned professional in the late Amiga- and 16-Bit scene. His text was edited by Rockstar's David McCarthy. While David never personally met up with the team, he was a close member thanks to avid e-discussions on style and orthographic subtleties. *P98, caption1, line 4: please write 'PSSST' instead of 'PSST'*: His lists of comments, later corrections were the micro-code behind the **Game.Machines** workflow. Consequently you may wish to count errors and send us comments and corrections at lit@game-machines.co.uk

While this book is far from complete or perfect, many helped to make it decent, at least: Thanks go to Frank Salomon of www.oldbits.de and Austrian TV game historian Dieter König, to John Stringer (www.jcec.co.uk) who wouldn't wait for the English edition, and sent us corrections which were already implemented in the first German reprint (early 2004).

Most people around Gameplan are male and quite computer minded, but not everybody: Magdalena for instance, who runs direct-sales and Gameplan stock in Kensington, just bought her very first computer. No, she didn't go to Shekhana, but visited Regent Street, to purchase the gear needed to handle our encyclopaedia of hardware.

Welcome to nerd's world and please enjoy this book.

Utting, January 2005
Winnie Forster

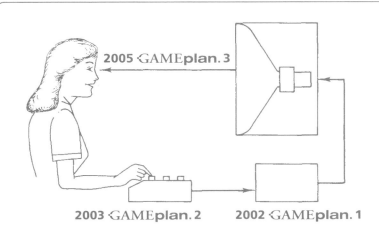

2005 ⟨GAMEplan.3
2003 ⟨GAMEplan.2   2002 ⟨GAMEplan.1

The Gameplan trilogy is made up of a book on hardware (GP1, of which you are holding the revised edition in your hand), a book on controllers and the human-machine interface (GP2 'Joysticks', at the moment only released in the German language) and the forthcoming GP3, dealing with game software and graphics.

For more information, please visit www.game-machines.co.uk or www.gameplan.de.

Gameplan 1.5

Gameplan 2

Explanation of hardware chapters

Gameplan gives the name, **country of origin** and **year of first model's release** at the head of each chapter. At the end of most chapters, there is a box listing all **variants and successors**, in chronological order of their original launch dates. Regional dates are mostly explained in the actual text.

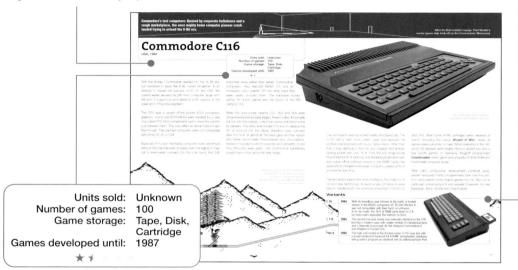

Units sold: Unknown
Number of games: 100
Game storage: Tape, Disk, Cartridge
Games developed until: 1987

The info box

… encompasses the whole hardware family and its games. Exclusions are the IBM PC and Apple Macintosh chapters. As it wasn't possible to squeeze all their variants from 1983 to today into one book, we've cut the date at an arbitrary point. The info given deals with DOS PCs and Motorola 68000 based Macs. The history of PC gaming is further told in introductory chapters (see pp. 144 and 170). These and three other chapters serve as an overview to the five eras we have split the history into and deal with temporary or new trends like Laser Disc coin ops, iMode games or MMORPGs.

The **number of units sold** is based on the manufacturer's information as well as news in related or official magazines (eg. the British Sinclair User, Germany's 64-Magazin, or the pan-european OPM). For Japanese platforms since 1985, we relied on the bi-annual sales figures found in the Japanese game magazine Famicom Tsushin. All figures have been rounded. For platforms still alive and kicking, these numbers are of course not final, but as of January 2005.

We've also rounded the **worldwide number of games developed** for the platform (US, Europe and Japan). We've ignored shareware and freeware games, pirate copies or just regionally marketed software, like Japan-only Pachinko and Mahjong simulations.

The stars found in each box are Gameplan's subjective rating of the quality and quantity of available software. Did/does the platform cover all game types? Are there adventures for the machine or just shoot 'em ups? What about support from third-parties and the availability of prominent titles: Are there any games by Rare and Square? Or just by Loriciel? A ★ ★ ★ ★ ★ ranking has been awarded to the PlayStation, which was continually supported with software from across the globe, been treated to all game types and even invented some of its own. The ranking ★ means: Only the hardware's manufacturer provided games, and a half ✦ : Apart from initial shipment there was no software support.

Games developed until gives the year in which professional developers finally dropped the platform. Of course, this figure also excludes shareware and similar, as well as any retro development activity. Noteworthy amateur games or new programmes for an old hardware are sometimes mentioned in the last text paragraph.

Speed and safety at a high price
Electronic media

Tintin on the Moon cartridge for Amstrad's game console, 128 K (Infogrames, 1990).

The European Top Gear 3000 cartridge has a DSP chip for graphics acceleration (Gremlin, 1994).

Cards for the Atari Lynx contain 128 to 512 K (Epyx, 1989).

The J-Cart with built-in multiplayer ports, a Mega Drive novelty by Codemasters, 1996.

Whilst most computers used magnetic media, video games were released on `mask-programmable´ ROM chips over almost three decades, and in some rare cases also on rewriteable EPROMs. A static storage medium (`solid state´) is recorded by electric charge, requires no power supply to store data (`non volatile´) and needs neither motor, nor mechanics – to date it's the fastest and safest, though most expensive storage medium.

Megashock for Neo Geo; with 3 to 100 MB, it's the biggest and most expensive `masked´ ROM for games (SNK, 1990).

Cartridges (carts) initially came with 2 to 8 K, during the Nintendo age with 64 K to 8 M of ROM plus often 8 K of RAM and a battery; today, only the Game Boy still uses ROM cartridges.

Cards: Japanese developer Hudson invented the super flat BeeCard for the MSX and enhanced it to become the HuCard, used by the PC-Engine console (mask-programmed) as well as Atari's early Portfolio (writeable). Only the front part contains data; the rest is plastic and makes the card bigger and easier to handle.

BeeCard is the rare predecessor to the HuCard; MSX computers required a special adapter to read it (Hudson, 1986).

Flash: Due to their miniscule format and low power requirement, EEPROMs are perfect for mobile games. Today, they are available as SD, Compact-Flash and Multimedia-Cards on the mass-market and as Memory Cards for video games. The media are rewriteable, not `masked´ and shift data slower than cartridges.

`Double Ender´ cartridge for the Atari VCS, two times 8 K with connectors on both sides (Xonox, 1983).

SmartMedia-Card (SMC), a Flash format developed by Olympus and Fuji for mobile equipment. Shown here as game medium for the Korean GP32 handheld (Gamepark, 2001).

Which media were used for game storage?

Recordable and cheap but sensitive
Magnetic media

Microdrive: Sinclair's digital, recordable magnetic tape in a miniature cartridge reached transfer rates of 5 K/s (1984).

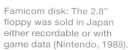

Famicom disk: The 2.8" floppy was sold in Japan either recordable or with game data (Nintendo, 1988).

3" Compact Disk, Maxell's unusual floppy variant for British and Japanese home micros (1983).

The principle of disks, hard-drives and removable drives is based on rotating, magnetically layered discs, on which data is stored by polarisation. Unlike static storage, the read/write heads of the drives are mechanical and thus sensitive to shock and temperature.

Tapes: In the early '80s, standard audio-cassettes were the cheapest and popular media for games and other hobby applications. Smaller, digitally recordable successors like Sinclair's Microdrive could not establish themselves.

Disks: While IBM's original 8" format was never used for games, the **5.25"** floppy became the standard computer game medium. In the mid-'80s, the **3.5"** disks replaced it with its 1 MB of storage space. An uncommon **3"** format was marketed by Maxell, a **2.8"** Quick Disk (QD) by Sharp and Nintendo in Japan.

Zip-related: The pioneering format introduced in the '90s by Iomega serves in this context as our wild card for all exchangeable disks sized 25 to 100 MB. Zip-related media were for example used by Nintendo as 64DD, containing 64 MB of game and user data.

5.25" disk, double-sided, about 100 K on each side: Floppy disk for C64 and Atari 800 (Sierra Online, 1985).

3.5" disk, 800 K single-sided. Despite the label, the disk was formatted either for ST or Amiga – not recorded with two Star Glider 2 versions (1988).

Audio tapes with ten minutes of running time were often pre-recorded on both sides, just in case – an analogue storage medium (Psion, 1983).

64 DD disk, a partially recordable Zip variant for the Nintendo 64's Randnet expansion (1999).

Stable storage giants
Optical media

GD-ROM: The special CD-ROM format for the Dreamcast console holds 1 GB (Sega, 2000).

The Mini-DVD for the Gamecube, with a capacity of 1.5 GB, was developed by Matsushita (Nintendo, 2002).

Laser Disc: The rare '80s arcade medium stored animation and sound, not data. This Dragon's Lair picture disc was released in 1990 for the LD port of the Commodore Amiga.

CD-ROM and similar media carry data stored as blank or dark code pits read by a laser. Apart from ROM discs, there are also re-recordable discs (-R, -RW etc.). To store more data, optical media are sometimes recorded on both sides, sometimes double layered or with `double density´.

LD: The large picture disc was the analogue predecessor to the Video CD and was now and again seen as medium for interactive applications, multimedia and games. At the end of the '90s, the DVD replaced it as format of choice for home cinema couch potatoes.

CD: The CD-ROM was invented by Sony and Philips in 1985, as a cheap, but not re-recordable storage medium. It was established a little later by NEC and Fujitsu in Japan and on the western Hemisphere by Apple. Sega's variant with more than 1 GB of storage was the Dreamcast **GD-ROM**.

DVD: The CD-ROM successor multiplied the storage capacity up to a maximum of 17 GB (double-sided and layered) and is today the medium for all PC and PlayStation games. Matsushita developed a miniature variant for Nintendo's Gamecube as well as Sony, which uses a 60mm `Universal Media Disc´ (**UMD**) for its PSP handheld.

Game storage in comparison

Technology		from	until	data transfer M/s	access ms
Cartridge	electronic	1976	today	> 5	< 1
Tape	magnetic[1]	1977	1990	< 0,001	> 1000
Disk	magnetic	1978	2000	< 0,1	> 100
LD	optical[1]	1983	1990	unknown	unknown
Card	electronic	1987	1996	> 5	< 1
CD	optical	1987	today	0,3 [2]	> 100 [3]
Flash	electronic	1994	today	> 1	~ 0,1
DVD	optical	1999	today	> 1	> 100 [3]
Zip	magnetic	2000	2001	~ 1	< 50

[1] Analogue storage.

[2] Video game consoles use either single or double speed drives, 150 or 300 K/s. Current PCs come with eight to 52-speed drives with transfer rates of several M/s.

[3] Depends on drive's speed: Fast spinning drives suffer from higher access times.

The birth of electronic games: Mainframes, arcades and TV games

All success stories have their forefathers. Naming the inventor of the video game is a controversial issue, but one thing is for sure: The medium whose Pac-Man, Mario and Solid Snake outperformed other entertainment forms, was not born in a garage, but in American high-tech laboratories. At the time, there were no disks, no colour display, no RAM chips. Only some elite universities and research centres had access to computer technology – and to the visionary brains that thought up the concept of on-screen action. Instead of wasting time with `teaching machines´, early users loved the competition and tests of skill against the computer. Four of these visionaries, three experienced US scientists, and half an electronics engineer from Stanford University, independently invented the first and only interactive entertainment medium.

Willy Higinbotham was a physicist working at Brookhaven National Laboratory, the famous radar and nuclear research facility. In 1959, the Nobel-winning institution had planned an open day for visitors and laboratory head Higinbotham had prepped the oscillograph a little. In order to gain the interest of the visitors, the nuclear expert invented a kind of interactive tennis game: Visitors used two controllers to move a glowing point, while a vertical line dividing the screen posed as the net. By playing around with the

equipment, visitors learned a lot about technology – and had fun. Higinbotham improved his invention, but didn't file for a patent. The first video game never left the halls of Brookhaven.

But it's Steve Russell who is considered to be the true father of computer games. After all, Higinbotham's oscillograph was no computer. In the early '60s, Russell was programming at the Massachusetts Institute of Technology (MIT), the most important research lab of the computer age. He was both a science fiction and Godzilla fan, and a member of the Tech Model Railroad Club, which was portrayed in Steve Levy's history of computers `Hackers´. Prior to Russell and his cohorts, a few specialists (known as `operators´) had fed the huge '60s machines with punched cards. Lesser scientists and students had no way of even touching these analogue monsters. Then came the PDP-1 – the size of two refrigerators, ironically being celebrated as the `Minicomputer´. The first of the $200,000 units went to MIT. From 1961, Russell, Alan Kotok and others spent days and nights in front of the PDP-1.

These hackers were serious scientists but at the same time they were gamers: When Russell moved abstract spaceships instead of numbers on the display, the event

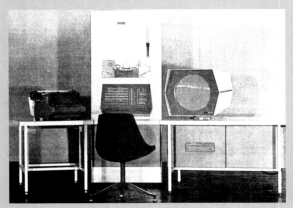

MIT scientists Alan Kotok and Steve Russell saw the first computer with screen and keyboard as a toy and technical challenge. Unlike IBM's mainframes, the DEC PDP-1 was hands-on programmable. Inspired by E.E. Smith novels, they wrote the science-fiction shoot 'em up Space Wars.

The first game computer:
Digital Equipment Corporation PDP-1

In 1959, the `Programmed Data Processor` (PDP) by US manufacturer DEC was the first commercially available computer with keyboard and graphic display. It was used by scientists and students of research institutes and abused to become a games machine. The original version of Space War (the first computer game) ran on a DEC PDP-1 in 1961 – making DEC a proud part of the history of interactive entertainment. In 1971, two Stanford students, Bill Pitts and Hugh Tuck developed a Space Wars arcade machine based on the PDP. The machine stayed on campus until 1979.

Before home and personal computers had established themselves and PDP power had shrunk to typewriter size, the hardware influenced the evolution of computer games several times. At the end of the '70s, William Crowther devised his dungeon simulation Advent on a PDP-10, in 1980, one of the Advent fans, British scientist Roy Trubshaw, released his Multi User Dungeon on the very platform – his MUD is the predecessor to all MMORPGs. Further PDP milestones were Richard Greenblatt's MacHack chess game from 1967 (PDP-6), Ken Thompson's PDP-7 conversion of Space Travel (as legend goes, this led to the invention of Unix), as well as Walter Bright's Empire from 1978. Around 1980, VAX machines replaced the PDP family of computers. In many parts of the world, PDP computers remained in use. And thus, enter Alexey Pajitnov, who programmed a simple puzzle game on a Russian PDP-11 variant, Electronica. He called it Tetris.

Computer Space, 1971

marked the birth of **Space Wars**, the first computer game. The `gameplay`: Two MIT students shot torpedoes at the others' space ship, each hit resulted in an on-screen 'explosion' – the vehicle was replaced by a scramble of dots, representing the debris. Space War was then enhanced by flabbergasted colleagues, based on astronomy data and spread among PDP users. This wasn't much of a business model however: According to Steven Levy, Russell didn't earn `a single penny` with his invention.

The legal father of the video game was German-born, US-educated Ralph Baer: As the R&D manager at the military research company Sanders, the radar expert was thinking about alternative uses for the black & white TV. He developed golf and shooting games for the TV set, which he filed for patents in 1966. Baer was an ingenious inventor but no salesman. It wasn't until 1970 that his patent ended up with the US subsidiary of electronics manufacturer Philips. In 1972, Philips turned Baer's TV toy into the first games

The arcade boom: Science fiction becomes reality

Year	Coin-op game releases/year	
1969	–	First man on the Moon – where no man has gone before
1971	–	First microchips by Intel (4004, 4-Bit) and by Texas Instruments
1972	2	First games console: Odyssey. First arcade game: Computer Space
1975	25	Computer DIY kit Altair 8800. William Gates quits Harvard
1976	30	Text adventures running on the PDP-10
1977	50	Star Wars at the cinemas, VCS and Apple 2 in the shops
1978	75	Space Invaders, RPG boom in the USA: Dungeons & Dragons
1979	80	Philips and Sony invent the CD
1980	85	Portable player: Sony Walkman

Most consoles of the '70s were not programmable, but played Pong variants only. The controllers were hard-wired, the score counter worked mechanically.

console and launched the Magnavox Odyssey. Magnavox offered licences for any company wishing to participate in the game business. So paying for development licenses arrived before Nintendo.

Nolan Bushnell, an engineer who played Space Wars as a student, spotted the potential and future of video games: Before the Odyssey shipped in 1972, Bushnell had created a variant of the shooting game. While Russell fed the academic world with game action and Baer put the TV game into living rooms, Nolan Bushnell made his game for public places, bars and pinball arcades. In 1971, his

Nolan Bushnell's Computer Space was basically the Space Wars idea gone public. But it was to be the simpler Pong (pictured) that became a hit across arcades and bars.

Computer Wars coin-op couldn't return his investment and Bushnell replaced it with the simpler **Pong** – a ball game similar to Higinbotham and Baer's experiments. Pong turned out to swallow coins by the bucketloads and Bushnell set it up across the US. In 1972, he founded the first video game company and called it Atari – which is the threat to capture a stone in the eastern board game of Go. The name seemed to provoke the copycats: By 1973, there were dozens of Pong clones from Japan.

From 1972 on, the new entertainment form became many-sided, evolving in three categories: Universities brought forth ideas from science-fiction, D&D role playing games, from `Star Trek´ and `Lord of the Rings´. They were abstract programs, living off the huge storage capacity of networked computers, displaying the stories in letters and numbers. The strategy game **Star Trek** was a Klingon hunt through space quadrants; **Adventure** (1976) was a cave simulation by scientist William Crowther. Students and scientists around the globe fell in love with the first adventure game. At MIT, Mark Blank and Dave Liebing expanded the game to become the `great underground empire´ **Zork**. At the University of Essex in England, the concept was turned into MUD – a **Multi User Dungeon** for many players.

The game evolution unfolded even faster in public arcades. By now, Atari and pinball manufacturer Midway were competing with their Japanese challengers Taito and Sega for new game concepts.

Breakout, the ingenious youthful sin of later Apple founder Steve Jobs and Steve Wozniak was countered by Taito's **Space Invaders**. Initially, it was supposed to become a game with tanks rolling left to right across the screen, turning around, continuing in the other direction a line beneath. But turning the vehicles around was something Taito's engineer Toshihiro Nishikado couldn't achieve on early Intel 8080 CPUs. So he decided to create symmetrical monsters instead. At the bottom of the screen, the player moved a cannon and fired it at the alien armada that got closer and closer to the earth – add to that a hypnotic stampeding sound, two crackles that got faster and faster. In Japan, Space Invaders led to the first video game hysteria and also inspired home console manufacturers. From then on, new machines simply had to be capable of playing ball and shooting.

The charming novelty of the TV game was all but forgotten. Despite a second generation of 'programmable' consoles, the market was heading for a dive. It wasn't until Atari released a home conversion of Space Invaders and ported other action arcade games for its VCS 2600, that the cartridge consoles experienced a boom.

Before Breakout, most games were played mechanically, without a CPU and memory: In Submarine a light-torpedo was shot at enemy cruisers. With every hit, the background lit up.

The machines of the early and mid '70s mark the beginning of our history of home consoles and micros: Apple, CBM and Tandy laid the foundation for the software industry; the Atari VCS started the console business. 'Star Wars' had arrived on the big screen, as did Bandai's 'Battle Ship Yamato'. Music too, was turning digital. Jean-Michel Jarre dreamt his synthetic fantasy 'Oxygene' and in the year of Atari and Apple, Germany's Pop-Robots Kraftwerk took a ride on the 'Autobahn' as 'Mensch-Maschine'.

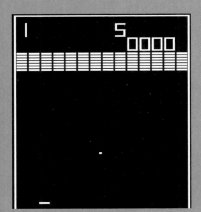

With novel ideas like Breakout, Atari stayed ahead of Japanese copycats, for five years.

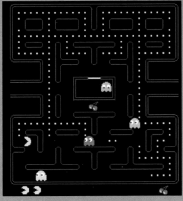

From 1980, pixels were coloured and enemies got clever: Ghosts with googling eyes were after Pac-Man, ...

... insectoids dived at the hero's ship in shooting frenzy Galaga (1981). Both classics were designed by Namco.

Magnavox Odyssey

USA, 1972

US Engineer Ralph Baer invented his TV game while working for arms supplier Sanders and first showed it to electronic manufacturers in 1969. After talks with RCA, General Electric and others, Sanders sold the TV game licence to Magnavox, the American consumer subsidiary of Dutch Philips.

The Odyssey was not a computer like other machines found in this book. It had no micro processor or memory chip, but was made out of conventional capacitors, resistors, transistors and diodes. Despite this, the Odyssey was programmable and game variants could be exchanged – the six included Game Cards were used to rewire and power up the machine.

The hardware displayed three squares (ball and bats) and a line on the TV screen, but no colour or details. To improve the image, overlays were used, and game add-ons ranged across dice, plastic coins, board and cards.

While Atari's electronic games thrilled the arcade scene, the Odyssey could not break into the mass market. The TV game was retailed only through Magnavox dealers and misleadingly advertised: Many customers believed that the Odyssey worked only on Magnavox TV sets. The first video game for private households wasn't a flop – but it was no tremendous success either. In 'The Ultimate History of

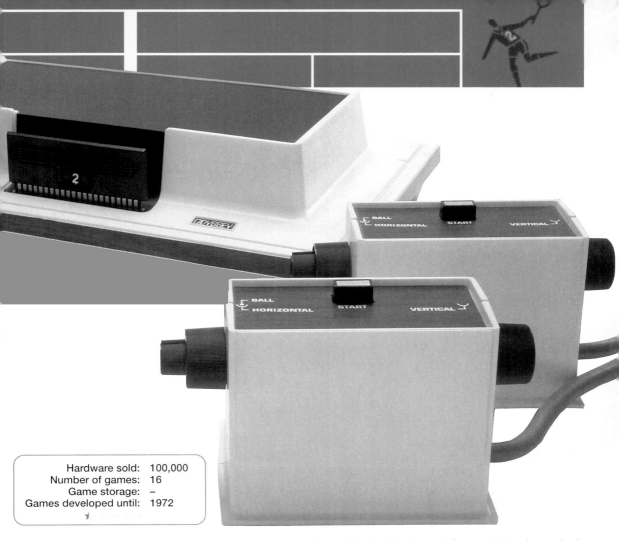

Hardware sold:	100,000
Number of games:	16
Game storage:	–
Games developed until:	1972

Instead of a joystick, the controllers sported analogue wheels left and right, plus a button on top.

Together, the console, two controllers and a lot of accessories retailed for $100.

Video Games' Steven Kent claims 100,000 units were sold in two years, and Ralph Baer believes that 360,000 games were sold before early 1975.

Magnavox didn't realise until late on that the TV game patent was key to establishing the future interactive entertainment industry. Nolan Bushnell and Atari were conquering the arcades with the new hobby (and quickly found themselves up against Japanese imitators) whilst Philips began cashing in on the manufacture of home consoles. In the beginning, licences and the near-monopoly were hardly exploited. It wasn't until 1975 that Magnavox closed an agreement with Atari and began selling licences as a revenue source. The lawyers had entered the games industry.

Fairchild Channel F

USA, 1976

Units sold:	Unknown
Number of games:	26
Game storage:	Cartridge
Games developed until:	1979

When asked for the first home video game, many computer and game historians object to the prevailing view that it was the Odyssey and point instead to chip pioneer Fairchild Semiconductors. Under the management of Robert Noyce and Gordon Moore (who later founded Intel) the company set up in 1957, mass-producing integrated circuits and quickly grew to several thousand employees, turning Californian Sunnyvale into Silicon Valley. Moore's prediction of chip integration and computing power progressing in 12 or 18 month steps was later defined as 'Moore's Law'.

Fairchild's heyday was long gone (as were its founders), when the company created a TV game. As a leftover product of chip development, the Channel F used Fairchild's 8-Bit CPU F8 and lots of solid state memory: For the first time, games came on exchangeable cartridges. This pioneering effort had little effect on the dawning market: Due to the puny hardware, the logic behind

The forgotten pioneer: As the first programmable and CPU equipped console, the Channel F and licence-built Saba Videoplay couldn't touch the Atari offensive starting 1978.

exchangeable games wasn't obvious to consumers, and within months, the machine was technically obsolete. When the market finally kicked off, more powerful second-generation consoles, focused on audio-visuals, blew the Fairchild away. Nevertheless, Channel F already had colours and didn't need the overlays used with the Odyssey and '70s arcade machines.

The oddest Channel F elements were the two controllers pulled from underneath a cover in the machine. The gamepilots (Saba) could be moved left and right, up and down, but also be pushed, pulled and twisted. The black controller had no fire buttons.

Like the consumer, Fairchild lost interest in the console soon and handed the marketing rights over to Zircon, who released five final games along with the externally slightly modified Channel F II, retailing for $100.

The Telematch Processor by ITT was a pretty Channel F variant including built-in Pong and controllers with blue and red button.

Variants and successors

Channel F	1976	Apart from the cartridge slot, the first US model had no ports or connectors. Both controllers, antenna and mains lead were firmly wired. In the first version, sound came from the console; later machines like the German-built Saba Videoplay output audio through the TV.
Channel F II	1979	After Fairchild pulled out, Zircon began selling a revised model with newly positioned, removable controllers and sound via TV.
German Variants		While the Saba Videoplay appeared in Channel F case, the Teleplay by Nordmende came in a slim, metallic coloured case and used the original controllers. The ITT Telematch Processor was also slimmer and sleeker than the chubby US original and sported a front panel in aluminium look.

After the takeover of Radio Shack, Dave Tandy's 1919-founded leather factory grew to an US-wide electronics sales chain. With the market in deep crisis, Tandy looked out for new products and predicted computers as the industry's future.

Tandy TRS-80

USA, 1977

Units sold:	1 Million
Number of games:	200
Game storage:	Tape, Disk, Cartridge
Games developed until:	1979

★ ★

After the first personal computer, the MITS Altair, was sold as a DIY kit, Tandy's managers John Roach and Don French came up with a new concept – a complete system consisting of central unit, screen, tape drive and software, featuring a keyboard instead of switches and a monitor instead of lamps. The TRS-80, devised by Steve Leininger, saw the light of day in August 1977. Going head to head with Apple and CBM, the home computer boom ignited.

Despite technical weaknesses, the affordable system rose to become a computer for the masses and launch pad for early software classics like **Temple of Apshai** by Automated Simulations (later to become Epyx) and **Galactic Empire**, the debut of Brøderbund founder Doug Carlston, both written in 1979. Scott Adams programmed his legendary text adventures on the TRS-80; others used the hardware as development system for their Atari or Spectrum software.

In 1980, Tandy mixed colour into the game by producing the Color Computer in collaboration with Motorola. The CoCo was still inferior to the competition, but was treated to over 1,000 programs, most of them published by semi-professionals or in a few cases by companies like Activision, Infocom and Sierra. It had a cartridge port that was used by 70 ROM-Packs. Steve Bjork's **Mega-Bug** and conversions of **Arkanoid** and **Rampage** (which weighed in as a 128 K ROM and ran only on the CoCo III) were good examples of late TRS-80 development.

How it all began: In 1978, Adventureland by Scott Adams was the first adventure game for home computers.

Variants and successors

TRS-80	1977	Model I (Z80, with 1,78 MHz, 4 K RAM, 128 x 48 Pixels) retailed for $600 including a 12" monitor and tape drive. A year later, Level II was launched with 16 K. 250,000 units were sold before it was replaced by Model II and put out of production in early 1981. The new system had a 4 MHz CPU, 32 K, improved text display and Microsoft BASIC, monitor and 8" disk drive and was aimed at professional users. Alternatively, the entry-model III had a 2.03 MHz CPU, 16 K, a monochrome 128 x 48 resolution graphics and retailed for $700 with monitor and datasette.
Color Computer	1980	Improved hobby computer with Motorola CPU 6809E (0.89 MHz) and 256 x 192 resolution graphics in 8 colours but with only 4 K as standard. Sold for $400 and replaced by a smaller, multi-tasking model for $240 in 1983.
Color Computer III	1986	Despite improved hardware (1.78 MHz MC68B09E CPU, 128 K, 80 character display, 640 x 225 resolution in 64 colours) and a $220 price tag, the final step in the Tandy evolution never had a chance against the 16-Bit generation Amiga, Atari ST and Mac. It went out of production in 1991.

The legendary Apple II was the second attempt by young hardware designers
Steve Jobs and Steve Wozniak. It made computers sociable and was the most
important games micro of the '70s and early '80s

Apple II

USA, 1977

Units sold:	5 Million
Number of games:	1,000
Game storage:	Tape, Disk
Games developed until:	1991

★ ★ ★ ★

The Apple II europlus debuted
at the end of 1978.

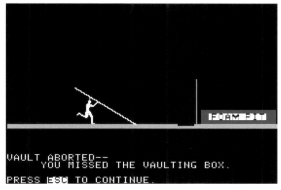

VAULT ABORTED--
    YOU MISSED THE VAULTING BOX.
PRESS [ESC] TO CONTINUE.

Before DOS, Microsoft published Apple II games like the minimalist Olympic Decathlon.

Duellists under the deck: Swashbuckler defined the beat 'em up in 1982. Below: Sierra's film conversion Dark Crystal (1983).

The Apple II enjoys an exceptional reputation among computer historians. Classic programs like the first spread-sheet application VisiCalc are considered to be funda-mental for the software industry. With 4,000 bytes of memory, BASIC operating system and (from 1978 on) an external disk drive, the two young hardware architects Steve Wozniak and Steve Jobs came up with the first Per-sonal Computer. Unlike the self-assembled contemporary machines, it worked straight out of the box and shipped in a sleek case. A price tag of $1,300 (without monitor and drive) made it unaffordable for young users. Nonetheless, the Apple II heavily influenced the game industry.

It was no coincidence: The Apple II was devised with gamers in mind and two paddle controllers were included. Both Jobs and Wozniak had previously worked for Atari. In his history of Apple computers ('...And Then There Was Apple'), Jack Connick quoted hardware designer Wozniak: `A lot of features of the Apple II went in because I had designed Breakout ... That was the reason that colour was added in – that games could be programmed. ... I got this ball bouncing around, and I said, "Well it needs sound," and I had to add a speaker. It wasn't planned, it was just accidental... Obviously you need paddles, so I had to scratch my head and design a minimum-chip paddle circuit, ... these features that really made the Apple II stand out in its day came from a game ...´ Wozniak and his early customers' lust for games propelled many innovations for the computer industry. The Apple II drew in the first generation of consumer software creators like a magnet.

At the time standard, today rare: Analogue paddles with Apple logo.

BEFORE JEN CAN ACT, A MYSTIC APPROACHES AND SAYS, "URSU, WISEST OF OUR RACE, IS DYING. HE HAS SENT FOR YOU. COME QUICKLY!" THEN THE MYSTIC WALKS AWAY.

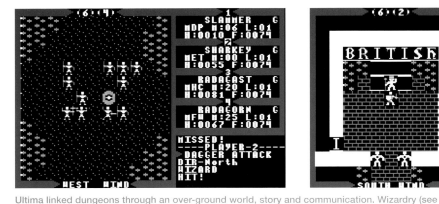

Ultima linked dungeons through an over-ground world, story and communication. Wizardry (see box right) reduced RPG life to survival in caverns – two leads for other fantasy games to follow.

Many game designers started their careers on the Apple II: Early Apple games were Dan Bunten's debut **Wheeler's Dealers** (1978) and **Dungeon Campaign**, an RPG by Robert Clardy. To market strategy and RPG games, Joel Billings founded Strategy Simulations Incorporated (SSI) in 1979. Doug Carlston gave up his job as a lawyer to start Brøderbund, quickly touching base with the Japanese software scene. With **Mystery House** in 1980, the married couple Roberta and Ken Williams created the graphic adventure: She told the tale, he coded it. What started as a spare time venture quickly grew to one of the biggest publisher of computer games for many years to come, Sierra On-Line.

The impact of Apple RPGs in particular, was substantial: In 1979, Richard Garriott laid the foundation for the **Ultima** series with **Akalabeth**; over the years, **Ultima** transformed

In this promotional shot, Apple presented its hardware as all-round serious micros. To the right, the Apple III is shown, a short-lived, not 100% compatible successor.

The portable Apple IIc is one of the best designed and prettiest 8-Bit systems: The costly computer featured a floppy drive fitted to the right, and both...

...monitor and TV output. It was quickly set up and took up little space. The handle converts to a stand – a practical office and games machine.

from simple dungeon crawling to an adventure world in the vein of J.R.R. Tolkien. With plenty of imagination and technical talent, the son of a NASA astronaut populated his continent Britannia, installed towns that switched to a different scale upon entering, laid secret passages and commanded in peasants, wizards and hordes of monsters. In the centre of adventure, enthroned the creator himself, granting experience levels as Lord British.

Dungeoneers Robert Woodhead and Andrew Greenberg went straight in the other direction: In **Wizardry**, the overworld was reduced to inn, temple and weapon shop, the rest was hack'n slash, a rough rumble for survival in the dungeons. A six-strong party cast spells, fought and puzzled its way through the underworld while collecting experience points.

Even after the introduction of the audio-visually more powerful competitor Atari 800, Apple remained the leading computer format. According to the American trade magazine 'Computer Gaming World', half of all games before 1982 were either available for Apple or Apple-exclusives. It wasn't until 1984 that the popularity of the Apple II noticeably dropped in the face of competition from the C64 and Atari 800, soon also from IBM compatible PCs. Only a quarter of new games were now released for the Apple II. Despite manifold revisions, Apple itself abandoned its 8-Bit veteran to focus on the 16-Bit successor Macintosh.

Regardless of Apple's world wide excellent reputation, the platform remained an American phenomenon: In Japan, it had covered only a small niche and in Europe, the

expensive Apple II europlus and its successors were left without a chance against the C64. Cheaper platforms like Sinclair Spectrum and Amstrad CPC ruled the UK mass market, while Acorn kept Apple out of the educational sector. Local gamers discovered classic Apple software years after release as conversions for those platforms. In 1986, Apple launched the technically overhauled IIgs, a 16-Bit machine that was backward compatible with the 8-Bit oldies.

A late Apple success was Jordan Mechner's **Prince of Persia**, which perfected the body animation of his early '80s hit **Karateka** and added more cut-scenes and cinematic sequences. As combination of Hollywood drama and pixel-perfect jump 'n run it was later ported to every platform. Other last generation Apple games were Paul Neurath's **Space Rogue** (co-designed by the young John Romero) and **Keef the Thief**, the amusing debut of Crash Bandicoot creators and PlayStation evangelists Jason Rubin and Andy Gavin. In 1993, John Carmack converted **Wolfenstein 3D** to the IIgs. The same year, Apple stopped the production of the classic computer.

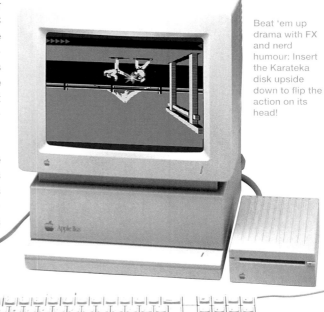

Beat 'em up drama with FX and nerd humour: Insert the Karateka disk upside down to flip the action on its head!

The Apple II gs was the first Apple with 16-Bit CPU. With this backward compatible machine the Apple scene managed to survive until the mid '90s.

Apple II variants and successors

Apple II	1977	The first model, initially with 4 K RAM and two analogue game paddles, retailed for $1,300. The tape drive was the primary storage medium.
Apple II+	1979	The technically revised successor with Applesoft on board and 16, 32 or 48 K RAM retailed from $1,200. Specific to school use, it was also sold in a black case (Bell & Howell) and in Europe as `europlus´.
Apple IIe	1983	Revised successor with 64 K RAM as standard, 80 row text and `Double Hi-Res´ graphics in 16 colours. The first Apple with 65c02 CPU sold for an initial $1,400.
Apple IIc	1984	Technically revised 128 K Apple II (resolution up to 520x192 pixels) in a white mini tower with handle and internal disk drive. Next to the mouse port, the portable Apple had serial ports, RF and (via adapter) RGB output, but could hardly be upgraded. Starting price: $1,300.
Apple IIgs	1986	The completely revised personal computer with separate keyboard, new 16-Bit CPU (Motorola 65816), 3.5" disks (800 K) and a maximum resolution of 640x200 in four of 4,096 colours, retailed for $1,000. Its new sound chip (15 synth voices, built-in memory) was designed by R. Yannick, who engineered the famous SID-chip inside the C64.
Apple IIc +	1988	The revision of the 'portable' Apple IIc retailed for an initial $675. The 65c02 was now clocked at 4 MHz; the computer came with internal 3.5" drive, power supply inside and mini-DIN 8 port.
Apple IIe LC Card	1991	The rare expansion card made the 16-Bit computer Macintosh LC (see page 102) compatible with its 8-Bit predecessor's software and was thus the final Apple II hardware to be produced.

CBM Pet

USA, 1977

Units sold:	Unknown
Number of games:	30
Game storage:	Disk
Games developed until:	1982

★

Together with the Apple II and the TRS-80, the 'Personal Electronic Transactor' kicked off the home computer industry. It was built around the 6502 processor by Chuck Peedle's MOS Technologies, a company that Commodore took over in 1976, and although the name Pet had to be dropped after the first model due to legal reasons, it remained a nickname among users.

The Pet came ready to run straight out of the box, not as a construction kit. Computer enthusiasts forked out a mere $600 for a 4 K computer, keyboard, Datasette and monitor. Young professionals bought Pets because they were cheaper and looked more serious compared to Apple or Atari hardware. It's said that schools loved the Pet because the massive 20 kg colossus could hardly be stolen or damaged. Our own belief is that the text mode display was uninviting for playing games.

Despite the professional image, the Pet was no quality product. It was poorly manufactured and appeared dated. Commodore replaced the Datasette and the too small keys in 1978 with external storage media like the double floppy CBM 3040 and with a real keyboard. Pet printers were supplied by Epson.

There were games released for the device, even though it wasn't capable of producing sound and high-res graphics. Among them was Chris Crawford's debut **Tanktics** and Epyx founders Jon Freeman and Jim Connelly's **Temple of Apshai** and **Starfleet Orion** in 1979. In the UK, Mike Singleton controlled his PBM game 'Star Lord' via a Pet.

Unlike Apple and Atari, Pet game development never got professional. Apart from Scott Adams and Avalon Hill, very few companies supplied software.

Variants and successors

2001 (PET)	**1977**	The first model with green monitor, Datasette and 73 symmetrically ordered Mickey Mouse keys could be memory expanded through a sideward port. Peripherals like the dot matrix printer 2020 were connected via the 8-Bit user port.
2001 (N, B)	**1978**	A new case (professional keyboard instead of Datasette) and maximum of 32 K RAM. The 2001B had a smaller numerical pad (only 11 keys) and lacked the Pet logo.
3001 (3016, 3032)	**1979**	Like the 2001, but with enlarged numerical pad, BASIC V2 and machine language monitor integrated in ROM and 16 or 32 K as standard.
4001 (4016, 4032)	**1979**	For the first time shipped with a 12" monitor. The unit had an improved BASIC V4 and a number pad with 11 keys. An example of an IEE-488 add-on was the 340 K drive CBM 4040.
8032, 8096	**1981**	The Pets developed in Germany used BASIC 4.0 with a doubled text mode display (80 characters) and with 96 K from 1982 on. The same year, the 8032SK was shipped, wrapped in curved plastic and with a separate keyboard as well as rotating and tilting monitor.
MMF 9000	**1982**	The 'Micro Mainframe' in an old(ish) angular case represented the final stage in the computer's lifespan. It was equipped with 96 K, an RS232 port, an additional Motorola 6809 CPU, two operating systems and a switch. Extras were the double floppy and the hard-drives CBM 9060 (5 MB) or 9090 (7.5 MB).

Atari VCS

USA, 1977

Units sold:	30 Million
Number of games:	500
Game storage:	Cartridge, Tape
Games developed until:	1992

★ ★ ★ ☆ ☆

Clear design, simple control and 500 games:
The first VCS featured wood imitation on the front panel.

The Atari VCS represented the biggest step in the history of electronic games. Introduced in 1977, it superseded Atari's (and roughly a dozen other competitors') Pong consoles and made use of exchangeable cartridges, founding a billion dollar industry in the process.

In spite of some tough competition, the 'Video Computer System' became synonymous with videogames. In the early '80s, every teenager and all young families wanted to own an Atari.

But the VCS initially experienced a slow start and even Atari failed to see the potential of its exchangeable ROM games. Fairchild, RCA and Magnavox/Phillips were also marketing 'programmable consoles', but Atari, with its well-known brand of arcade games and strong design team, was in pole position. The breakthrough came when the company extended the choice of games by adding VCS conversions of Japanese arcade games – in particular Taito's hit **Space Invaders**. Halfway through 1981, this arcade conversion had already sold more than a million copies.

All Atari games were developed by Atari itself – until the programmers wanted more money and credit: In 1980, a team of developers left Atari and founded Activision, led by marketing pro Jim Levy. Atari was not amused seeing their in-house stars David Crane, Larry Kaplan and Alan Miller walk out, but it wasn't long before it became clear that independent development companies rejuvenated the industry. Following the creation of Activision other 'third-parties' were founded. Apart from more Atari deserters

(such as Rob Fulop who co-founded Imagic), traditional toy manufacturers began producing VCS cartridges. Monopoly maker Parker licensed and converted Japanese games by Konami and Nintendo as well as prominent movie and comic brands (**Star Wars**, **James Bond**). Competitor Tiger had to stick to lesser known arcade machines from Taito and Orca, also producing VCS versions of computer games by Sierra Online.

The broad spectrum of games and world wide brand awareness left Atari's competition without a chance. In 1980, the Intellivision was introduced and 1982 the Colecovision. Despite advanced technology and several million buyers, both left only a scratch on Atari's market share. The two competitors were forced to bow before Atari's success and began humbly converting their own games for the VCS. Then, smaller companies, often new to the video game market, joined the industry. In 1982, the market witnessed twice as many new game releases as in all the years before. Gamers' trust diminished in the face of quickly put together and primitive games.

Whilst third-parties repeated old formulas again and again, without introducing any innovation, the price for new cartridges dropped to ten dollars. VCS development consequently became unprofitable, and an array of recently founded companies were forced to close down. In 1984, the Atari market was crushed under the weight of several million unsold games, taking down with it all other platforms. The industry had its first crash. In the west, it seemed as if the hobby had come to an end.

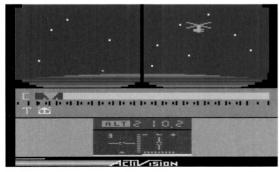

As the most complex cart, Steve Kitchen's Space Shuttle simulation utilized all control switches found on the console.

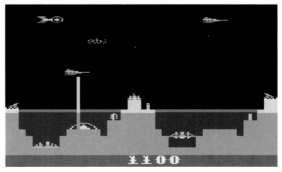

The Imagic logo stood for visually perfect, fine tuned VCS games: Atlantis from 1983.

In the time-span of eight years, only minor modifications were made to the case:
In 1980, the two difficulty levers were moved to the machine's back...

By the time the 8-Bit market began to take off again, spearheaded by Nintendo, Atari's era of triumph was over. The VCS successors, the 5200 and 7800, both failed, and only the old-timer VCS remained on the shelves. In the early '90s, the final series was shipped.

With an estimated 30 million sold units, the Atari VCS was and still is a worldwide classic. Collectors and retro fans look out for the first of four variants – the wood imitation on the front reflecting the taste of the '70s. Atari's joystick, included with every console until 1986, is legendary – consisting of a simple design with rubber clad stick and red fire button. Despite contacts wearing out, the straightforward joystick is one of the best controllers of all time. Eight directions, fire: The minimal functionality was better suited to the mass-market than the complex controllers by Intellivision and Coleco.

Atari itself shipped only the most important peripherals, making way for a flourishing add-on industry of deluxe joysticks with massive arcade technology or the clever feet-controlled Joyboard by a then little known company called Amiga. External keyboards and BASIC cartridges upgraded the console to a home computer, ROM jukeboxes like the Videoplexer or Game Selex helped gamers to organize their collection; even copying systems were sold in Europe.

...in 1982, Atari gave up the wood-look and produced the successful console entirely in black.

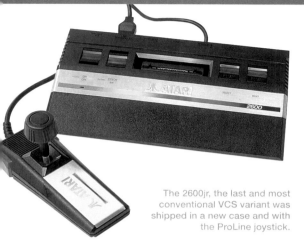

The 2600jr, the last and most conventional VCS variant was shipped in a new case and with the ProLine joystick.

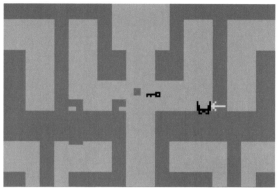

Fantasy journey via joystick: Adventure (1978).

The most ambitious and interesting add-on was the Supercharger adapter, which gave the VCS' tiny 128 bytes of internal memory another 6 K and allowed the development of complex games on cheap audio tapes. Later, the engineers behind the Supercharger turned into an in-house team of famous C64 publisher Epyx.

In 1983, the GameLine modem appeared, not for head-to-head action, but for software download. It wasn't a success but left behind it a legacy: While the video game market collapsed, the game distribution venture became C64 internet provider Quantum Link, which gave birth to the first online community Habitat. Quantum Link later changed its name to America Online (AOL).

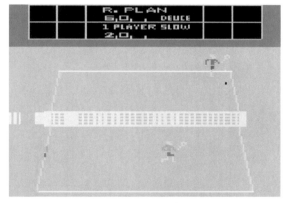

Excellent action for two players: RealSports Tennis (1983).

Atari VCS variants and successors

Atari VCS 2600	1977	The first version with rustic planks on the front and three toggle switches to the left and right of the cartridge port (power, colour, left and right difficulty level, select and reset) retailed for $200 and shipped with two joysticks and Combat cartridge. The six-switch version was sold world wide, in the US also by Sears (under the name of Telegames Arcade), in Japan by Epoch. The Epoch Cassette TV Game was released in October 1979 for an audacious 57,300 yen.
Atari VCS 2600A	1980	The new version retained the wooden look, but had only four toggle switches to the left and right of the cartridge port. The two other switches were moved to the back of the machine – bad for games like Space Shuttle, which used all switches for additional functionality. Also sold as Sears Telegames Arcade.
Atari 2600	1982	Features a black case with four toggle switches. Identical to the 2600A, apart from the colour and dropped wood look. The console retailed for $100, available either with two games and joysticks, or with just one game and joystick.
Atari 2800	1983	Sold for 24,800 yen from May 1983, this was the Japanese version of the VCS 2600 with six toggle buttons, a modified case and new controllers. Apart from that and the logo, it was externally identical to the US licensed Sears Telegames Arcade II.
Atari 2600jr	1986	The last version sold for below $50 in an overhauled and compact case and with new joysticks. The machine stayed on the shelves as a low budget alternative to Nintendo and Sega right until the '90s.

Interton VC 4000

Germany, 1978

Units sold:	Unknown
Number of games:	40
Game storage:	Cartridge
Games developed until:	1982

★ ☆ ☆ ☆ ☆

The end of the '70s saw the Interton VC 4000 as the only alternative to Atari available to European gamers. It was the successor to non-programmable Interton TV games, but it lacked the sheer voluminous software library of its American rival. Only Interton itself produced and sold games, while a mere four colours and mono sound made it technically weaker than its more prominent contemporary.

The exterior of the only German-produced games machine had an uncluttered appearance, without any bells or whistles. Two removable controllers were embedded in the sturdy case and, apart from its silver label, the machine was completely black. The controllers were pointing to things to come, combining analogue sticks with two fire buttons and a grid of twelve function keys, which were covered using a

Solid technology, an excellent analogue stick and an explosive painting on every cartridge box: The European Atari rival Interton VC 4000.

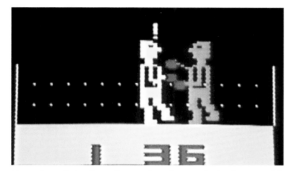
Charming minimalism: The exclamation marks in Cassette 18 Boxfight later returned in Metal Gear Solid.

game-specific paper overlay explaining the controls. The idea was borrowed by Bandai Japan for its Supervision 8000 – and ultimately established itself with the Intellivision, Colecovision and other consoles of the third generation.

In terms of technology, the Interton was a hybrid of the analogue games of the early '70s, and the digital future. Hans-Heinz Bieling, Author of cartridges 14 and 34, explained the graphical functions of the hardware: *'Next to the four objects, there's a programmable background. It consists of a base colour and a matrix with lines in different widths … a score counter was integrated, using four figures displaying either a four-figure number or two two-figure numbers, either in the top or bottom quarter of the screen … many games used their own counter built from objects that could appear anywhere on the screen.'* Early arcade games and the contemporary Microvision handheld used

screen overlays to display and colour game areas – Philips subsidiary Signetics, supplier of the 2650 processor and the graphics chip 2636, electronically integrated this as well as the mechanical counter of early arcade games. Signetics provided the hardware with four 'real' colours, four sprites including four-step zoom and a noise generator for explosions.

Like the first VCS games, Interton cartridges held either 2 or 4 K. Several ball and shoot 'em up games as well as simple edutainment titles were released, followed in 1982 by parlour games (Chess, Checkers) and clones of prominent arcade games (Space Invaders was **Invaders**, Pac-Man was **Monster-Man**) and very early 3D experiments like the flight simulator **Cockpit** by Martin Greiner. In addition to German productions, Interton games were also developed in Asia but the PAL console left larger game publishers unimpressed.

While the library of games grew to a considerable but not competitive 40 Interton cartridges, the console was already obsolete, and was (like its license-built Grundig Superplay 4000) shunted out of the market by US machines. The VC 4000 meant the end for the Interton company – the early licensee of video game inventor Magnavox had little luck with the transition from manufacturing hearing aids to producing consumer electronics. The family business went bankrupt and the Türk brothers never built the announced VC-4000 successor – instead, Hanimex and other Signetics licensees did.

Variants and successors

Elektor 2650 TV	1979	The DIY computer kit published in the 100th issue (April 1979) of German magazine Elektor was based on the Signetics chips 2650 and 2636, contained more RAM (2 K) as well as BIOS by Signetic's owner Philips in a 2 K ROM. Unlike the console, the `TV Spiel-Computer´ was expandable to 4 K RAM and could read and write audio tapes. Interton programmers used it as a development kit and also programmed games for it. After some VC 4000 conversions, Elektor had tape games programmed until 1984.
Grundig Super Play 4000	1979	The only Interton compatible console lacked modulator and conventional TV out. Using a special plug, the Super Play could only by connected to Grundig TV sets; the adapter was plugged into a front jack in the TV and delivered a better picture thanks to a direct signal input. Other than the chrome look, the Grundig's case and controllers were identical to the original.
Other variants	from 1979	Numerous consoles on the European and Asian market were code- but not cartridge compatible. The machines by Rowtron (Television Computer System), Audiosonic, Radofin and Hanimex (1292, 1392) were supported by Interton games in a different cartridge form, often renamed. Additionally, there were isolated variants (not compatible with other systems) like the French ITMC MPT-05. In the UK, an adapter appeared that allowed local 'Database' console games to run on the Interton.

The first cartridge-based console by patent-holder Philips looked like a home computer.
But already towards the end of the '70s, the technology sheltered
by a membrane keyboard struggled to be competitive.

Philips G7000

USA, Holland 1978

Speak to me: The US version
of Terrahawks supported
'The Voice'. In Europe it was
re-released in
enhanced Plus guise.

Units sold:	2 Million
Number of games:	50
Game storage:	Cartridge
Games developed until:	1984

★ ↗

With membrane keyboard and hard-wired joysticks, Philips G7000
attempted to close the gap between toy and computer.

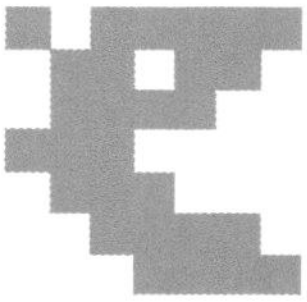

It wasn't Atari who produced the first video game console but Magnavox, the US subsidiary of the Dutch Philips group. In the early '70s, Magnavox purchased the rights to a patent owned by German-born inventor Ralph Baer and began production of the Odyssey, a television game with 12 game variations built-in. In 1975, Magnavox introduced the Pong machine Magnavox 100 to counter growing competition and then in 1978, Odyssey 2, the first cartridge console. In contrast to the Atari VCS, the G7000, as it was called in Europe, had two joysticks as well as an alpha-numerical membrane keyboard to allow educational games and even programming the console.

Apart from that, the G7000 was technically conventional and in terms of sound and graphics, weaker than Atari's VCS. Its main disadvantage wasn't technology though, but the lack of software: At the beginning, Philips had neither third-party support nor the catalogue of Atari's tried and tested arcade games. Both the formidable sports games of the Intellivision system and the prominent Sega and Nintendo licences purchased and used by Coleco in the early '80s were sadly missed. Towards the end of the

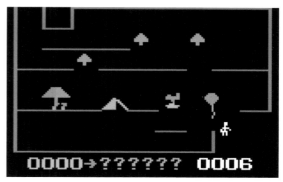

For PAL consoles only: Looney Balloon +

G7000's days, only two third-parties, Imagic and Parker, rolled out a few VCS and arcade conversions – and in the case of Parker, did so merely in Europe.

With around 50 games, Philips itself kept the machine alive until the video game crash in 1984. The games included the unique Master Strategy Series: The tabletop/cartridge hybrids **The Quest for the Rings**, **Conquest of the World** and **The Great Wall Street Fortune Hunt** were sold in large

The Master Strategy series mixed board game with onscreen fantasy and adventure: The Quest for the Rings

Pickaxe Pete

The rare G7200 was the deluxe update of antique technology. The built-in monitor was practical, but stripped the sparse graphics of any colour. The large dial to the left sets the contrast in seven levels.

boxes containing game board and tokens. Other complex products were the **Chess** add-on with additional RAM and processing power and the external speech synthesis 'The Voice of Odyssey 2'.

The shake out of the console market killed the G7000's successor: The G7400 was backward compatible but also ran improved revisions of older games and G7400-specific cartridges. Like the console, the Plus games with their detailed background graphics and the five carts developed exclusively for the G7400 were only released in Europe.

Hardware update for better graphics: The G7400.

G7000 variants and successors

G7000	**1978**	The first programmable console by video game licence owner Magnavox/Philips was launched as the Odyssey 2 in the States, in France under the name of C52 and in the rest of Europe as the G7000 – also as variants by Schneider and Radiola.
G7200	**1981**	The daring combination of G7000 and 9" monochrome monitor was launched in multiple variants (eg. in the form of the black Radiola Jet 27), but only in small numbers. Today, the 5.5 Kg machine is a popular collector's item on both sides of the Atlantic. It has buttons and knobs to adjust contrast, volume and brightness. Both joysticks can be unplugged.
G7400	**1983**	Updated with better graphics (but backward compatible to older cartridges) the G7400 ran exclusive titles Norseman, Helicopter Rescue, TransAmerican Rally and Moto Crash + by French company Jopac, as well as a home computer program. Launched in France alone were the Videopac G7401+ (with Péritel RGB output), the Radiola Videopac+ Jet47 in a slightly modified case and the Brandt JO7400, tucked inside a distinctly altered case. Licensed builds by Schneider (+74, +741 with RGB output) were also available.

Japan's largest chip manufacturer invented the 'Personal Computer':
With their own processor and BASIC, NEC PCs
dominated the local industry long way into the '90s.

NEC PC-8001

Japan, 1979

Units sold:	Unknown
Number of games:	2,000
Game storage:	Tape, Disk
Games developed until:	1992

★ ★ ★ ★ ✦

Devised as a direct challenger to western computers created by Apple and Commodore, Nippon Electric Company (NEC) developed its own Personal Computer. The CPU was a Z80-related µPD 780C; to display Kana characters, the PC-8001 was equipped with video RAM along the main memory.

As with the Sharp MZ, the first games were black and white or ASCII based. In 1982, developers began using the 'Programmable Character Generator' to display spaceships and pixel-sportsmen. Graphics and sound programming experienced a surge and magazines were full of BASIC listings. In 1983, the technically improved MkII and PC-88 appeared and each month 20 new adventures, RPGs, shoot 'em ups and simulations arrived as well as conversions of US games by SSI, Avalon Hill, Sierra and Brøderbund. The floppy drive replaced the 1200bps Datasette.

Software company Enix started the 'Game Program Contest', enticing hobby coders to the keys: Winning programes were sold across the country, and the competition became a springboard for professional careers. In 1982, Yuji Hori placed first. He joined Enix and became famous as the creator of Dragon Quest. Ascii, Pony Canyon, Tecno and Systemsoft were PC pioneers; thanks to

Dragonslayer (1984), Xanadu (1985) and Ys (1987) Nihon Falcom grew to become an RPG specialist. Koei released text simulations and adventures and in 1983 Nobunaga's Ambition, which graphically represented Japan's medieval provinces. Koei started further strategy series and remained loyal to the PC-88 until the '90s.

Even more successful than historic simulations were adult games: Nearly 1,000 PC-88 games with erotic, dating simulation or raunchy RPG content were released. The culprits were again Koei and Enix, who did two shady hits in the early days of the PC-88: Nightlife (1982) and Lolita Syndrome (1983).

With mini keys, cart slots and joystick ports, the PC-6001 tried the low budget and entry sector.

After the PC-8001 had sold 100,000 units in 1981, more memory, sound chips and better graphics were added, making the platform Japan's market leader.

Variants and successors

PC-8001	1979	The compact keyboard computer was shipped with 16 K and 2 K VRAM and retailed for 168,000 yen; it was superseded by the MkII (64 K + 16 K VRAM, 320x200 pixel, colour). In 1985, the model MKIISR came with a new BASIC and the YM-2203 sound chip, replacing the previous chirping audio.
PC-6001	1981	The hobby version came with rubber keys, but was seen with a solid typewriter keyboard in the USA (PC-6001A alias NEC Trek). It was replaced in 1983 by the MKII with a second µPD 8049 CPU, 64 K and 96 K ROM. The last variant was the 6601SR with built-in 3.5" floppy and YM2203 sound chip.
PC-8801	1981	The desktop computer with a minimum of 64 K and 48 K VRAM seamlessly replaced the PC-8001, successful as both office and home computer. The keyboard was separate, the central unit housed one or more tape or floppy drives (eg. PC-8801FH, 1986), as PC-8801VA the YM2203 chip, as VA2, VA3 and FA the sound wonder YM2608 with the PCM, FM, PSG and ADPCM channels from its mighty 16-Bit relative PC-98.

Under the management of media group Warner, Atari turned into a computer
manufacturer: Four joystick ports, two cartridge slots, great graphics
and sound made Atari computers the best games machines of the early '80s.

Atari 800

USA, 1979

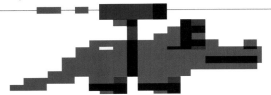

Units sold:	Unknown
Number of games:	1,000
Game storage:	Cartridge, Disk, Tape
Games developed until:	1990
★ ★ ★ ★ ✦	

From 1972, Nolan Bushnell's Pong arcade machines and consoles paved the way for a global market of electronic games. Within the entertainment industry his company quickly became the hottest thing since sliced bread. In 1976, prior to the release of the Atari VCS console, media giant Warner gobbled up Atari, pumping it with millions of dollars for the next step in the process: Atari's goal was to capture the nascent computer market. Instead of a new console, Warner's manager Ray Kassar presented the 8-Bit computer Atari 800 and its smaller brother Atari 400.

With two cartridge slots, four joystick ports and a custom circuitry focused on graphics and animation, the Atari 800 shone as the perfect games machine. Arcade conversions made up a good portion of the early software, but at the same time, games exclusive to the 800 appeared. Doug Neubauer's 3D space odyssey **Star Raiders** lit the fire of the development scene: When asked today, many designers name this game as their major influence and the reason for buying and programming the Atari 800 instead of an Apple or CBM micro.

The bulky, lavish Atari 800 had a flap
covering the cartridge slots, internal expansion
possibilities and four joystick ports as standard.

The powers of light versus darkness: Bizarre chess pieces cast spells and battled it out in real-time with Archon (1983).

The Atari 400 was the small and cheap alternative to its big brother Atari 800.

In 1982, Bill Stealey and Sid Meier launched the company Microprose to produce and sell Atari games. Other star designers of the 8-Bit era were Paul Edelstein, Bill Hogue, Jon Freeman and Chris Crawford, who attracted attention with the strategy game **Eastern Front**. The start line-up of the company freshly founded by former Apple employee Trip Hawkins was devoted to the Atari too: Hawkins marketed Freefall's **Archon** and Dan Bunten's **M.U.L.E.** as Electronic Arts.

The 8-Bit hardware was devised and developed by Jay Miner, Joe Decuir, Steven Mayer and Douglas Neubauer, the team that previously invented the VCS. Responsible for

the graphics was Lyle Rains, one of Atari's most experienced arcade game developers. The external company SMI provided the BASIC operating system; later project manager Paul Laughton came up with AppleDOS.

The team conceived a revolutionary concept: Three special chips supported the 6502 CPU. The Alpha-Numeric Television Interface Circuit (Antic) was a graphics processor with its own command set and DMA access to RAM. It controlled Rain's patented TV interface chip GTIA, which took care of colour, animation and collision detection. With its 'player-missile' graphics, the Atari 800 had beaten the 'sprites' of later computers and consoles to it. The third chip 'Pokey'

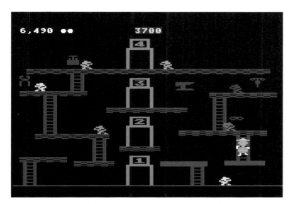

The Atari's powerful hardware sprites and colours were not only of use for action games like Miner 2049...

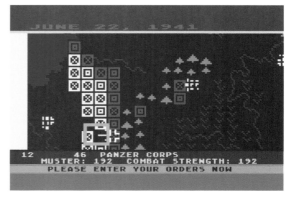

...but also for joystick-driven strategy simulations: Eastern Front by Chris Crawford (1981).

In 1982, the XL range appeared with a new case and high-quality add-ons like the trackball.

combined I/O functions (keyboard and controller supervision) with sound and random number generation.

With its Multi-LSI architecture, the Atari 800 replaced the year-older Apple II as best games computer. However, it had merely one year of dominance, before the Commodore C64 took over the world market.

Looking back, the Atari 800 was in no man's land: As a pure games machine it was too expensive, but on the other hand it was unable to establish itself as a serious computer alternative. Hardware power, typewriter keyboard and expansion possibilities contrasted sharply with the Atari image: For many potential buyers, the logo stood for toys, not for reliable micros.

Bruce Lee chopping his way through: The game by Datasoft was a successful blend of Kung-Fu and action adventure.

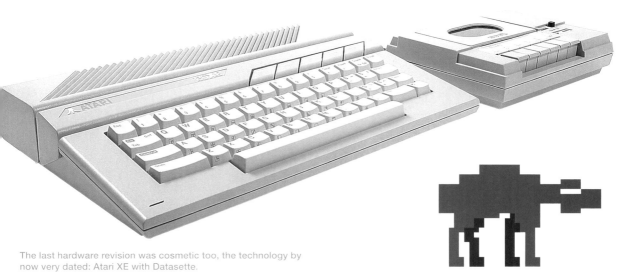

The last hardware revision was cosmetic too, the technology by now very dated: Atari XE with Datasette.

Even after Warner split the computer business from the games division, winding down the latter, Atari was unable to find a consequent product strategy. The badly thought-out Atari 1200 XL was dead on arrival, the succeeding variants 600 XL and 800 XL were revised or stripped and boiled down to the computing and graphics standards of 1979. Both were boldly advertised but could not win over gamers or programmers from the C64 which was streaks ahead. The technically related but cartridge-incompatible game console Atari 5200 suffered an uninspiring launch and ran fully into the video game crash.

After the success in the '70s, Atari's 8-Bit development in the mid '80s was ill-fated. Warner could no longer take such large losses and sold Atari's computer business to Commodore founder Jack Tramiel, who replaced the XL series with the technically barely improved XE computers, whilst at the same time pulling back from 8-Bit development in favour of the first 16-Bit computer Atari ST.

Atari was no longer of relevance in the computer market or the console sector – and with the introduction of the last 8-Bit machine the company was still apparently undecided

The best Atari games were created in the early '80s in the US: Fort Apocalypse gave depht to the Choplifter idea ...

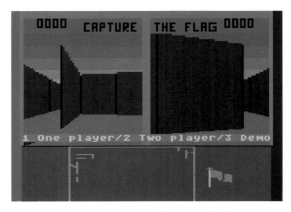

... Paul Edelstein's Capture the Flag brought 3D and colour gradients to the two-player split screen.

between creating games machines or hobby computers. The Atari XE Game Console shipped with a light-gun, integrated **Missile Command** on one hand and keyboard and BASIC on the other. It was inferior to all machines of that period. In 1992, Atari stopped production and shut down the entire 8-Bit development.

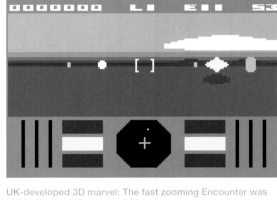

UK-developed 3D marvel: The fast zooming Encounter was written by Paul Woakes in 1984.

Rounded function buttons in pastel colours refurbished the grey Game System. The GS sometimes sold as a programming kit with keyboard and BASIC.

Atari 800 variants and successors

Atari 800	1979	The first Atari computer shone with 8 to 48 K of RAM, four joystick ports, two cartridge slots and four expansion ports for RAM and video add-ons. Earlier models contained a CTIA instead of a GTIA chip – the BASIC Poke 623,64 led to a blue, instead of a black screen. The machine retailed for $1,000.
Atari 400	1979	Smaller brother of the Atari 800 with only one cartridge port and cheap membrane keys instead of a proper keyboard. This introductory computer initially shipped with only 8 K RAM and had an RF connector, not a composite video output as standard.
Atari 1200 XL	1982	Revised successor with updated CPU 6502C, 64 K and a new black/white case, Help and four separate function keys but only two joystick ports. The missing expansion port, the incompatibility of its cartridge port with many games and the starting price of $1,000 were the nails on the coffin for the machine.
Atari 800 XL	1983	Successor to the 1200 XL with a middle sized case and separate keyboard, five function keys (Reset, Option, Select, Start, Help) and power LED. It had BASIC integrated in its ROM, a PBI port and on the back, composite video output as standard. As some other XL variants never went into series, the 800 XL remained the flagship of the range. The starting price was $250.
Atari 600 XL	1983	A small version of the 800 XL with only 16 K RAM and RF instead of composite video output.
Atari 65 XE	1985	Under Tramiel's management this XL successor retailed for $99, with a new case, 64K RAM and larger ROM, yet without the expansion port of its predecessor. The Atari 800 XE version was released in Europe only.
Atari 130 XE	1985	The big brother to the 65 XE had 128 K RAM and the 'Freddy' MMU from the 65 XE. The expansion port of previous XL machines was modified.
Atari XE GS	1987	Compatible games console in a grey case with colourful function keys (Reset, Option, Select, Start and Help) and optional keyboard (see picture above). Missile Command was included in the ROM.

Japanese manufacturers neglected the western computer market, except for Sharp:
With a series of practical 8-Bit micros, the office-equipment specialist
dared to target the European market.

Sharp MZ

Japan, 1979

Units sold:	Unknown
Number of games:	150
Game storage:	Tape, Disk
Games developed until:	1987

★ ★

A few weeks after the arrival of the PC-8001 from NEC, Sharp's Z80-equipped MZ-80 entered the scene. Whilst NEC and Fujitsu computers were seldom seen in the west, Sharp also marketed its hardware in Europe.

The MZ case was eye-catching – a 10-inch monitor, keyboard and Datasette were put together into one square-edged terminal. Earlier models had an ample 48 K of memory but no graphics. In spite of that, development blossomed. In fact, the company Hudson started out working on HuBASIC and ASCII character games.

From 1983, Sharp shipped most models with CP/M, creating a huge family of flexible office computers: The MZ-700 and MZ-800 were available without monitor, but with built-in Datasette and in some cases with a plotter. They had a faster CPU and were supported by Micronet, Micro Cabin, Thinking Rabbit and other game companies. Hal converted Namco's **Rally X**, Tecnosoft produced

The clunky MZ was not trendy but reliable. In Europe, the computer was welcomed as the Volvo among micros. Shown here is the first MZ with high res graphics built in, the 80B.

Thunderforce and Hudson was allowed to program and sell two exclusive **Mario Bros.** games. Development took place in Europe too, where Andreas von Glyszynski coded for the MZ, before founding the local subsidiary of Hudson.

But the MZ remained an unlikely games machine outside Japan, with gamers only 'accidentally' playing on them. As software on tape was not the hottest thing in Japan either, Sharp pushed the Quick Disk (QD) in its last marketing campaign in 1986: The MZ1500 was released with a QD floppy drive as standard and saw a final wave of 100 disk-based games.

Variants and successors

MZ-80	1979	Keyboard, monitor and Datasette in one case: Following DIY kits, Sharp released a complete micro for 200,000 yen. The 80C sold with 48 K and improved keys for 270,000, later variants retailed at 150,000 yen. In 1982 the 1200 came with 9" monitor, Datasette and typewriter keyboard. It was called 80A in Europe.
MZ-80B	1981	Retailing for 280,000 yen, this 16 kilogram colossus was one of the most successful Sharp computers, spearheading Japanese Z80 development. It used a 4 Mhz CPU and drew graphics in 300 x 200 pixels.
MZ-2000	1982	This machine featured an integrated monitor and Datasette, and had the faster B-CPU, 64 K and a solid keyboard; and retailed for 220,000 yen. It was the flagship model of the series. From the more compact, cheaper keyboard model 2200 Sharp derived the specifications for the X1 computer.
MZ-700	1982	This bright computer without monitor, sold for less than 100,000 yen, had a Datasette and integrated plotter (731 model only) and weighed less than 5 kilograms. TV and RGB output were standard; high-resolution graphics were realised using an additional PCG card.
MZ-800	1984	The last important step in the MZ evolution brought high-res graphics as standard and 'near-backward' compatibility with the 80 and 700; according to the manual some games that used the joystick didn't run. In Scandinavia and Japan, the machine was sold as a black 1500 with QD as standard medium.
MZ-2500	1985	The professional machine (6 MHz CPU, 256 colours, hard-drive) was sold in Japan only and thanks to a switch beneath the small front panel, was compatible with the 80B and 2000. Apart from the two 3.5" floppy drives, the case featured the good old Datasette. Looked quite bizarre.

Mattel Intellivision

USA, 1980

Units sold:	3 Million
Number of games:	125
Game storage:	Cartridge
Games developed until:	1990

★ ★ ⅃

The IntelliVoice made the console talk. Games were plugged in this adapter from the side.

Up until 1980, the Atari VCS alone ruled the market of programmable consoles. Then a big-name rival turned up. At the end of 1979, the toy conglomerate (and Barbie inventor) Mattel presented its `Intellivision Master Component´ in limited numbers. A year later the machine was distributed to dealers across the country. The slim, golden-brown unit was technically superior to Atari's hardware and was to bridge the gap between TV game and family computer. *'Begin with the Master Component (available now) for entertainment and education, then add the Keyboard Component (available 1981)'*, read the blurb on the US brochure from 1980. *'A range of programs designed to put a whole new world at your family's fingertips. And right on your own television screen!'* Mattel promised educational, accounting and simulation programs: *'Update your finances and unload an NFL*

While Intellivision provided realistic sports games, third-party developers...

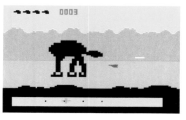

...handled conversions of well-known brands: Empire Strikes Back...

...by Parker and Imagic's Demon Attack however, came too late.

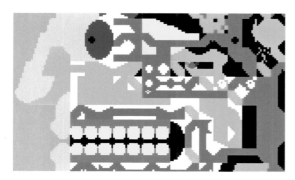

The Intellivision had sophisticated games with explicit but static graphics: Imagic's Microsurgeon from 1982.

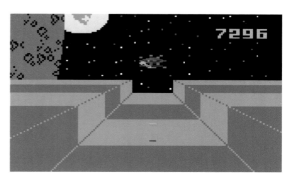

Luke Skywalker's trench battle was the inspiration for early 3D shooting games like Star Strike by Mattel (1981).

bomb.' But the release of add-ons (keyboard, Datasette, microphone, printer and modem) was delayed a number of times, and the most ambitious expansions were dropped altogether. The few hundred keyboard units shipped for testing expanded the memory to 64 K, but were twice as expensive as the console. Today they are very rare.

The Master Component was a powerful piece of equipment, whose 16-Bit CPU shone thanks to a series of visually realistic sports games. Apart from the potential computer upgrade, Mattel's biggest selling-point was improved game graphics: Compared to Atari's flat playing fields, Intellivision games such as **NHL Hockey** and **NBA Basketball** offered realistic perspective thanks to pseudo 3D graphics.

Atari's prominent arcade games were missing, so Mattel concentrated on sports licences and later published RPGs and adventure games. Generally speaking, Intellivision games were not as fast-paced and simple as VCS

The Intellivision II was compact but not more powerful than its predecessor. Both controllers were removable.

cartridges. The controller too was more complex: Thumb placed on the paddle, fire buttons on both sides of the pad. The top half of the pad held 12 membrane keys, with a coloured overlay used to reveal the game's functions. The controllers felt unusual and inaccurate and because they were wired to the Master Component, there was no way to connect alternatives.

Other than a conventional joystick, the Intellivision also lacked software. Not until 1983 did third-parties like Activision, Imagic and Parker begin with cartridge production and marketing. Atari also ported some of its own and Japanese coin-ops by Namco, Nintendo and Sega. The Intellivision's worldwide release was as late as the third-party software support: In Europe, the machine was released 1982, the same year Bandai launched it in Japan.

Stateside, Mattel released a speech expansion and the Intellivision II in a new case: The second unit was compact, seemed more serious and modern than the predecessor's glamorous wood and gold appearance. In the middle of 1983, Mattel finally kept its promise of a home computer expansion: The ECS cartridge was a half-heartedly marketed combo of 49-key keyboard and a `CPU Module´, which contained 2 K RAM and 10 K ROM for BASIC programming, a three-channel sound chip and joypad ports. The same year, a 49-key piano keyboard was released.

In 1984, Mattel took advantage of the fall of the video game industry to quit: Hardware, games and patents were sold to Mattel's manager Terry Valeski whose new company INTV marketed the black System III and 35 new games between 1985 and 1990. The last Intellivision carts were **Stadium Mud Buggies** and the volleyball simulation **Spiker!**.

Few computer modules made it to the shops. The alpha-numerical keyboard and a piano were connected to the expansion port.

Intellivision variants and successors

Intellivision Master	1979	The heart of a planned computer system was bundled with `Poker & Blackjack´. In 1980 the price was lowered to $269 from $299 for the country-wide release. There were variants by Sears (`Telegames Super Video Arcade´ with removable controllers), Radio Shack (`Tandyvision One´) and GTE (`Sylvania Vision´) and in Japan by Bandai (June 1982, retailed for 49,800 yen).
Intellivision II	1983	A compact successor with removable controllers, external power supply and status LED for an initial $150. The dull console was not marketed in Europe; in the US, it was quickly dropped in price and just before Mattel Electronics closed down, bargained for $70. Unlike the first version, it was compatible to Atari VCS games thanks to the `System Changer´.
INTV System III	1985	The license built `Master Component´ in black was sold for $70 and should not be mixed up with the unreleased Intellivision III. Later, it was also called the `INTV Super Pro System´. It had no removable controllers and wasn't `System Changer´ compatible.

Three years before his Vectrex, Jay Smith invented the portable games console. The concept was weird: The CPU was not located in the machine, but inside each cartridge.

Milton Bradley Microvision

USA, 1979

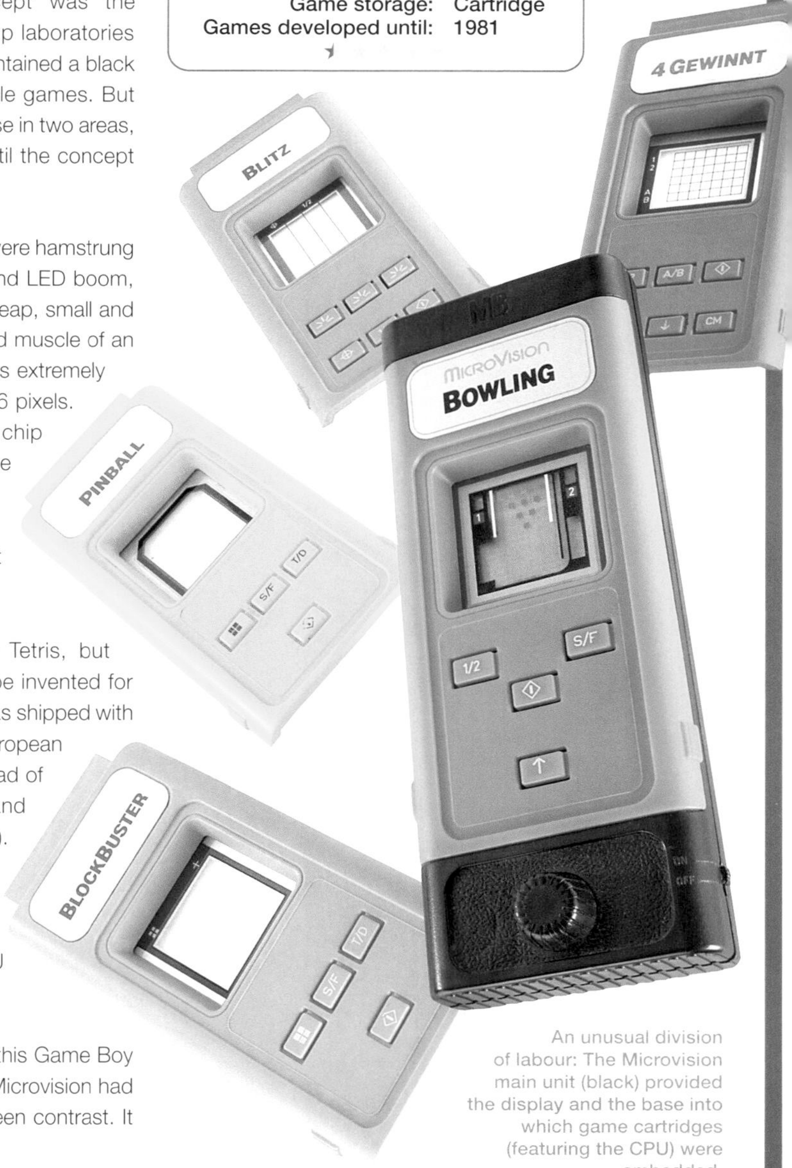

Units sold:	Unknown
Number of games:	12
Game storage:	Cartridge
Games developed until:	1981

The history of electronic games is full of clever inventions that were technically ahead of time or too early for the mass market. One such overambitious concept was the Microvision: The machine by American chip laboratories Smith Engineering was battery powered, contained a black and white display and played exchangeable games. But because Jay Smith's team had to compromise in two areas, the first handheld was soon forgotten – until the concept was reanimated by Nintendo ten years later.

Smith and toy manufacturer Milton Bradley were hamstrung by the technical realities; before the LCD and LED boom, there was simply no technology that was cheap, small and saved power whilst offering the graphics and muscle of an Atari computer. Hence, Smith's machine was extremely minimalist; the tiny screen was just 16 by 16 pixels. The unit contained little technology, just a chip driven LCD and a control paddle. The game cartridges, which contained the CPU and game program, were nearly as large as the base unit, fitting over the top of the main part of the machine.

The technology would have sufficed for Tetris, but unfortunately, that puzzle game wasn't to be invented for another half a decade. Thus, the machine was shipped with the simple Breakout clone **Block Buster**. European game carts had better buttons (plastic instead of a membrane) and came in little jackets, and different colours (red, green, yellow or blue). US games had a dull colourless plastic appearance. The first game chips were provided by Intel or Signetics, while later games used the 4-Bit chip TMS1001 CPU (clocked at 0.1 MHz) by Texas Instruments.

Both the processor and the case design of this Game Boy forerunner were spartan, but effective: The Microvision had a voltage control on its back to change screen contrast. It was powered by two 9V batteries.

An unusual division of labour: The Microvision main unit (black) provided the display and the base into which game cartridges (featuring the CPU) were embedded.

Sinclair ZX 81

GB, 1981

It was the early '80s and the young computer market was subject to domination by American companies. But against the might of transatlantic giants were arrayed the plucky spirit of some indomitable Brits, holding out against invaders and ready to battle the likes of Apple, Tandy and Atari with home-grown micros. The most successful among them was inventor Clive Sinclair, who was later knighted for his life's work. He marketed his first computer as a DIY electronics kit in 1980.

The ZX 80 did not have colour or sound and possessed merely 1 K of memory – but it was affordable for anyone. This tiny computer connected to ordinary TVs and used cheap and simple audio-tapes for data storage. The most sensational feature was the size and light weight of the system: instead of a proper keyboard, Sinclair decided to fit the plastic case with a 40-key membrane, making it nearly as thin as a calculator. A year later, the pre-assembled ZX 81 went into mass production. Another miniature computer, located at the lower end of the price scale, it became a big

As the ZX 81 shipped with only 1 K memory, most users plugged an additional 16 K into the rear port.

Units sold:	1.5 Million
Number of games:	100
Game storage:	Tape
Games developed until:	1984

success in Europe and – even without colour, sound or joystick – an important platform for early computer games.

The predecessor of the million-selling Spectrum played classics like Chess, Star Trek or simple shoot 'em ups but also gave birth to groundbreaking new concepts: Long before Doom, Malcolm Evan's **3D Monster Maze** presented claustrophobic tunnels in blocky 48x48 pixel resolution. Among the talented programmers who began their career on the ZX 81 were Charles 'Broken Sword' Cecil, Andrew Glaister, Costa Panayi and Digital Integrations founder Dave Marshall. Plug-in cartridges were used to expand the hardware with an additional 16 K or 64 K, HiRes graphics and a cute mini printer, which used thermo rolls instead of normal paper to draw simple graphics and text.

3D Shock in black and white: Monster Maze was the first survival horror game (1981).

US versions

Timex Sinclair TMS-1000	1982	The upgraded 2 K version for the USA was incompatible with the ZX81 and available for the bargain price of $45 at the end of 1983.
Timex Sinclair TMS-1500	1983	Released for $70 this TMS-1000 successor had internal 16 K memory and was a complete failure. An additional 16 K RAM pack could be purchased for $30.

Texas Instruments TI99/4a

USA, 1980

Before Intel flattened the semiconductor market, Texas Instruments was the leading developer and producer of chips. Even today, it's not clear which company was first to merge processor functions (ALU, Register, Control Unit and Bus) on a single chip: Intel with its 4004 or TI, who had their microprocessor patented the same year, 1971.

From 1973, millions of TI's 4-Bit chips were used in calculators and TV games. TI's kid's learning machine 'Speak & Spell' came with a patented speech-chip and a TMS1000 CPU, just like electronic games by Milton Bradley.

Already in 1975, TI produced the first 16-Bit processor, but facing the cheap 8-Bit alternatives on the market, the demand was low. And so TI built its own computer around the new CPU. Four further TI chips assisted the TMS9900. Software also came on solid state ROMs.

TI manufactured all components but it underestimated the importance of independent software developers: There was no floppy drive and no assembler. The TI99/4a was difficult and slow to code for. When TI finally released the 32 K memory expansion and 'Extended BASIC' ROM, it was too late. The price war was lost to Commodore. Its VC 20 was technically weaker but better positioned, marketed and supported by developers.

A chip behemoth: the graphics and sound processors of the TI99/4a (pictured with plugged-in speech module right) were later incorporated in MSX, Coleco und Sega consoles.

Units sold:	2.5 Million
Number of games:	100
Game storage:	Cartridge, Disk
Games developed until:	1985

★ ★ ☆ ☆ ☆

But amid the silicon frenzy of the early '80s, even a peripheral platform was treated to cartridges. Atari ported its arcade hits **Dig Dug**, **Pole Position**, **Pac-Man** and **Joust**; Parker made **Popeye** and **Frogger**; Imagic **Fathom** and a talking **Microsurgeon**; Tigervision shipped **Miner 2049** and **Espial**. The **Adventure** cartridge by Scott Adams required separate scenario tapes (later floppies).

The best game was the science fiction shoot 'em up **Parsec**, a killer application for TI's speech synthesiser. An even more unusual peripheral was Milton Bradley's 'MBX Voice Recognition System' – the first speech input for games.

Alas, from 1983 the company was losing money with every unit sold. In October, TI announced that the 99/4a was being discontinued and in March 1984 production ceased.

Variants and successors

TI99/4	1980	With a metal case, 40 little plastic keys and a programmable 'Equation Calculator' in ROM, this first version had similarities to a pocket calculator. The price of $1,200 for the inflexible unit with a bundled 13" monitor (without add-ons or third-party support) made it too expensive. Unlike its successor, the machine had a headphone socket and sometimes a mono speaker.
TI99/4a	1981	For the world market, TI turned the keyboard into a typewriter but kept the basic design. To the right, the large cartridge port, on the side and back the joystick port, tape recorder and TV connector. The video chip was slightly better (TMS9918A instead of TMS9918). In the States, 1983 saw a second, beige variant selling at $100. It contained a new operating system as a protection against unlicensed development.

With an affordable computer for the masses, Commodore challenged the posh Apple and Atari hardware. In the US, the VC 20 broke the 300 dollar barrier, in Germany, the C64 predecessor became the 'Volkscomputer'.

Commodore VC 20

Japan and USA, 1981

Following its PET office computer, US company Commodore introduced its first home computer. Based on the tried and tested 6502 processor, the VC 20 was already a rather dated piece of hardware when it launched, but much cheaper than the competition. Retailing for less than $300, the machine was a hit both stateside and in Europe. Prior to its debut in the west, the VC 20 was sold in Japan, where HAL (today a strong Nintendo partner) provided early VIC software.

Beneath the white case with its professional keyboard, the Video Interface Chip VIC sat next to the CPU, drawing graphics with eight colours and also providing three channel sound. With 5 K of memory, the VC 20 was feebly

With cartridge and 9-pin joystick ports, the VC 20 was designed for games.

Units sold:	2 Million
Number of games:	200
Game storage:	Cartridge, Tape
Games developed until:	1984

★★┙

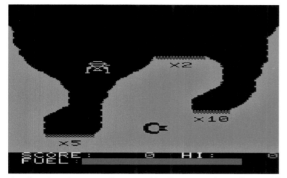

Jupiter Lander was the graphical conversion of an old mainframe simulation and even switched…

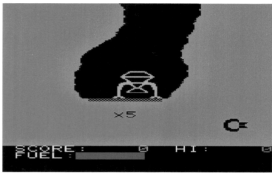

…to a new scale when approaching the ground. Apply just enough thrust to land the probe safely inside a crater.

specced; BASIC users had a mere 3.5 K at their disposal. But its low price, reliability and expansion possibilities made it a brief success between 1981 and 1983. Whereas in the US nearly 200 games appeared on cartridge, British and German companies published games and applications on cheaper audio tapes. The 16 K RAM expansion and the analogue paddle were connected via a 9-pin port – using this standard the VC 20 was compatible with all Atari controllers.

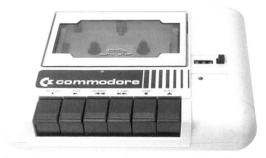

As most software appeared on tape, the add-on Datasette was a must.

After the release of the more powerful C64, the VC 20 managed to hang on for a few years. Later users connected a disk drive to the serial port, getting the most out of the machine with the VC1020 box. Up to five expansion carts could be connected, such as the Machine Language Monitor VC1213, Super Expander VC1211A, Programmer's Aid VC1212 and IEE-488 interface VC1112.

Around the world, about 400 games and applications were released, including arcade hits, ports of Apple and Atari games by Sirius, Epyx and Brøderbund, Scott Adams' adventures and – the most prominent European development – **Gridrunner** by Jeff Minter (1982).

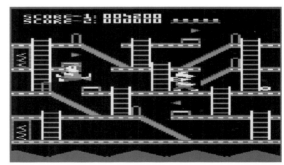

With action games like Congo Bongo, German developer Kingsoft jumped right into the British software charts.

Japan version

VIC-1001		1980	As the first product for Commodore's home computer division, the VC 20 was developed by teams in the US (hardware) and Japan (software) and released in the Far East before introduction in the west, much like the games developed by HAL for Commodore. As HAL held the computer licence for Namco games, Jelly Monsters and Star Battle were released with their correct names Pac-Man and Galaxian. The VIC-1001 had a modified keyboard (Katakana instead of western characters, Yen instead of Pound character) and was the first home computer for less than 10,000 yen. It was quickly put out of the market by platforms from NEC, Hitachi and Sharp.

The videogame crash and home computer success story

Little cartoon animations lured gamers into the Congo-Bongo jungle. Sega, 1983.

From 1980 onwards, the videogame scene began getting crowded. An intriguing situation which led to 50 different platforms being launched within a few years – not all exclusively, but each one just as enthralling for gamers. Consoles became more expensive whilst home computers dropped below the $500 price level. Apple, Atari and IBM, Compaq, Thomson, Texas Instruments and Amstrad all devised their own sets of standards; their machines were not compatible with others.

While the computer competition grew fast and inspired a drive to new technical heights, the console market stagna-

Handhelds and tabletops put the arcade in your pocket. The popularity of LCD and LED machines by Mattel, Parker and Bandai and two dozen other manufacturers culminated in 1982: Puckman by Tomy, 1981.

Q*Bert was the cutest US arcade hero, but also rude. After a wrong jump, he cursed! Game mechanics were influenced by Pac-Man and M.C. Escher drawings.

ted. The old Atari VCS remained number one even after the introduction of more powerful machines, but it had lost its sparkle and offered little in the way of new experiences. Cartridges from competent companies had made the most of this limited hardware, but were buried under a pile of inferior and rushed software. Games became cheaper and cheaper but at the same time, worse.

Whereas Nintendo later regulated the market, Atari had little control over third-parties at this stage. The Time Warner management started messing up, producing twelve million **Pac-Man** cartridges (with an installed base of ten million consoles) and directing $20 million from game development over to Hollywood. The Spielberg licence **E.T.** was rushed in time for Christmas and turned into a commercial disaster. Dealers were in no position to sell the huge amount of cartridges by Atari and more than twenty third-parties. It is rumoured that Time Warner buried a few million games somewhere in New Mexico.

Humour and dynamics on optical disc: Disney's apprentice Don Bluth produced a playable fantasy movie. Dragon's Lair, 1983.

Like contemporary arcade games, Atari's Crystal Castle utilised a 6502 chip, the CPU used by many popular micros.

In 1981, the US market was still making $500 million from videogames, and a year later twice as much, culminating in revenues of over $3 billion in 1983. Then within two years, the business collapsed to just a quarter of that sum. In 1985, it was `game over´ for most new companies – although some (such as Starpath) saved themselves by moving over to the computer industry.

Battered but technically and creatively still in shape, the coin-op market survived. Both before and after the crash, the arcades remained a reliable source of new game concepts and technology. From jump 'n runs to racing, from shoot 'em ups to football, all action genres were increasingly arcade oriented. More memory for sprites and landscapes, a crisp RGB picture, special controllers and hydraulics; in terms of gameplay, arcade games were a generation ahead of home entertainment, and often

copied and imitated. In 1980 and 1981, more than 100 new coin-ops were launched, including the shoot 'em up milestones **Phoenix**, **Missile Command**, **Defender**, **Battlezone** and Scramble, **Centipede**, **Galaga** and **Tempest**. Those who preferred to puzzle and laugh played **Pac-Man**, **Qix** and **Lady Bug**, or leaped about with **Frogger** or Mario in **Donkey Kong**.

In 1983, the arcade industry discovered the Laser Disc. Don Bluth and his team painted and animated traps and enemies in cinematic quality for **Dragon's Lair**. Gamers interacted with the on-screen adventure using a joystick, jump and fire command, but they couldn't take direct control of the pre-animated hero and action sequences. Dragon's Lair had limited gameplay, yet overwhelming audio visuals. Coleco and Atari announced Laser Disc players and adapters, while Hasbro took aim at a VHS-based game console.

But the interactive movie soon lost its magic, and the LD and VHS consoles collected dust as prototypes. Ten years later, the 20 or so American and Japanese LD games were dug up and re-animated to fill the 600 MB of the CD-ROM.

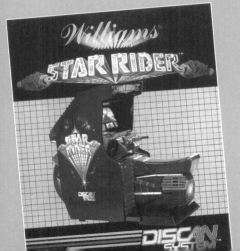

Neither remake, nor MAME emulation can bring back Midway's Star Rider. The LD racer disguised its linearity with 3D models and 3D landscape: Shaded, prerendered and stored on LD as a computer film. Only a small view of the space panorama was shown, the player's steering scrolled it slightly. Giving full throttle made the CAV disc play at double-speed and the space bike accelerate. Racing across galactic beams, the gamer crouched on a bike seat, watching others in the rear mirror as they overtook at breakneck speed.

Unbeatable technology, strong expansions and arcade hits from
Sega and Nintendo: The Colecovision was the console to own
in the early '80s – but was soon blasted by the videogames crash.

CBS Colecovision

USA, 1982

Units sold:	4 Million
Number of games:	100
Game storage:	Cartridge
Games developed until:	1985

★ ★ ✦

The Colecovision did well thanks to conversions of Japanese and American arcade hits.

At the beginning of the '80s, the Atari VCS had reached its maximum popularity but also its technical limits. Cute cartoon games from Namco, Sega and Nintendo were impossible to convert and it was just as futile to port computer games to the VCS.

Having gained experience with numerous Telstar consoles in the '70s, US company Coleco spotted a gap in the market and launched a new generation of programmable consoles. The unit was based on a fast Z80 processor, could draw graphics in 256x192 resolution and displayed up to 32 sprites. This technical benchmark wiped the floor with the VCS and the Intellivision to boot.

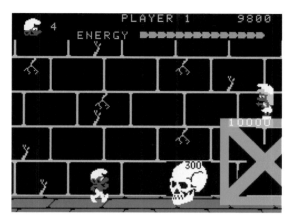

Visual splendour versus Atari's chunky graphics: At the end, a loving Smurfette awaited you in Gargamel's Castle.

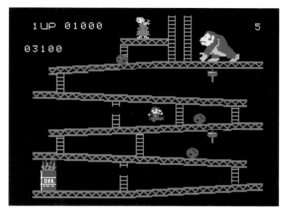

Mario on Colecovision: The first home version of Donkey Kong lacks one of the four original levels.

To beat the competition, Coleco bought licences for the home versions of popular Japanese games like **Donkey Kong** and **Zaxxon**. These and other innovative arcade titles made the Colecovision the only western console to offer near perfect conversions of both Sega and Nintendo games.

For development, the close affinity to other Z80 machines (coin-ops, MSX and Sega hardware) proved to be a blessing, and successful American computer games like **Apshai** and **Montezuma's Revenge** were ported to the Colecovision.

Thanks to an Expansion Module 1 plugged into the front, the console became compatible with Atari VCS games.

Prominent games were accompanied by Coleco's add-ons for the mega console: A trackball (`Roller Controller'); the bold `Super Action Controller´ with a proper joystick, four triggers, keypad and a small revolving shuttle; as well as the `Expansion Module 2´, consisting of steering wheel and gas pedal, which was initially bundled with the Sega game **Turbo**. One strategically important adapter was the `Expansion Module 1´ that allowed Atari VCS games to run on the Colecovision.

But in spite of superior hardware and software, Coleco was denied long-term success. Eighteen months after launch,

Hollywood's power punch: The characters of Rocky (1983) were pixellated after their alter egos from the big screen.

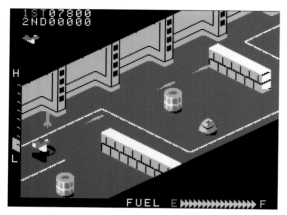

Zaxxon didn't scroll flat, but added a new dimension to space with its isometric perspective. A shadow showed your height.

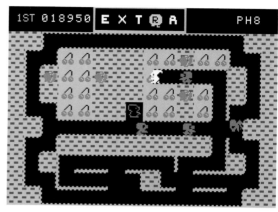

Coleco hired almost all arcade heroes under licence. This is Universal's clown Mr. Do digging it on the Colecovision (1983).

the American videogame market collapsed. Coleco attempted to save its skin with a move to the booming computer market, and consequently ceased development of its Colecovision update `Super Game Module´, presenting the home computer Adam instead.

But the Adam's release was put back several times, which, together with technical problems made it a disaster. Like many manufacturers, Coleco left the computer market and surprisingly triumphed with its `Cabbage Patch´ dolls for

small kids instead. As Coleco was drawing its last breath in 1988, Telegames inherited the hardware and sold the console for a few years as the `Personal Arcade´. A second licence-built version was the Dina 2-in-1 by Bit Corporation that sported two cartridge slots. The second cart slot swallowed Sega SG-1000 console games. When this machine went out of production, emulators saved the Coleco heritage: Telegames released the `Personal Arcade´ for PC and the `Coleco Hits Volume 1´ compilation with Z80 games by Activision, Konami and other third-parties.

The console's technology was put into a white case and repacked with keyboard, magnetic twin drives and more RAM: The result was called Adam and failed miserably.

The successor

Coleco Adam	1983	Because of the console crisis, Coleco canned the planned update `Super Game Module´ in favour of a backward compatible home computer and created an unheard-of bundle: Retailing for $600, Adam came with 16 K VRAM, a professional keyboard, keypad controllers, text processing, printer and two integrated tape drives. The exotic storage medium, technical problems and several delays as well as a price increase to $750 closed the Adam case: Only about 100,000 units were shipped prior to Coleco disappearing from the hardware market.

Handheld-specialist Entex used LEDs, a mirror and an early Intel chip
to build a technically peculiar mini arcade machine.
It was supported by a mere four games and today is a rare collector's item.

Entex Adventurevision

USA, 1982

Units sold:	50,000
Number of games:	4
Game storage:	Cartridge
Games developed until:	1982

As a hybrid of mechanical, optical, electronic, digital and analogue parts, the Adventurevision was unique but was left without a long-term strategy.

In the early '80s, portable electronic games shared the booming success of consoles and computers. Console conversions of well known brands like Donkey Kong, Frogger and Zaxxon were frequently followed by pocket sized LED or LCD games. Entex made the combination: The Adventurevision was formed like an arcade cabinet, though portable and not dependent on mains power or TV set. Like a console it used exchangeable cartridges.

The plastic case was a lot smaller and less heavy than the Vectrex, the display more intricate: A motor powered a spinning mirror which multiplied 40 red LEDs to a 150x40 resolution. Instead of drawing fine lines like the Vectrex, the Adventurevision showed flickering dots. Due to the low frame rate, the animations were similar to the stuttering images of the silent movie era.

The miniature arcade was operated using four batteries. It featured a plastic knob as joystick and four buttons on each side – for both left- and right-handed gamers. Headphones were connected using the stereo jack; the covered expansion port on the right side was never used.

A quartet of high-quality games was released with the Adventurevision: The horizontally scrolling **Defender** and **Super Cobra** by Williams and Konami, **Turtles** and the Asteroids clone **Space Force**. Even if the conversions were technically stripped down, Entex had made the best of the arcade licences. Sadly, further cartridges never appeared; the machine itself disappeared from shelves by 1983.

All-around neat design: The four cartridges available were bolted into the rooftop of the console.

Vectrex

USA, 1982

Units sold:	Unknown
Number of games:	25
Game storage:	Cartridge
Games developed until:	1985

★ ★

The Stone Age of videogame technology saw two display and telescreen concepts in competition: The conventional television utilises an electron beam shot from the top left to the bottom right of the screen line by line to create images. The vector-based screen on the other hand allowed the beam to roam freely, creating an afterglow, which draws lines and in effect geometrical objects. True vector graphics were useful for fast movement and hence for 3D arcade games such as Battle Zone and Star Wars by Atari. Colour was possible, but filled-out areas (known as shaded vector graphics) could not be rendered.

With his company western Technology, American Jay Smith, creator of the innovative Microvision handheld, developed the only home videogame using vector technology. The Vectrex came with a built-in monitor, the excellent Asteroids clone **Mine Storm** and a fold-out joypad (featuring an analogue stick and four fire buttons) serving as a front panel of the machine. A second joypad could be connected separately. The Vectrex required no additional cabling, merely power, and was easy to carry thanks to its grip shaped top.

Originally, the Vectrex was manufactured by US company GCE and sold for $200; later international marketing was taken over by Milton Bradley (MB). The toy giant lowered the price to $150 and finally, shortly before the video game crash, to $100. The dark year of 1984 represented the end of the short career of the Vectrex. At this stage, the unusual system only offered 30 cartridges, all developed by GCE.

Without support by Atari, Activision and or any third-party, the list of games lacked recognisable names. On top of that, Vectrex games were just different: the monochrome software was coloured using screen-overlays which shipped with the games. This was used to create the impression of a green football pitch in games

such as **Blitz!** for example. Similarly, the '3D Imager' promised a true 3D effect and is today one of the most sought after collector's items. It was supported by three games, distinguishable by the '3D' suffix. A second unusual add-on was the Light Pen, also supported by three carts only, among them the drawing program **Art Master**.

Three versions of the Vectrex exist: The first with a GCE logo, the European model by Milton Bradley, and a licensed Bandai version, which appeared in Japan selling at 54,800 yen. Today, a used Vectrex can be purchased for €100.

Beam me up! The Vectrex only needs power for its instant vector magic.

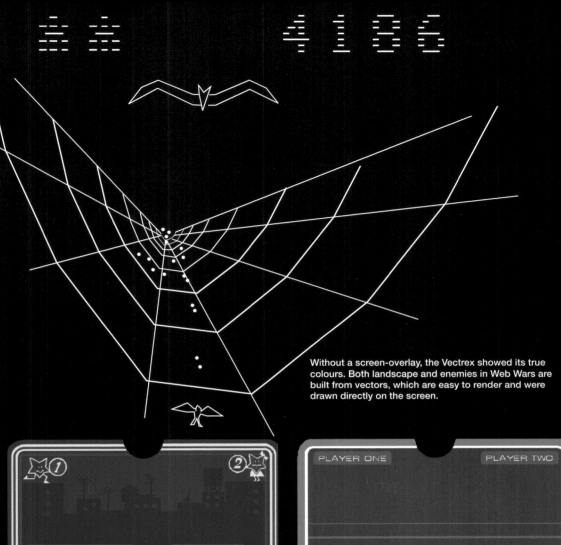

Without a screen-overlay, the Vectrex showed its true colours. Both landscape and enemies in Web Wars are built from vectors, which are easy to render and were drawn directly on the screen.

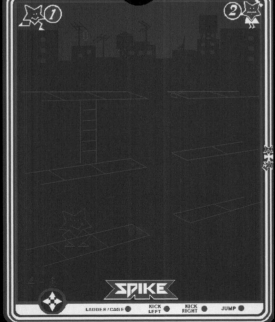

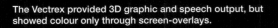

The Vectrex provided 3D graphic and speech output, but showed colour only through screen-overlays.

War of the vectors: Action on the Vectrex lacked details but scrolled and moved much faster than Atari games.

Hanimex HMG 2650

Origin unknown, 1982

A short lifespan, false marketing promises and more international variants than you can shake a stick at, all obscure the history behind the second Hanimex console. For videogame historians, a tough case indeed.

With different names and in varying guises, the Hanimex 2650 was released in all three big markets (USA, Japan, Europe), but it arrived too late to make a difference to the first console race. Whatever it lacked in terms of charm and technical flair, it made up for it with a compact case and low price. To no avail however: The console and its exotic CPU Signetics 2650 was the least popular machine of the 'third generation'.

Twenty years after its debut (and 19 years after its just as spontaneous disappearance), game collectors have acquired an interest in the system, discovering about two dozen compatible variants: In the US, the machine was sold as the Arcadia 2001, in Europe as the Schmid TVG 2000 and Hanimex Home Arcade among others. It is most likely to stem from the Far East and was probably not developed and manufactured in Japan (where it appeared as the 'Bandai Arcadia' in March 1983), but in Hong Kong.

At the start of the '80s, no one cared for the small, cheap console. The hard-wired joypads rested on the sides of the case. With their direction disc and twelve buttons, they were reminiscent of the Intellivision controllers but were not quite as useless. Thanks to a thread it was possible to fasten a tiny joystick into the disc.

With its red fire buttons and a clean case-design, the Tele-Fever by German retailer Tchibo was an elegant HMG 2650 compatible in two parts.

Units sold:	Unknown
Number of games:	30
Game storage:	Cartridge
Games developed until:	1983

★ ﾉ

The small HMG2650 console packed normal sized, but also longish game cartridges. A similar model manufactured by Schmid is shown in the background.

The strange '70s chip used in the Hanimex as CPU also worked in a handful of coin-ops and pinball machines by Italian manufacturer Zaccaria. It was in the older Interton VC 4000 too – this German machine is the technical predecessor to the Hanimex and Arcadia family. But German game developers no longer programmed the Hanimex – engineers in Hong Kong did, including Andrew Choi, who wrote the Galaxians clone **Space Attack** and, prior to that, three Interton cartridges.

Technically, the machine was more powerful than the Interton VC 4000, but audio-visually it stood little chance against the Colecovision. The software library was spiced up a little thanks to the carts' internationality: Unlike the contemporary Colecovision and Intellivision, the Hanimex had some Japanese products, including **Macross**, **Doraemon**, **Gundam** and even **Dr. Slump**.

Nearly all games were clones of well-known Japanese coin-ops: Space Invaders became **Alien Invaders**, Pac-Man turned into **Cat Trax**, Phoenix was **Space Vultures**. Hanimex however did actually license eight official arcade games: **Turtles** and **Jungler** by Konami, **Red Clash** and **Pleiades** by Tehkan (later Tecmo) as well as Sega's **Happy Bug** (alias **Jump Bug**) which was the most diverse and best Hanimex cartridge.

Variants

Various	from 1982	The Emerson Arcadia 2001, released at the end of 1982 in the US, and the Japanese Bandai Arcadia (1983) were the best known of more than 20 Hanimex variants.
		Other manufacturers of compatible hardware in Europe were Intercord, Schmid, Palladium, Polybrain and Tchibo. Next to Hanimex, Rowtron was the second manufacturer to make HMG clones (Rowtron 2000 or MPT-03) after building Interton compatibles (around 1980).

Sinclair presented its colour successor to the ZX 81: Stripped down to the minimum – neither sound nor graphics chip, no joystick port and no proper keyboard – the Spectrum became England's most successful home computer.

Sinclair Spectrum

GB, 1982

Simultaneously to its rival C64, the Spectrum bestirred the second wave of home computers. Unlike the Commodore, Clive Sinclair's invention was a local phenomenon though. British gamers and developers loved the cheap and transparent hardware but on the continent, the Spectrum played a secondary role. Stateside, only a half-hearted attempt at marketing the Z80 based micro was started, while in Japan no one bothered.

After the first version was shipped with 16 K RAM, 1983 saw 48 K become the standard. CPU, memory and one expansion port on the back – no components to write home about. Instead of a professional keyboard the Spectrum only had tiny keys. Indeed, many users covered those rubbers with a new case containing a mechanical keyboard, and as the Spectrum lacked a joystick port, adapters became the most popular add-on.

To beef up the low-budget computer, little black boxes for various needs, including memory, sound and speech modules, popped up all over the place. Sinclair itself released two expansions: The Interface 1 was an adapter for the `Microdrive´ storage device, magnetic tapes with a capacity of 80 K. The Interface 2 provided the Spectrum

Units sold:	5 Million
Number of games:	2,000
Game storage:	Tape, Cartridge
Games developed until:	1992
★★★★	

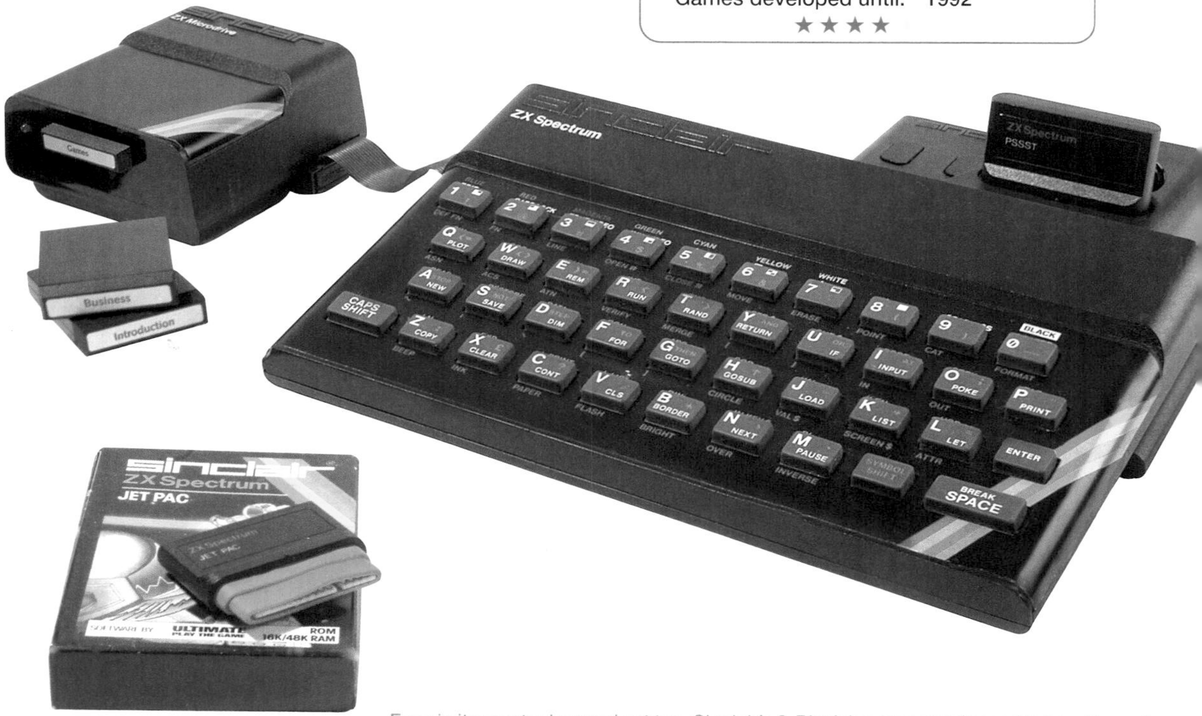

Even in its most advanced set tup, Sinclair's 8-Bit vision was smaller and lighter than other micros. Unlike the actual computer, the Interface 1 and mass storage device (left) were ignored. Only ten games appeared for the Interface 2 (cartridge and joystick ports), among them the tiny 16 K ROM versions of Jet Pac and PSSST – Rare's debut titles.

Named Plus, the Spectrum earned an improved keyboard. Two years later the +2 even featured RGB video output and a sound chip.

with two joystick ports and a slot for ROM cartridges. As neither met with significant success, conventional audiotape remained the main medium.

While Sinclair's storage decisions were ill-fated, its selection of software partners was excellent. Without dictating a strict third-party policy (like later console manufacturers did), Sinclair cleverly took the best developers under its wings and began selling games by Melbourne House (today the Australian part of Infogrames/Atari), ROM conversions of Chris and Tim Stamper's debut titles, and even imported Japanese software to Europe – tiny 10 K programs by a new company named Hudson.

Its closest partner (a `second-party´ according to today's standards), was Psion, founded by physicians David Potter and Charles Davis. David wrote Britain's premier **Flight Simulator** and, as development manager, produced the F1 simulation **Chequered Flag**, and a year later, **Match Point** tennis and **Psion Chess**. Davis took part in restructuring Psion when it became an early PDA developer; he is now a board member at Symbian.

In the USA and Germany, the Spectrum was bashed for missing graphics and sound chips but for the creative English coders, the minimalist components provided an advantage. Sprites and scrolling were hardware supported on other micros. Whereas C64 programmers followed their fixed routines, Spectrum game design had to be conceptualized and done from the scratch. The result was a tremendous gameplay and graphical variety:

The wireframe 3D of **Stargate** and **Dark Star** was followed in 1985 by the shaded polygons of Realtime's **Starstrike 2**. Isometric graphics were popular on the Spectrum too, and adventures with icon control as well as unusual strategy RPGs like Mike Singleton's epic **Lords of Midnight**. Experimental `interactive movies´ such as Automata's **Deus Ex Machina** or **Mugsy** by Melbourne House (1984) anticipated Cinemaware's subsequent Amiga games.

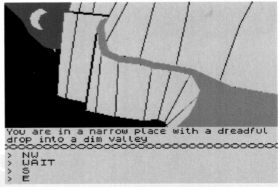

You are in a narrow place with a dreadful drop into a dim valley

> NW
> WAIT
> S
> E

Across the Misty Mountains: The drawings in The Hobbit adventure (shown above) looked charming and naive, much like J.R.R. Tolkien's own water paintings; its parser spoke Inglish. Not Tolkien-based, but influenced by his ring trilogy was Mike Singleton's masterpiece Lords of Midnight, shown left.

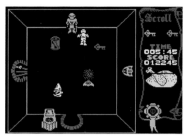

The simple hardware didn't force programmers to follow routine; but called for manifold game and graphic styles. From the left to the right: One of the 20 caverns in Manic Miner, the action adventure Atic Atac and Sandy White's bow to M.C.Escher, Ant Attack.

Spectrum games paved the way for the stars of the Amiga and PlayStation generation, for David Perry, the Gollop brothers (**Rebel Star Raiders**, later renowned for X-Com) and Steve Kelly, who became a Bitmap Brother in 1986. Melbourne House's design lead Phillip Mitchell unleashed a Tolkien boom among micro users, when he told **The Hobbit** as an illustrated adventure and invented 'Inglish' in the process – a smart parser to compete with Infocom's.

While coin-op conversions looked and played a sad part on the Spectrum, the best original games mixed fresh ideas and technical competence: Malcolm Evan's **Trashman** turned the Frogger concept into a human race through suburban gardens, David Reidy's **Skool Daze** was a satire on classroom situations. Early Britsoft was explicit, very eccentric and mostly funny.

Several hardware updates helped the Spectrum format into the '90s but the era of ingenious software had already faded by the mid '80s. After that, coin-op, C64 and even Amiga conversions appeared looking pretty paltry on the Spectrum. One of the last revolutionary Speccy games was the 3D adventure **Driller** in 1987, incorporating a massive 3D architecture that anticipated Ultima Underworld and Castle Wolfenstein 3D.

Amstrad built the last Spectrum with a solid keyboard and exotic 3" disk drive.

Spectrum variants and successors

Spectrum	1982	The two versions with 16 and 48 K were released shortly after each other and retailed for £125 and £175 respectively. The 16 K version was no longer marketed after 1984.
Timex TMS 2068	1983	The technically enhanced US licence retailed for $199 with a new case, cartridge port, two joystick ports and sound chip and wasn't compatible with European Spectrums. 20 games were released on tape, six on cartridge. The predecessors TS 2000 and 2048 were planned but never sold. In 1984, Timex stopped production.
Spectrum +	1984	The compatible successor in a new case and with an improved, QL-similar keyboard and (finally) a reset button, retailed for £180 and was bundled with six games and applications before the price was dropped in 1985.
Spectrum 128	1985	Released in Spain first, it arrived in 1986 in England (£180) and the rest of Europe. A split keypad was available separately. The prettiest Spectrum had 128 K RAM, RGB output, RS232 port and – at last – the well known sound chip AY-3-8912A.
Spectrum +2	1986	The new Sinclair owner Amstrad treated the Spectrum to a CPC-similar case with a better keyboard and integrated Datasette which retailed for £150. The 128 K machine had a combined RS232 and MIDI port, RGB, composite and RF output and two nine-pin, non-standard joystick ports.
Spectrum +3	1987	The new case with 3" floppy drive (173 K), 128 K RAM and AmsDOS in 64 K ROM shipped for £249 initially, but was reduced in price the same year.

Computing power for the Kingdom. An 8-Bit computer from
Cambridge prepared British youngsters for the digital era,
turning academics into game programmers in the process.

Acorn BBC B

GB, 1982

Units sold:	1 Million
Number of games:	200
Game storage:	Tape, Disk
Games developed until:	1990

★ ★ ★ ★ ★

Cambridge graduate Dr. Hermann Hauser founded his company, Acorn, in 1977 and is reckoned as a pioneer of British computing along with Sir Clive Sinclair. Hauser took on Sinclair's salesman Chris Curry and distributed computer DIY kits via mail order. He chose the MOS 6502 as CPU for his babies. The Atom was superseded in 1980 by the BBC, which derived its name and was advertised in cooperation with the broadcasting giant.

Professionally marketed, backed by the government, quality-built and easily expandable, the `Beeb´ established itself as a more serious alternative to the Spectrum. The higher price suggested a different target group, too, namely affluent users, schools and scientific institutions. The 16 K variant A retailed for £250, but was underpowered for most applications and games. The BBC B cost £100 more, had 32 K and better ports: It became the most popular model in the range and became standard at British schools. From 1983 on, it was heart of the educational `Econet´.

Owing to the Beeb's graphical capabilities, many games were released, including coin-op conversions like **Zalaga** by Nick Pelling and many original titles. In 1983, David Braben pushed the Beeb to its imits with **Elite**. This 3D space opera is one of the few rewarding cross-genre experiments.

Robert Schmidt compares to other micros on 'BBC Lives!': *The only thing missing was sprite graphics, and this is where BBC games lost out on some of their competitors. …*

this shift of emphasis resulted in a number of innovative, mathematically powered blockbuster games which started ... on the BBC, but were ported to most micros around.' Smith names Geoff Crammond's **Sentinel** and the **Aviator** and **Revs** simulations as examples. *'The BBC Micro had two very obvious advantages over most micros in the '80s. It had an Operating System ... and it had an inbuilt assembler'*, praised Gary Partis (beebgames.com). *'This allowed anyone to develop software for the BBC without much additional cost for development tools. I used it to develop games for the C64!'* Chris Roberts, the (later) ST specialist Peter Johnson and Reflections founder Martin Edmondson were all taught coding by the BBC B.

Physics and simulations were the Beep's field of specialisation. The last ingenious BBC game, Exile used the enhanced Master hardware to let particles fly in 1988.

Variants and successors

BBC A, B	1982	Fast CPU, three channel sound and neat ports in a sturdy case. The A had 16 K of RAM, the more successful B model 32 K. The maximum resolution was 640x256 pixels. In 1985, the BBC+ was released with 64 or 128 K. Production was stopped in 1986.
Acorn Electron	1983	The Electron had a new case and a CPU clocked at 1 MHz. It retailed for £200 in August and established itself as a cheap alternative despite weak graphics and sound and missing ports. Before Olivetti dropped home computers in 1986, BBC games were often accompanied by simplified Electron versions, in the beginning even on cartridge for the Plus-1 adapter.
BBC B Master	1986	The last series had 512 K RAM, expanded BASIC, improved graphics, a second 6502 CPU (Master Turbo) or an additional 32-Bit processor (Master Scientific). Other variants were the Master ET online-terminal and the last model, the Master Compact with a 3.5" floppy in a desktop case.

Last, but not least: Five years after the Apple II and three years after the Atari, Commodore released the middle class computer C64. With its sprites, scrolling and the sound beast SID, the C64 ploughed through the market, unfolding as a success story.

C64

USA, 1982

"CAPTAIN, WE'VE CAPTURED
COUNT DE TOLEDO AND
A 6 GUN PINNACE
OF 20 TONS. WE HAVE
SPACE FOR 79 TONS IN THE
HOLD. SHALL WE KEEP HER?"
YES, SEND A PRIZE CREW
NO, PLUNDER AND SINK HER

When Commodore demonstrated the successor to the cheap and million-selling VC 20, its games reputation was still negligible. Programmers and gamers disapproved, with Apple and Atari veterans in particular criticising the C64 technology and distrusting Commodore's marketing strategy. But in spite of the huge software libraries of Atari and Apple, the C64 quickly established itself – especially in the gaming sector.

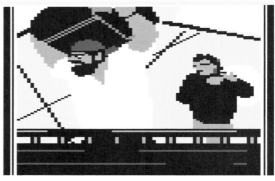

Romantic high sea travels and artillery duels in real-time: Without the map (shipped within each Pirates! box) you were lost.

commodore
64
POWER

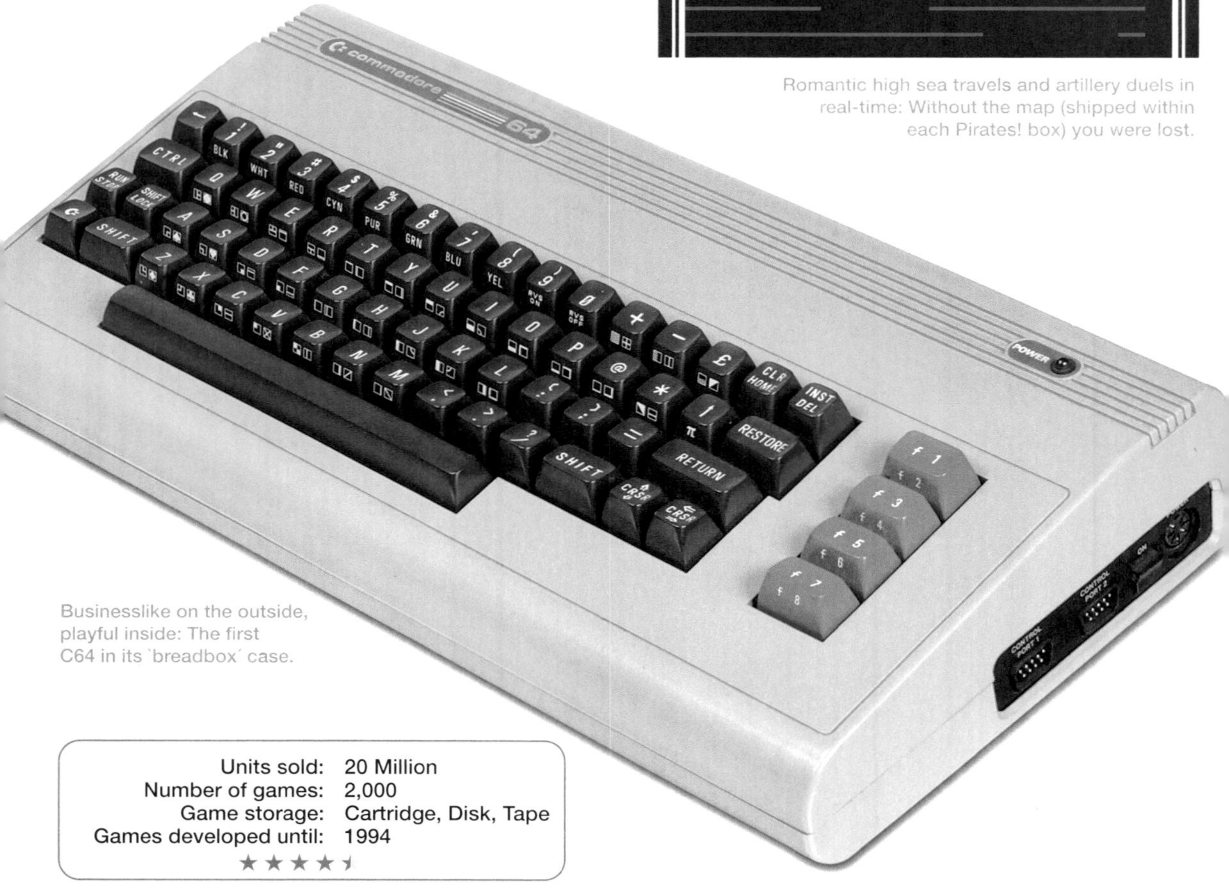

Businesslike on the outside, playful inside: The first C64 in its 'breadbox' case.

Units sold:	20 Million
Number of games:	2,000
Game storage:	Cartridge, Disk, Tape
Games developed until:	1994

★★★★½

The 1541 floppy drive for double-sided disks was quite slow and retailed for £300 or more, yet quickly became the fave storage for C64 gamers, crackers and developers.

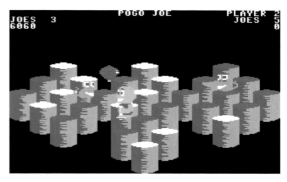

Cute sprites, smooth shaded pillars and multi-channel sound effects: Pogo Joe (1983).

Commodore chose to save budget on the CPU and used a 6502-related chip by Commodore's subsidiary MOS, but treated the C64 to graphics and sound chips that were more powerful than the competition. Sprites, hardware scrolling, an exquisitely programmable 3-channel sound generator, cartridge and two joystick ports: The home computer bowed to all the desires of creative and playful users. The 1541 disk drive was expensive at first and not particularly fast, but became a must-have, as most software developers picked the 170 K floppy instead of tapes or cartridge ROMs.

The C64 won the race against Atari 800 and Apple II: 'America's fastest selling home computer reached one million US homes in its first year', wrote Electronic Games magazine in 1984. Access and Accolade were the first companies to dedicate themselves to the C64 – and Microprose, Electronic Arts and Origin also changed their priorities. **Ultima**, **Bard's Tale**, **Archon**, **Fort Apocalypse** – classic Apple and Atari software became known outside the US thanks to C64 conversions.

Which was the best micro for games? Epyx programmer and **Jumpman** inventor Randy Glover answered this question in January 1984, in Electronic Fun magazine: 'I admit: The Commodore 64. I don't like it nearly as much as the Atari, but it's got many nice features.' He meant it was straightforward to program, making it easy for experienced coders to move to the C64 while simultaneously bringing on a new breed of game developers. The amateur scene turned out to be a blessing and curse at the same time: Especially in Europe, the boundaries blurred between

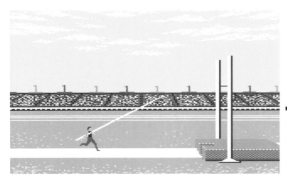

Great animation and national anthems performed by the SID-chip: Summer Games by Epyx was the champ of 8-Bit sports.

Adventure games took no advantage of sprites and scrolling: Interplay's Borrowed Time looked a lot like on the old Apple 2.

Snobs and hackers relied on the SX 64. The screen is small, but displays graphics and text perfectly. The cartridge port holds International Soccer.

creative users programming their own graphics and sound demos and the malicious crackers that copied whatever they got their hands on. The evil of the industry saw `cracking´ as a kind of sport or science, not as data theft.

Stateside, game development and marketing had already reached a professional level prior to the C64. Academics wrote software, which was sold aplenty by visionaries like Trip Hawkins (Electronic Arts), Ken Williams (Sierra) or Harvard graduate Doug Carlston (Brøderbund). In the European development countries Germany, Spain, Scandinavia and Benelux, professional structures and ties to Silicon Valley were missing. Consequently, a plethora of software came from the underground.

Only in the UK did an industry with long-term experience, its own trade shows and professional press exist. As local platforms by Acorn and Sinclair survived as alternatives to the C64 into the '90s, the few British Commodore specialists became world renowned: Andrew Braybrook

dropped his Dragon 32 to do six C64 games before 1988, including the clever **Paradroid** and the technically and graphically exceptional horizontal scrolling **Uridium**. The eccentric Jeff Minter moved from VC 20 to the C64 to develop fast and furious Defender and Centipede clones featuring sheeps and Llamas, as well as inventing the colour

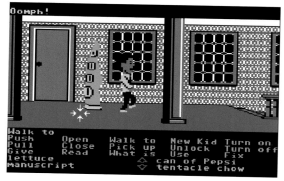

For the C64, LucasArts released funny adventures like Maniac Mansion and founded the first online community Habitat.

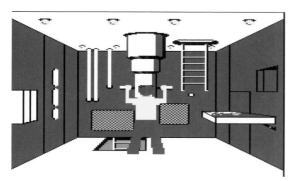

Most strategy and simulation experts did their training and first mission an a C64: Silent Service by Sid Meier, 1985.

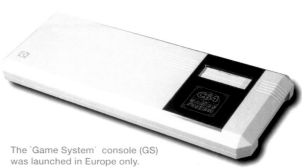

The `Game System´ console (GS) was launched in Europe only.

synthesizer **Psychedelia**. And Anthony Crowther turned out to be the most diligent and prominent C64 programmer, creating 20 games including several jump 'n runs starring **Blagger** and **Monty Mole**.

At first, game soundtrack and effects were done by gifted programmers. But because the SID chip was more flexible and powerful than the sound generators of other machines, creative users began specializing in C64 music and took this task off the main designers' hands. Rob Hubbard was the first star of the 8-Bit music scene, composing virtuous melodies that turned three channels into a twelve-headed orchestra; the SID maestro later became sound boss at EA. In Manchester, Martin Galway arranged sounds for conversions of Japanese coin-ops – in many cases, his samples and tunes were the only highlights of Ocean's dull mass-produced games.

Hubbard, Galway and Co. were inspired by electro pop musicians like Thomas Dolby, Tangerine Dream and Jean-Michel Jarre, and soundtracks by Georgio Moroder, Phillip Glass or Jerry Goldsmith, while they themselves became idols of for the second generation of C64 musicians. Jeroen Tel (alias Maniacs of Noise) bridged the gap between videogame sound and '80's dancefloor.

Whereas the Commodore scene still flourished in Europe in early '90s, stateside, IBM compatible computers put a sudden end to the 8-Bit era in the late '80s. The C64 made its biggest mark in an area it is not normally associated with: The C64 network Quantum Link was later renamed AOL, its online experiment **Habitat** (developed by LucasArts for Quantum Link, enhanced by Fujitsu in Japan) heralded a watershed for virtual net communities. The first avatars were American C64 users.

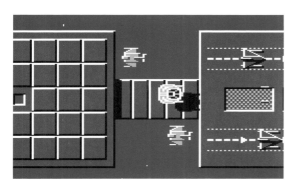

Andrew Braybrook became Europe's most talented C64-developer. Shown here is his chart-topping Uridium (1986).

Melbourne House's Way of the Exploding Fist was an excellent beat 'em up.

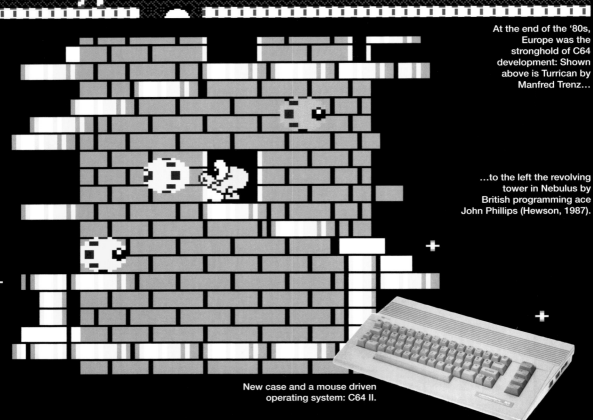

At the end of the '80s, Europe was the stronghold of C64 development: Shown above is Turrican by Manfred Trenz...

...to the left the revolving tower in Nebulus by British programming ace John Phillips (Hewson, 1987).

New case and a mouse driven operating system: C64 II.

C64 variants and successors

C64	1982	The first C64 looked like a brownish VC 20. It retailed for an initial $595 in the US, £350 in the UK and quickly became a classic. Most users bought a 1541 for fast game access.
Maxmachine	1982	The technical transition model from VC 20 to the C64 was sold mainly in Japan, in Europe as the VC 10 and announced in the States as Ultimax. Instead of a professional mechanical keyboard, it had 66 membrane keys, only 4 K RAM, no multi-colour mode, and neither a serial nor User-port. Connecting a floppy drive was not possible, BASIC was available on cartridge.
C64 SX	1983	Retailed for $995, the C64 with built-in screen was a dream-come-portable. The lid doubles as mechanical keyboard, the handle becomes the stand for a posh desktop computer. Disk drive, cartridge port and two joystick ports were standard with this games compatible portable computer. A power lead is all that's needed.
C128	1985	The high-end C64 in a new case had a second processor (Z80), disk drive and improved BASIC. Despite CP/M, manifold ports and a good text mode, the C128 was never accepted by office users. The model D was an elegant desktop version with separate keyboard and built-in disk drive which looked a bit like the Amiga 1000.
Gold Edition	1986	To celebrate one million units sold, a `golden´ C64 appeared at the Consumer Electronics Show (CES) in 1984. Two years later, a similar machine was presented at the German CeBit show. The golden `breadboxes´ were limited and numbered and boasted an acrylic plate with the words: 'To celebrate 1,000,000 C64s in Germany 5th December 1986'.
C64 II	1986	The C64 successor had identical ports, operating system and chipset, yet presented itself in a slimmer, C128-inspired case. An alternative to the operating system was the mouse driven GEOS. Also known as C64 C.
C64 G	1987	Internal update (smaller board, identical power) inside the original `breadbox´ case. Brighter colour, white keyboard.
C64 GS	1990	The keyboard-less console retailed for £100 in the UK. Internally identical to the computer version, it lacked serial, user and Datasette interfaces. Software companies supported the system with ROM cartridges only for a short time.

Half TV game, half hobby micro, this creative hybrid from the Far East arrived at just the right time – to be smashed under the weight of the console crash.

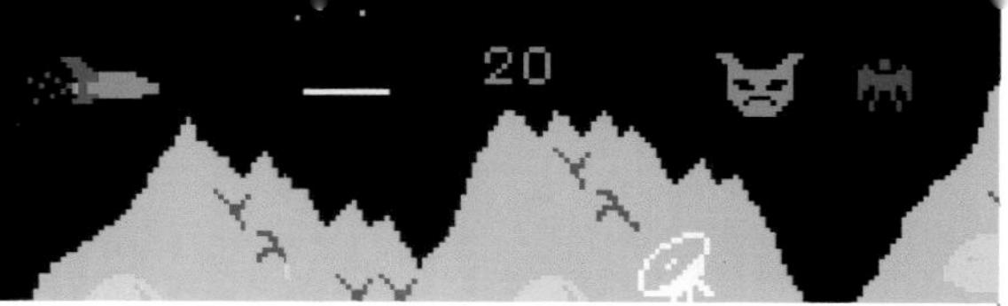

VTech Creativision

Hongkong, 1983

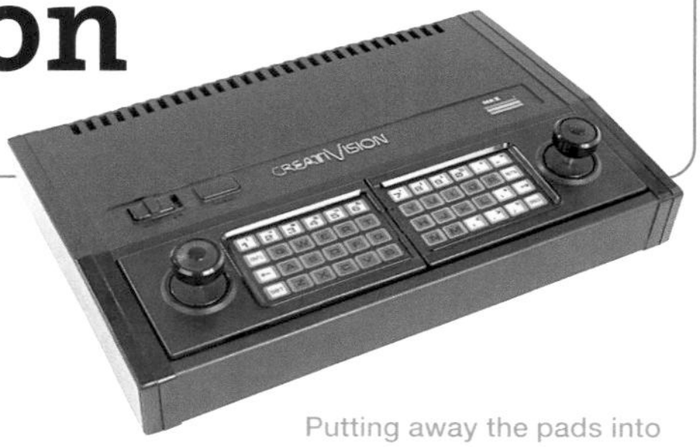

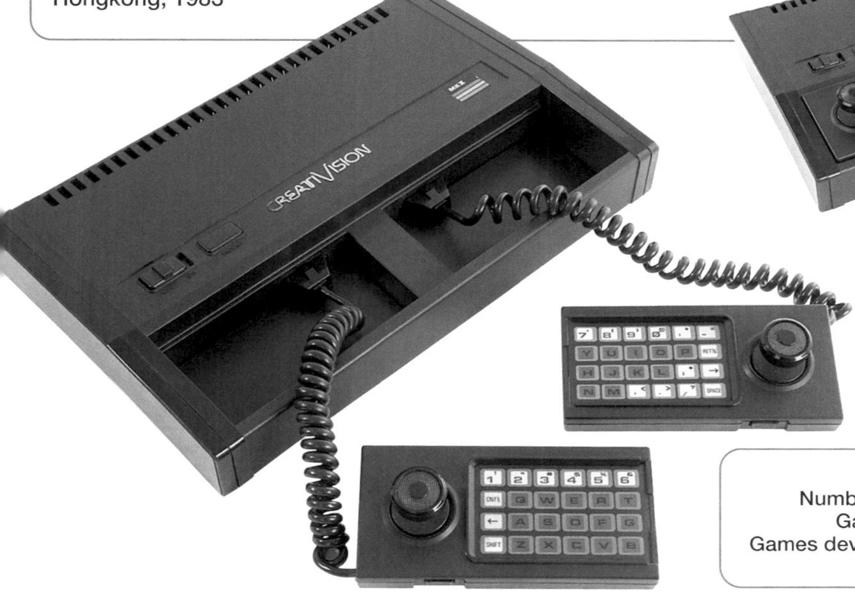

Putting away the pads into the case turned the TV game into a computer – the pads formed an alphanumerical keyboard.

Units sold:	Unknown
Number of games:	20
Game storage:	Cartridge, Tape
Games developed until:	1984

★½

At the beginning of the '80s, the gaming world was divided into east and west, and Asian computers and consoles stood little chance against the machines from Atari, Commodore and Amstrad in Europe and North America. The time had not yet come for the global breakthrough of Nintendo and Sega.

The first eastern consoles surfaced in 1983, in smaller quantities and with slender advertising. They arrived just in time for the great crash. VTech, founded in 1978 in Hong Kong as a home computer developer, did just that, being hit directly by the fall of the industry whilst launching its machine in Europe. The Creativision was announced, presented at shows and for the press and then vanished into thin air.

It wasn't ugly or simple though. On the contrary, the two Colecovision-inspired controllers fitted in the base unit to form a cute membrane keyboard. Indeed the Creativision posed as a compact computer with add-ons like the Datasette matching form and colour, and BASIC available as a 12 K cartridge. You could also impose a larger rubber keyboard on the Creativision case.

As to its exterior, the Creativision and its peripherals seemed down-to-earth and well designed. Had it not arrived as late as 1984, it would have had some technical merits to boot: Its CPU was technically similar to that of the NES, and its chips and capabilities were used by the Z80-contemporaries Colecovision, MSX and the first Sega consoles.

As the Creativision was not compatible with any of these machines though, the software on offer was limited. There were clones of games like Pac-Man (**Crazy Chicky**), Space Invaders (**Sonic Invader**) and Donkey Kong (**Police Jump**), the Combat-clone **Tank Attack** (with a river landscape and foliage shadows), and the innovative (if pretty useless) **Music Maker**. Nope, good, original concepts it had not.

Computer variant

Laser 2001	**1983**	Sanyo distributed this home computer with Z80 CPU, two 16 K RAMs and a mechanical keyboard in Europe. It was cartridge and tape compatible with the Creativision (which was also marketed as the Laser 500). An adapter for Colecovision games was shown in 1984, but probably never shipped.

Atari celebrated the video game rush with a deluxe VCS successor and it wasn't taking half-measures. The `SuperSystem´ contained everything gamers dreamed of, but lacked compatibility with other Atari formats.

Atari 5200

USA, 1982

Units sold:	Unknown
Number of games:	70
Game storage:	Cartridge
Games developed until:	1986

★ ★ ★ ★ ★

Technically and aesthetically, Atari's biggest console had the potential to become a bestseller. When not being used, the two controllers were deposited beneath a flap over the rear part of the machine.

A noble among common consoles: After a prosaic VCS generated sales of many millions, Atari showed off with the glamorous super console 5200. The third generation games machine was based on Atari's micros and technically identical to the Atari 800 and XL – computers that were considered to be state of the art by gamers.

On the exterior, the 5200 outdid all competition: Two controllers were hidden behind a black flap while the four metre RF cable was rolled around a cable bracket on the underside of the machine. The Atari logo and power switch were the only asymmetrical elements within the clear black and silver design.

Space Dungeon was 5200-exclusive and came with an adapter that connected two pads to form a twin-stick.

The 5200 conversion of Gremlins was well done, but delayed two years until 1986.

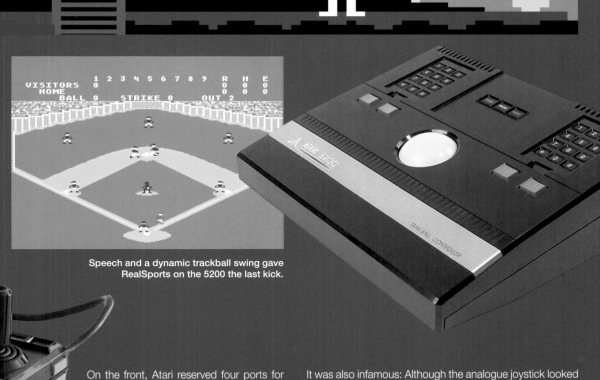

Speech and a dynamic trackball swing gave
RealSports on the 5200 the last kick.

On the front, Atari reserved four ports for the controllers: Multiplayer as a standard feature. Later machines only had two ports.

The controllers were partly responsible for Atari's misfortune: By not implementing 9-pin ports (which would have allowed for controller exchange between other Atari and Commodore machines) but instead wider 15-pin ports, gamers were forced to use the new joypad. Start, pause and reset buttons were positioned above the short stick, a number pad with four by three keys beneath. Two red thumb buttons on each side served as fire. The stick and 19 buttons in total made the 5200 pad the most complex controller in 8-Bit days.

It was also infamous: Although the analogue joystick looked pretty cool with its rubber casing, it didn't work very well. In practice, it was a catastrophe: Games that demanded precise control ended in frustration for many gamers – to get **Pac-Man** munching for instance, you'd need to always centre the stick manually instead of just tapping in the right direction. That stressed out both player and controller. By the time you got used to the pad, it was usually already in tatters.

Neither brilliant arcade conversions (**Berzerk**, **Defender**, **Gyruss**), nor well-known originals like **Ballblazer** and **Rescue on Fractalus** by Lucasfilm, could stop the 5200's demise. As early as 1984 the machine had been replaced by the (just as ill-fated) Atari 7800. Some 70 cartridges appeared for the 5200, nearly half of them by third-parties Activision, CBS, Parker and Sega.

A dream come true: By order of George Lucas, computer scientists and Atari engineers developed interactive science fiction. In 1982, Loren Carpenter implemented realtime anti-aliasing. To smoothen irritating `jaggies´, Ballblazer interpolated between edging pixels.

Sharp X1

Japan, 1982

Units sold:	Unknown
Number of games:	500
Game storage:	Tape, Disk
Games developed until:	1989

★ ★ ★ ♪

The X1 had the full RPG and adventures, sports and strategy treatment, but also boasted the...

...complete range of action and shooting by Konami, Namco and even Nintendo. Shown above is the X1 port of Nemesis

Sharp's multimedia range X1 was related to the MZ but wasn't compatible and wasn't sold outside of Japan. The hobby computers were housed in nice red, white or metallic cases and featured the technical specs of the MZ-2000 (Z80, 64 K RAM, 620x200 resolution graphics) plus AV capabilities that were missing in the expensive office variant:

The three-channel sound chip AY-3-8912A, sprites thanks to programmable character generation (PCG), as well as up to 48 K Video RAM. X1 computers connected to RGB monitors and NTSC TV screens and could be upgraded with an additional `Image Board´ for analogue video digitisation in 3-Bits (8 colours).

Sharp brought its computers up to a par with the current games technology. The CZ-801C shown here was shipped as the second X1 in October 1983 and could be expanded with a plotter.

X1 computers were sold in one case or, shown here, with a separate keyboard. This model was also available in red or with floppy drives instead of the internal Datasette.

In Japan, the range was up against MSX, FM-7 and the NEC PCs, which established themselves as market leaders and dominated the scene into the '90s. In the mid '80s, the systems were still nearly equal, and popular 8-Bit games like Falcom's **Legend of Xanadu**, Enix's early **Door Door** and the RPG **Black Onyx** were released for all platforms.

As usual, Sharp's closest ally was Hudson, providing most software and helping Sharp take its next step in the late '80s, when the two companies dropped the X1 and moved on to the 16-Bit X68000. The old Z80 wasn't dumped, but used by Sharp for another decade. Sharp shipped millions to Nintendo alone, as CPUs for the Game Boy.

Variants and successors

X1	1982	Until 1987, Sharp sold computers for between 200,000 yen (for the first floppy model X1D in October 1983) and 70,000 yen (for the Datasette equipped model 10 in July 1986). The last variant was the mini-tower X1 Twin with integrated PC-Engine and HuCard slot, shown to the right.
X1 Turbo	1984	The successors had 48 to 64 K RAM as standard, as well as improved graphics and accelerated VRAM. Apart from the entry model 10, all Turbos (20, 30, 40) came with one or two 5" floppy drives with 320 K capacity. Replaced by the Turbo II in December 1985 and Turbo II in 1986.
X1 TurboZ	1986	The three final models utilised a 12-Bit colour palette (4096 colours) and the stereo sound of the X68000; the YM2151 chip with eight FMchannels was also available as a sound card for older X1micros. With 128 K RAM, the TurboZ retailed for 170,000 to 220,000 yen.

There was no room for yet another home computer in the kingdom.
The small Oric leaped across the channel, sparking off the 8-Bit development in France.

Oric-1

GB, 1983

Units sold:	350,000
Number of games:	200
Game storage:	Tape
Games developed until:	1985

★ ★ ★ ★ ★

This white and blue BASIC micro was small, flat and with its miniature keys, aimed at the cheap home computer end of the market, like the Sinclair Spectrum. The Oric-1 was also technically similar to its local rival, initially shipped with 16, later with 48 K of memory. It lacked sprites but featured the 3-channel sound chip AY3-8912 and even RGB output. The CPU was the tried and tested MOS chip 6502A, clocked at a rather tame 1 MHz.

There was no need for a further 8-Bit platform in the UK, but the gold rush mentality of 1983 still helped the sell-through of 100,000 hastily manufactured and badly marketed units. Just like the Dragon 32, the Oric-1 enjoyed a year of support by British developers. Twenty companies, including Tansoft, Softek, PSS and Virgin programmed clones of Pac-Man, Galaxian and Manic Miner, followed by a few Spectrum and

BBC conversions, before things came to a halt. Oric replaced the slim version with the black and red Oric Atmos, but few cared: The small scene had long moved across the channel to France, gaining minor momentum in the process. Roughly half of all Orics were sold in France.

And so, in spite of its short career and minuscule hardware, plenty of new software was released in 1984 – more than 100 games in fact. A glance at the Oric software reveals tapes by Infogrames and Ere Informatique (later called Cryo) – the roots of the French software industry. Puns in software titles were en vogue: History software was called **Historic**, diet software served as **Caloric**.

The most diligent developer was Loriciel, which published dictionary, graphic tools, Logo and a French BASIC. Many

Flat, light and with
little calculator keys:
The Oric-1 was designed
with the Sinclair
Spectrum in mind.

SCORE 005480   HI-SCORE 000500

Night Boat
AIR
SCREEN 08

Appuyez sur une touche

After the first wave of shooting games and clones of Manic Miner, French developers showed their talents...

...and their proximity to a strong national comic industry with gory graphic adventures.

Of the young amateurs who created games for Loriciel went on to later influence the industry. Titus founder Eric Caen programmed the Oric, just as Eric Chahi did, who was later responsible for the renowned 16-Bit adventures Another World and Heart of Darkness. The result was breath of fresh air for all types of games: French programmers developed Jules Verne and Arsene Lupin inspired games, yacht and sailing simulations, Carlo Perconti's culinary **Gastronen** and even **Don Juan**, the first flirt simulation.

Most games were adventures: Interactive books often bearing Maudite or Meurtre in their titles, testing various graphical methods like font icons (**Détective Story** by No Man's Land), painted portraits in comic panels (**Cobra's Meurtre à Grande Vitesse**), but mainly vector-based illustrations (such as **La Cité Maudite**). Themes like murder, thrills and buried treasures laid the foundation for Cruise for a Corpse and Alone in the Dark.

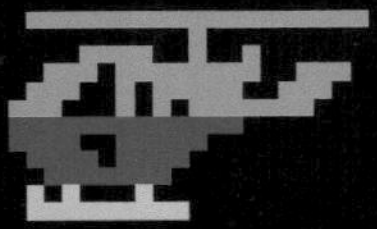

The Atmos had the exact same technology, size and shape as the Oric-1, but a proper keyboard and an improved operating system in ROM.

The Successor

| Oric Atmos | 1984 | The Atmos came in a racy black and red case and utilised a professional typewriter style keyboard. It was marketed mainly in the UK and France and just like its predecessor, for a short while in the rest of Europe. |

One operating system for all. Japanese entrepreneur Kai Nishi teamed up with young
Bill Gates to develop a multimedia standard. Sony, Mitsubishi and other electronics giants
followed their 8-Bit initiative, but MSX failed in the western hemisphere.

MSX

Japan, 1983

Units sold:	Unknown
Number of games:	1,400
Game storage:	Cartridge, Disk, Tape, LD, Card
Games developed until:	1992

★ ★ ★ ★ ↲

HitBit micros were Sony's first game machines.

Pace setter in the race to the British market:
The 64 K Toshiba HX-10 appeared as part
of the initial MSX wave in 1984.

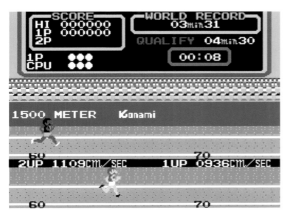

Many quality conversions of well-known arcade games made it to the MSX: Track & Field from 1984.

[女の子] フローラおねえちゃん！ そんなヤツにけんしさまなんて・・・。もしかして、あぶないヤツかもしれないのに・・・

In Japan, disk adventures and RPGs often displayed a scantily clad cast. Shown here is the PC-88 port X'na.

Ten years before Windows set a course for world domination, the market was devoid of a clear structure. A dozen different systems retailing for less than a thousand dollars cluttered the shelves. In 1982, entrepreneur Kai Nishi, founder of Japanese Microsoft distributor ASCII, embarked on a mission to cleanse the chaotic marketplace and to make home computers compatible with each other. Together with Microsoft, he laid down the specs and – based on MS BASIC 4.5 – developed a common operating system for the last 8-Bit generation, landing support from significant Japanese electronics manufacturers. On 16th July 1983, Nishi and Gates made their announcement: Sony, Yamaha, Mitsubishi, Sanyo and eleven other companies were to produce and market the hardware, with ASCII and Microsoft providing the operating system.

Home users, not professionals, purchasing at the lower price points were the target group for MSX. The compact computers had a keyboard with separate cursor pad, two joystick ports and two cartridge slots – ideal for gamers. Right from 1984, Konami converted a dozen arcade games, including the adorable penguin game **Antarctic Adventure** and shoot 'em up hits **Super Contra** and **Time Pilot**. Apart

from ASCII and Konami, developers Namco, HAL, Hudson and Takara published MSX games. Sony too joined the trend: With **Computer Billiards** and **Super Soccer**, the Walkman inventor made its first steps within the computer entertainment sector.

In autumn 1983, Panasonic rolled out the MSX onto the shelves. Before the end of 1984, 20 models by other manufacturers followed on its heels. All MSX computers were based on the Z80 CPU, used the TMS-9918 (or the 9928 and 9929) for graphics and the GI AY-3-8910 chip for sound.

With these tried and tested components (dated, according to detractors), the MSX was a close relative to Colecovision and Sega consoles – but not compatible with them. Memory was a minimum of 8 K, but most MSX machines shipped with either 32 or 64 K. All models featured a Centronics parallel port (for a printer).

A Chinese Fist Story:
Yie Ar Kung Fu featured bizarre enemies.

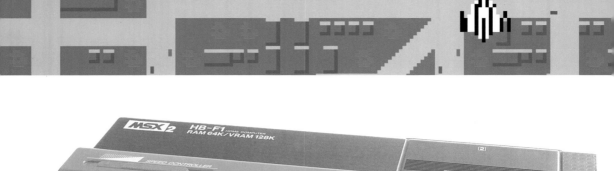

Machines of the second generation held more memory:
Apart from the main RAM, each MSX2 micro featured 128 K of VideoRAM.

Interestingly, the various MSX machines had their individual specialisations: The Sanyo Wavy came bundled with a light pen, whilst the PHC 30 featured an integrated Datasette instead of the second cartridge port. Sound specialist Yamaha released the computer with synthesizer cartridge and a port for an external music keyboard. Pioneer on the other hand, focused on video and treated the MSX to 'Superimposing', a technique of mixing computer graphics with a video signal. Much like Genlock did years later with

COMIC BAKERY ©KONAMI 1984

MSX is based on the same CPU as the Spectrum, but had dedicated ICs for animation, scrolling and sound.

the Commodore Amiga, superimposing bridged video editing with digital effects. Panasonic's computers were compatible with Laserdisc players and played the LD arcade games by Sega (**Astron Belt**) and Konami (**Badlands**).

These companies also provided the add-ons: Konami released the Hypershot controller exclusively for the button-killer **Track & Field** and a link cable for the MSX-2 game **F1 Spirit 3D**; HAL shipped a mouse, trackball and handy scanner; Panasonic a steering wheel cockpit. Hudson offered, among other things, an adapter for its own Bee Cards. The flat storage media were used by a handful of games and eventually turned into the famous HuCard for the PC-Engine.

While the MSX had penetrated the market in Japan, poor coordination and product delays hindered its success in the west. MSX Producers cared little for the US market (Spectravideo was the only American company to participate in the standard), Microsoft didn't make a move and only Activision developed a few games in 1983. In the UK, the 'MSX Working Group' (Canon, JVC, Hitachi,

Konami heroes made MSX users smile,
sweat and freeze at the same time:
Antarctic Adventure.

Sanyo PHC-28P,
a late computer of the
first MSX generation.

Mitsubishi, Sanyo, Sony and Toshiba) coordinated marketing and supported developers with hardware and technical information from early 1984 onwards. British software companies like Gremlin, Firebird and Mastertronic converted over 100 Spectrum and C64 games for MSX, although they didn't bother with original titles.

While the European market shifted from C64 to 16-Bit, there was no room for the 8-Bit machines from Japan. The most enduring scene turned out to be in Holland – Philips produced and sold hardware and add-ons right until the end of the '80s. In Spain and South America too, the MSX was widely spread.

In Japan the backward compatible MSX 2 were introduced, professional looking desktops with separate keyboard, new CPU, larger RAM and 128 K video memory. Instead of a tape deck, the units came with one or two drives for Sony's

new 3.5" floppies which were used in 1981 for the first time in a 'Typecorder', a year later for the CP/M editing computer SMC-70 and finally in 1983 as external HitBit storage media. In western countries, 16-Bit computers by Apple, Atari and Commodore established this drive.

The computer standard finally culminated in the MSX 2+ (1988, produced only by Panasonic, Sanyo and Sony) and the MSX 2 TurboR (1990, Panasonic).

Sound-wise, the hobby machines were competitive thanks to chips by Yamaha – like the FM synthesizers YM2151 and YM2413 (also known as MSX Music and featured inside the Japanese Sega Master System) and the Y8950 MSX-Audio – which provided the Panasonic FS-CA1, Toshiba HX-MU900 and Philips NMS-1205 with an additional 8-Bit ADPCM channel. The 24-voice Wavetable chip YMF278, known as Moon Sound card, was standard with the TurboR

Panasonic stayed loyal right into the '90s: The MSX2 micro
FS-A1 with integrated disk drive is shown left. To the right: A mighty
TurboR model with 256 or 512 K RAM, 128 K VRAM and digi sound.

computers. Konami used its own 5 channel sound generator for **Gradius 2** and **Snatcher**.

For Kai Nishi and for Japanese game developers and hardware suppliers like Yamaha, the MSX was a success story. But it was only a footnote in the history of American partner Microsoft. Armed with this experience, Bill Gates withdrew from the MSX in the mid-'80s, setting his sights on conquering the offices instead of the games market. It took more than a decade for Microsoft to return: Not with MSX but DirectX and the Xbox.

As the only European MSX manufacturer, Philips sold computers and peripherals until the end of the '80s.

MSX manufacturers and variants

Casio	With peripherals, games and affordable computers, Casio was an early MSX supplier. Machines like the PV-7 and the PV-16 were also shipped in Europe: featuring a cheap keyboard, only 16 K memory. Black or white case.
Daewoo	Approximately 10 Korean MSX 1 and 2 variants were sold in Europe through Yeno. From 1989, Daewoo and subsidiary Dyndata also produced three 'Zemmix' – game consoles without keyboard or computer-ports: The rounded model CPC-50 (blue/yellow, white/pink, bright blue/pink colour combinations) and the futuristic looking CPC-51 in red, black and white. The blocky CPC-61 console was based on the MSX 2, available in several colours. In Europe, neither the consoles, nor the add-ons (keyboard, memory expansion, joysticks) were available.
Hitachi	The Japanese electronics and chip conglomerate released six MSX machines as well as printer, disk drive and other peripherals. The small MB-H1 Hint had a pull-out carrying handle, the MB-H2 came with a built-in tape recorder, the MB-H3 with two times 64 K RAM.
JVC	This manufacturer sold multiple MSX machines from the beginning, featuring RGB output and Superimposing (eg. HC-7). From 1985, three MSX 2 computers followed: HC-80, HC-90 and the dual-CPU flagship HC-95, retailed for 200,000 yen.
Mitsubishi	After ten MSX 1 variants with between 16 and 64 K of RAM (the MLF-48 (48 K) and MLF-80 (64 K) at the end of 1984), Mitsubishi shipped several MSX 2 machines. The ML-G1 had a built-in drawing program, the G3 a 3.5" drive. Other machines were: G10, G30, H70.
Panasonic	The Matsushita subsidiary produced (among others) the CF-2700 (in Europe with 64 K RAM and 16 K VRAM) and – Japan only – the FS-3900 with built-in word processing and thermal printer. In 1985, came nine MSX 2 machines (FS-A1 series), including the A1Mk2 with numerical keypad above the cursor keys and bundled joypad, as well as the Floppy equipped models A1F and A1FM. The MSX 2+ models FX and WX (which were released near the end of the '80s) had a CPU that could be switched to 6 MHz, as well as the WSX which also had an S-Video output. Panasonic became the last MSX manufacturer, ending the series with its TurboR computers FS-A1GT and ST.
Philips	The only European MSX manufacturer delivered the VG-8010 (rubber keyboard) and the VG-8020 (mechanical typewriter keyboard). Philips sold an external 3.5" floppy already in 1984 and after 1985, released seven MSX 2 computers with separated keyboard and one or two disk drives. The NMS-8280 also featured Superimposing and video digitising. Peripherals were: Monitors, joysticks, memory and slot expansions, RS-232C port, printer and graphics tablet.
Pioneer	Optical media specialist Pioneer produced a computer with Laserdisc connectivity and Superimposing as early as 1984. The PX-7 was also the first MSX computer with a separate keyboard and professional look, which thanks to the respective connections, was useful if you had other audio and video equipment. In Japan, the unit was bright with a blue keyboard whilst the 1985 released UK machine was completely black. The PX-V60 variant had 64 K.

Sanyo

Sanyo was a diligent MSX manufacturer producing over 20 different machines. The first series (MPC-1 to 5) was sold in Japan, branded as Wavy. The MPC-2 (Wavy 2) had an unusual, asymmetrical case form, the Wavy 10 included a light pen. In Europe, Sanyo released the 64 K models MPC-64 and MPC-100, further MSX machines were the 200, X (improved graphics, 80 K VRAM as well as frame grabber, light pen and speech synthesis), and five PHC variants. The Wavy 23 was based on MSX 2 (case similar to the Wavy 2 but the keyboard had a numerical pad), as was the Wavy 77 with built-in printer and either 360 K or 720 K drive. The biggest model of the 1988 introduced MSX 2+ series was the Wavy 70 FD2 with two drives and two cart slots.

Sony

The Japanese electronics manufacturer gained computer experience with peripherals, software and more than 20 MSX machines. The first model HB-10 appeared in Japan only, while later HitBit computers like the HB-20 and the HB-75 (built-in address and schedule databank) were also available in Europe. The successors 101 and 201 had a rounded recession for a miniature joystick positioned in between the cursor keys and a pull-out handle. The HB-501 also had a Datasette. The MSX 1 machines with separate keyboard and integrated drive (500, 700) were rare. Most Sony versions were MSX 2 compliant: Various HB-F models, with up to 256 K RAM,128 K VRAM, two 720 K 3.5" drives, separate keyboard, built-in speakers and Superimposing. The HB-G900 had a port for modem and LD player, two models came with online-capability as standard. The MSX 2+ computer HB-F1XV ended Sony's involvement.

Spectravideo

After incompatible Z80 computers, the only American MSX manufacturer produced the SVI-728. This and the well-featured successor SVI-738 (360 K floppy, two joystick ports) were also sold in Europe.

Toshiba

At the end of 1984, the MSX 1 computers from the HX-10 Pasopia series were shipped with a maximum of 64 K RAM in Europe, just like the HX-20, with its built-in word processing software. The HX-20e variant of this machine had an RS-232C port, the HX-22 came with text-editor in ROM and an RGB output. Other variants were the HX-30, 31, 32 and 51. The HX-23 was an MSX 2 computer, the 33 and 34 variant in its desktop design and with a separate keyboard were updates.

Yamaha

The MSX computer series CX5M were music-machines and so even sold well in the US. Yamaha delivered three versions with the music expansion SFG-01, FM synthesizer, MIDI port and music keyboard connection. Sound tools came on cartridge. Several of Yamaha's 20 MSX 1 and MSX 2 machines had a music keyboard port, but only one cartridge port, the 'Music System' YIS-502 for example. The expansion could be connected to other computers via an adapter.

Other manufacturers

Canon, Dragon (64 K MSX 1 for the Spanish market), Fujitsu (FM-X with a port for FM-7 computers), General (three Paxon MSX 1 computers, two of which had RGB, one was a combination of computer and TV set with separate keyboard), NTT ('Captain Multi-Station', a MSX micro with 192 K + 128 K and internal modem), Olympia, Goldstar, Samsung, Radofin (Triton) as well as Radiola and Schneider, who licence-built the Phillips VG-8010 in another colour.

Unlike American computer RPGs, Japanese games switched to a 2D view when exploring the dungeons: Ys, a well-known Action-RPG by Nihon Falcom.

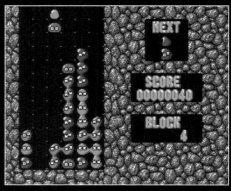

MSX games like Compile's Puyo Puyo were later converted for Sega or Nintendo consoles.

Sega SG-1000 & Master System

Japan, 1983 & 1987

Units sold:	10 Million
Number of games:	300
Game storage:	Cartridge, Card
Games developed until:	1995

★ ★ ★ ♪

Such is puristic entertainment: The first programmable TV game by Sega was shipped with one hard-wired joypad and a tiny 3 K of main and video memory.

In the mid '80s, European gamers got to know Sega for its arcade games. Action coin-ops like **Congo Bongo**, **Zaxxon** and **Hang On** made scaled-down appearances as licensed titles on western consoles and home computers. Finally, in 1987, four years after the Crash and two years after the NES debuted in the west, Sega entered the world market with its own games console, the Master System.

The first episode of the Phantasy Star RPG series was developed by Sega exclusively for its 8-Bit consoles.

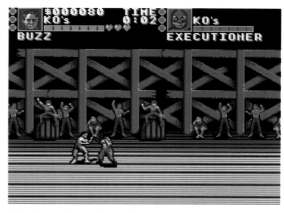

US software showed up at the end of the century. In most cases it was disappointing like this arcade port of Pitfighter.

Back home in Japan, Sega had already crossed joypads with Nintendo for a few years and the Master System marked not the beginning, but the end of a long-term hardware development: Technically, it was based on the SC-3000. The Z80 processor and 256x192 pixel resolution graphics put the machine on a par with the Colecovision and MSX computers. However, the three platforms were not compatible with each other. Like Nintendo, Sega defined its own standard.

The SG-1000 was followed by the SG-1000 II and Mark III (which featured slightly modified cases and more RAM) in 1984 and 1985 respectively. In 1987, the Mark III was thrown into a new case, with better sound, composite and RGB output and re-surfaced as the Master System. Sega's home computer ambitions were abandoned in favour of console development. Unlike its predecessor, the Master System was deprived of BASIC and keyboard.

Sega also didn't bother with a disk station like the Japanese Famicom's. Games appeared on ROM cartridges, and from 1985 also as flat `MyCards´, although these were limited to

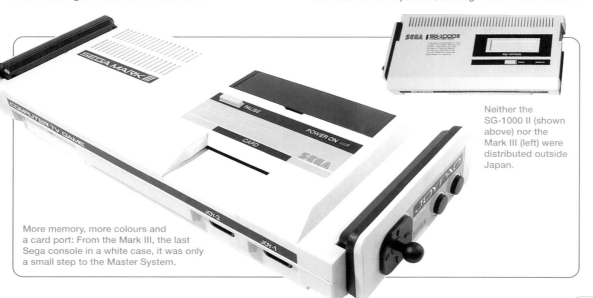

Neither the SG-1000 II (shown above) nor the Mark III (left) were distributed outside Japan.

More memory, more colours and a card port: From the Mark III, the last Sega console in a white case, it was only a small step to the Master System.

256 K, and a pair of 3D glasses was bundled with some European Master Systems.

Unlike Nintendo, Sega marketed the Master System in a design that was identical the world over: Slim, angular, black and red. Japanese, American and European variants differed by varying connections (like the additional Cinch plug in the European version) but all ran the same cartridges. Because western consoles lacked the FM sound channels of the Japanese Master System, PAL music in

Phantasy Star, Aleste and other games released after 1987, sounded worse than the original tunes.

As the Master System was not the only console in Japan, only Sega and its development partners Westone (**Wonderboy**) and Compile (**Aleste**) supported the machine with original software. More praise and support was to be found in England, where Acclaim, Codemasters and US Gold released more than 100 computer and arcade conversions for the Master System before 1992.

The small company TecMagic was ambitious enough to convert the 16-Bit hits **Populous** and **Shadow of the Beast** to the Master System. But as the machine was competing with half a dozen home computers and consoles, original or even exclusive Master System games were not being developed in the west.

In the early '90s, the compact and rounded Master System II replaced its predecessor. In view of the upcoming mobile Game Gear and the 16-Bit console Mega Drive, this last modification had to live without technical improvements, and thus, Sega closed the 8-Bit development case.

A late but impressive Master System cartridge was the port of Populous, shown to the left.

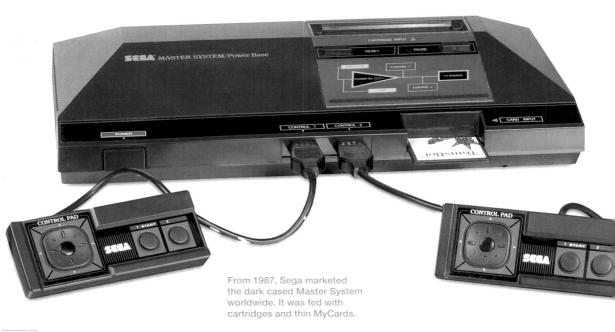

From 1987, Sega marketed the dark cased Master System worldwide. It was fed with cartridges and thin MyCards.

Sega challenged Mario with its own Wonderboy.

Smaller in size and without a card slot, the last and cheapest Master System was released in 1990.

Master System predecessors and variants

SG-1000	1983	Sega's first games console (white case, came with a wired joypad with a stick instead of direction pad) was technically related to the Colecovision and MSX. It had 1 K and 2 K video RAM, but no hardware sprites or scrolling. Start price: 15,000 yen, available only in Japan.
SC-3000	1983	The home computer brother of the SG-1000 was twice as expensive as the version without keyboard. There are versions with black, red and white cases; the French firm Yeno distributed the red one in Europe for instance. The SC-3000 was marketed with a mechanical keyboard, 18 K RAM and 16 K video RAM, and retailed for 33,800 yen.
Othello Multivision	1983	Tsukada Original marketed this rare SG-1000 licence built in Japan only. An alphanumerical keyboard (a to h, 0 to 9) specially designed for the board game Othello was let in into the white case. In 1984, a second Multivision version was released, this time with a small joystick instead of integrated pad and a keyboard connector on the back.
SG-1000 II	1984	Externally slightly redesigned console update with doubled memory, two controller ports and sideward holders for the pads. MyCards ran thanks to a `Card Catcher´ adapter and the optional keyboard SK-1100 expanded the console to a BASIC home computer.
Mark III	1985	Third Z80 console by Sega housed in a white case featuring sideward held pads, yet this time with a MyCard port on the front. Technically, the Mark III was a lot better: 8 K memory, 16 K video RAM, hardware sprites and scrolling. An optionally available FM-Sound-Unit expanded the acoustic capabilities. It was shipped with the OutRun conversion and implemented into the Japanese Master System as standard.
Master System	1987	Compared to the Mark III, the first Sega console for worldwide sale had a different case and ports. The Japanese variant launch price was 16,800 yen and unlike western machines, held an additional FM music chip. Later models contained the Sega game Hang On inside the ROM.
Master System II	1990	The final Master System variant was smaller and more rounded than all previous models. Stripped of the MyCard and expansion ports (hence not compatible with the 3D glasses), Reset button and operating LED. Alex Kidd in Miracle World or Sonic the Hedgehog was incorporated in the ROM.

83

Whilst US companies shifted their business to micros, Japanese toy manufacturer Nintendo unleashed a console and triumphed.

Nintendo Famicom

Japan, 1983

Units sold:	60 Million
Number of games:	1,400
Game storage:	Cartridge, Disk
Games developed until:	1994

★★★★★

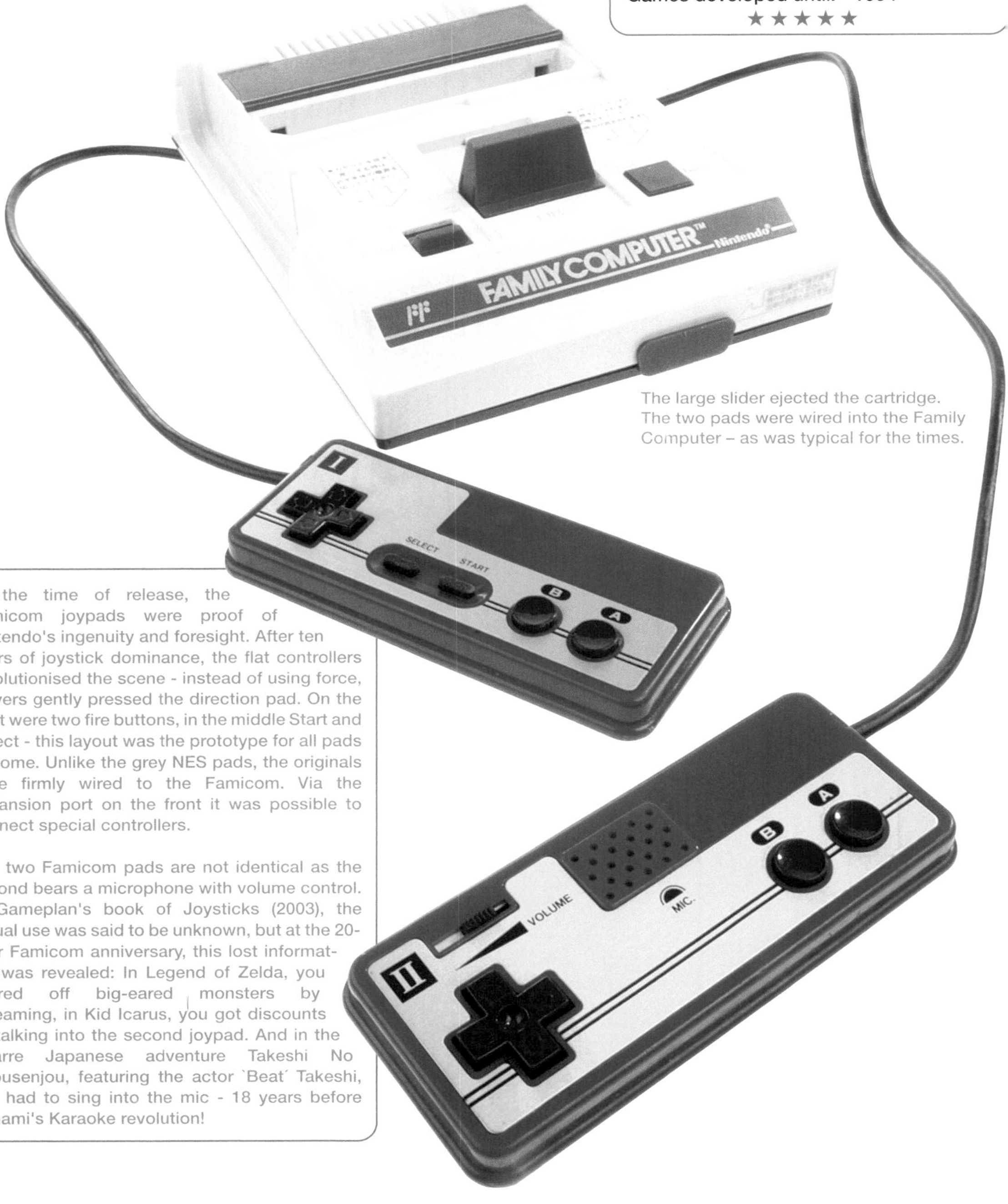

The large slider ejected the cartridge. The two pads were wired into the Family Computer – as was typical for the times.

At the time of release, the Famicom joypads were proof of Nintendo's ingenuity and foresight. After ten years of joystick dominance, the flat controllers revolutionised the scene - instead of using force, players gently pressed the direction pad. On the right were two fire buttons, in the middle Start and Select - this layout was the prototype for all pads to come. Unlike the grey NES pads, the originals were firmly wired to the Famicom. Via the expansion port on the front it was possible to connect special controllers.

The two Famicom pads are not identical as the second bears a microphone with volume control. In Gameplan's book of Joysticks (2003), the actual use was said to be unknown, but at the 20-year Famicom anniversary, this lost information was revealed: In Legend of Zelda, you scared off big-eared monsters by screaming, in Kid Icarus, you got discounts by talking into the second joypad. And in the bizarre Japanese adventure Takeshi No Chousenjou, featuring the actor `Beat´ Takeshi, you had to sing into the mic - 18 years before Konami's Karaoke revolution!

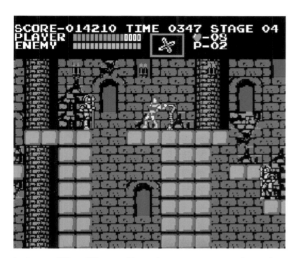

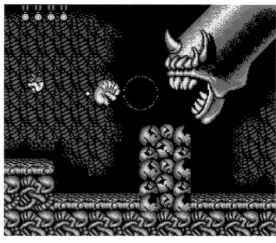

In Japan, US and Europe Konami games were popular and …   … successful. To the left, Castlevania, above: Probotector.

When the Japanese firm behind Game & Watch and the Donkey Kong coin-op released its first programmable console, the industry's rush had just turned into a hangover. Market leader Atari couldn't establish a successor to its ageing VCS in USA or Europe, and at the same time, the situation among independent game manufacturers was out of control; dealers were burdened under a landslide of low-quality releases. In 1984 the western console market crashed. In a state of panic, toy manufacturers Mattel and Parker withdrew; Atari and Coleco moved over to the computer business.

Japan was less affected: Of course, there were a lot of consoles, including license-built versions of Vectrex, Intellivision, VCS and VC 20, but there was no leading player to mess up the new business. Nintendo – like Sega – was just one console developer among many. Whilst other companies carefully monitored the home computer industry, company boss Hiroshi Yamauchi held on to his plan of a next generation console. The machine had to be better than older consoles in all respects, but it also had to be cheap enough for the masses.

Under the management of Masayuki Uemura, Nintendo's R&D2 team developed the no-thrills Family Computer. The Famicom was the result of rationalism and a visionary market perception: While Atari was squandering its market

share with the 5200, Nintendo released its practical toy in bright colours – white and red with gold trim. The Nintendo's functional appearance didn't show the specs R&D2 had put under its hood. There were no superfluous or irritating elements; the joypads were simple, with just two fire buttons, and instead of putting your left thumb on a joystick or disc, there was a modern looking, although technically primitive, direction pad – Uemura borrowed the minimalist design from Gunpei Yokoi's Game & Watch handhelds.

In July 1983, the release of the Famicom took place at the right place at the right time – 500,000 Japanese gamers

Japan-only
mass storage:
The Disk Station.

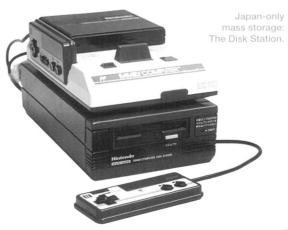

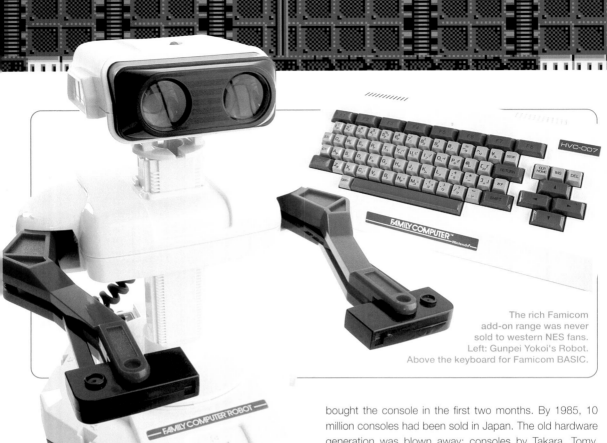

HVC-007

FAMILY COMPUTER™
Nintendo®

The rich Famicom
add-on range was never
sold to western NES fans.
Left: Gunpei Yokoi's Robot.
Above the keyboard for Famicom BASIC.

FAMILY COMPUTER ROBOT

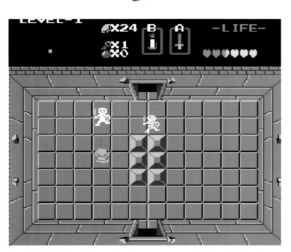

The first Zelda action adventure came on disk in 1986 and was
ported to cartridge.

bought the console in the first two months. By 1985, 10 million consoles had been sold in Japan. The old hardware generation was blown away; consoles by Takara, Tomy, Epoch, Bandai and Casio disappeared off the shelves within months.

Software sold hardware: Nintendo released jump 'n runs by Shigeru Miyamoto (four Mario games in the initial year) and in 1984, cartridges from Hudson and Namco appeared – the two companies were first to accept Nintendo's licensing model. Strictly speaking, all third-parties were only developers because every cartridge was tested and produced by Nintendo and then re-sold to its maker.

This production monopoly regulated the market and allowed Nintendo to control the content of the games to boot. Any content deemed unsuitable for kids was, for example, not approved by Nintendo.

Nobody's perfect, however. There was a product recall in Japan and to summarize the drama around the US launch told by David Sheff in his book `Game Over´ (1993) in one sentence: With all kinds of strategic tricks, marketing ideas and juristic skirmishes, Nintendo claimed and reformed the western market within 18 months.

THAT WAS A CLOSE CALL!

LIFE ▯

M. GUN

RANK ★

Konami novice Hideo Kojima wanted to program for the Famicom but had to implement his Metal Gear Solid on MSX first.

The first and most prominent US partner was Acclaim, which ported WWF roughnecks, **The Simpsons**, **Terminator** and other movie and TV brands to the NES. Konami remained the international number one in terms of quality and commercial success. Unlike Nintendo, Konami didn't give up its arcade business and instead delivered the best from the arcades along with original games (**Castlevania**, **Goemon**). Many Konami cartridges were pepped up with custom graphics and sound chips. Enix and Square were also successful, selling several million copies of each instalment in the **Dragon Quest** and **Final Fantasy** RPG series.

Sharp's TwinFamicom held a disk drive and was three times as big as the Nintendo console.

Capcom's Mega Man practiced his jumps and robot manoeuvres on the NES.

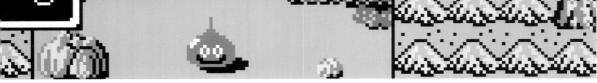

APG starring slime: Dragon Quest, 1986

A late NES game from the UK: Battletoads (Rare, 1991) is a raving cartoon beat 'em up for one or two toads.

In the west, the grey Nintendo Entertainment System (NES) was sold with the four-player adapter for some time.

In 1990, nearly every publishing company in Japan, USA and Europe held a Nintendo licence; some companies even produced their ROMs without it. Although it wasn't as prominent as the software range, the add-on industry played an important role in Nintendo's original strategy. The Famicom was released with the `Robot´ designed by Gunpei Yokoi, and though it wasn't particularly capable of much, it made the console stand out. From across the world, there came 3D glasses, light-guns, fitness mats and four-player adapters. In 1990, western gamers witnessed a

NES piano being released by Mindscape, as well as the Mattel Power Glove, a product spawned out of the Virtual Reality industry. The most complex peripherals never left Japan: With the Disk System, Nintendo slipped a 3" drive under the console. Nearly 200 games were released for the system before 1990. A Network Adapter connected the console with the telephone line in 1988. Nintendo's online service was supported by renowned Japanese companies, but unlike the Disk System, the expansion was not sold in millions but only 100,000 times.

Famicom, Variants and successors

Famicom	1983	Like many contemporaries, the Famicom had an RF connection and two unremovable joypads. The expansion port was used for special controllers, the cartridge port used for bigger add-ons: In 1984, keyboard and BASIC, in 1986 the Disk System and in 1988 the Network Adapter.
Sharp Famicom Televi	1983	The TV and Famicom combo was launched in October 1983, but Televi C-1 never was released in the west. The price is unknown.
Sharp Famicom Titler	1984	The most unusual variant weighs nearly 5 kgs and retailed for 43,000 yen at launch - four times the price of a normal Famicom. The Titler (AN-510) is a comfortably equipped computer for creating movie subtitles with English or Japanese characters. For this purpose, it had composite in/outputs and two S-video connections, the latter improving the console's picture quality to almost RGB quality.
Nintendo Entertainment System (NES)	1985	The Famicom for western markets (USA, Europe) had a new, rectangular grey case featuring two joypad ports. The cartridge slot is found behind a flap. Not compatible with the Famicom.
Sharp Twin Famicom	1986	Nintendo's hardware partner Sharp manufactured a Famicom with integrated disk drive and big red (later black) case under licence and shipped it for 32,000 yen in Japan.
Famicom AV	1993	The last variant was sold world wide in a new asymmetrical case with Super-NES style controller. The cartridge port is hidden beneath a flap.

Epoch brought the TV game to Japan but then lost track.
Like Tomy and Bandai, the former Atari distributor
had to make way for Nintendo.

Epoch Super Cassettevision

Japan, 1984

Units sold:	Unknown
Number of games:	30
Game storage:	Cartridge
Games developed until:	1984

★ ↗ ☆ ☆ ☆

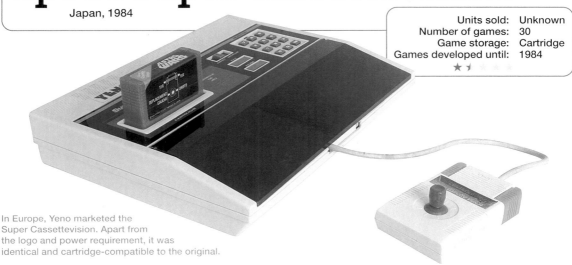

In Europe, Yeno marketed the
Super Cassettevision. Apart from
the logo and power requirement, it was
identical and cartridge-compatible to the original.

Japanese love the beauty of nature and mini skirts: Super Golf

In 1975, Epoch's wireless TV Tennis was the first TV game in Japan. The hobby boomed in the Far East, just as it did in the west, and by 1977, 30 different Pong machines and the first cartridge consoles appeared. Traditional toy manufacturers dominated the market (including Bandai and Tomy) until 1983, when the second wave of programmable machines rolled out. Nintendo launched the Famicom and Sega its SG-1000, and both were technically superior to Epoch's Cassettevision (see box below).

Epoch took a year to react with competitive hardware: The Super Cassettevision (SCV) had 16 K video RAM, drew 16 colours from a palette of 512 and moved up to 128 sprites. Like the SG-1000 and the Famicom, it launched at 15,000 yen, but it was obviously more expensive and complex to manufacture: Both joysticks were placed underneath a toned lid and Epoch built a numerical keypad into the top right of the unit. Besides antennae connection, the Super Cassettevision even had an RGB output – the first TV game with a such optimized picture quality.

Arriving late, the console lived a short life and had a compact software library that consisted largely of shoot 'em ups and jump 'n runs. There were **Pole Position 2** and **Mappy** by Namco, and US hits **Miner 2049er** and **Boulder Dash**. Three anime conversions **Dragonball**, **Doraemon** and **Lupin III** (who acted as Pitfall Harry for Epoch), came later. Points of historical interest include the action RPG **Dragonslayer** with its battery-backup for save games and a hardware variant Epoch made for girls: The rose-coloured `Lady's Set´ was sold in 1985 in a trendy travel case.

Predecessor

Cassettevision	1981	The first generation non-SCV-compatible cartridge console (NEC 4-Bit CPU, launch price of 13,500 yen) had 12 games. Graphically and gameplay-wise, it was on a par with the Interton 4000. Two miniature sticks, four buttons and two paddles on each side were integrated both left and right, all fixed to the case. In 1983, the machine was replaced by the heavily simplified and minimised Cassettevision Jr., which retailed for 5,000 yen – Japan's cheapest machine.

Commodore C116

USA, 1984

Units sold:	Unknown
Number of games:	100
Game storage:	Tape, Disk, Cartridge
Games developed until:	1987

★ ﾉ ☆ ☆ ☆

With the Amiga, Commodore headed into the 16-Bit era, but hesitated to leave the 8-Bit market altogether. In an attempt to repeat the success of VC 20 and C64, the market leader devised the 264 micro computer range, with the aim of supporting and replacing both classics at the lower end of the price segment.

The CPU was a variant of the proven 6502 processor; graphics, sound and IO functions were handled by a new chip called TED. Both components had to share the system bus between them. The cost-effective design had a major flaw though: The planned computers were not compatible with either VC 20 or C64.

Especially in Europe, the hobby computers were advertised without the manufacturer or press ever managing to map out a reasonable concept: On the one hand, the 264 machines were better than earlier Commodore computers, they featured BASIC 3.5 and an increased colour palette. On the other hand they were clearly stripped down: The hardware lacked sprites for action games and the sound of the SID-carrying C64.

While the announced variants 232, 264 and 364 were dropped even before sales began, three models did actually roll out onto the shelves – only to be quickly reduced in price by retailers. The entry level model C16 was to replace the VC 20 and put into the classic breadbox-case, coloured dark this time. A glance at the back gave another reason why these micros were misconceived and unsuccessful: Instead of standard ports for joysticks and Datasette, round mini-DIN ports were used – old Commodore peripherals couldn't be connected to the new range.

Athletic original developments for the fizzled hardware came from German company Kingsoft: Winter Olympiad aka Winter Events by Udo Gertz (1986).

The C116 was a shoddy flop,
popular only in eastern Europe.

The successors were launched nearly simultaneously: The C116 had a new, more stylish case, but replaced the professional keyboard with lousy rubber keys. Other than that, it was identical to the C16, but cheaper and similarly lacking power with only 16 K. Only the top range model Plus/4 had 64 K of memory and tempted potential buyers with some office software stored in the ROM. Sadly, the applications included were weak and pretty useless without an external disk drive.

Gamers and programmers were startled by the crude mix of old and new technology. At least simple conversions were easy to handle due to the technical similarities to the VC 20 and C64. After some ROM cartridges were released at launch (including the classic **Wizard of Wor**), nearly all games were published on tape. Most originated in the UK, whilst US releases were largely Infocom adventures plus a few sports games. In Germany, Kingsoft programmed the **Grandmaster** chess game and a handful of action titles for the ill-fated computer range.

After 1987, professional development crumbled away, Eastern European hobby programmers took over the platform and created some original games into the '90s, but in particular, unlicensed ports and sequels of western hits like Barbarian, Revs, Atomix and Total Eclipse.

Variants

C 16	1984	With its breadbox case (shown to the right), it looked similar to the BASIC computers VC 20 and C64 but it was not compatible with their hard- or software. In hi-res mode, the 16 K of RAM came down to 2 K, so most users expanded the memory to 64 K.
C 116	1984	The second low-end model was internally identical to the C16, but had a modern case with rubber instead of mechanical keys and a separate cursor pad. As the cheapest Commodore it was shipped in Europe only.
Plus/4	1984	The high-end model of the ill-fated range (C116 case but with a proper keyboard) featured 64 K RAM, spreadsheet, database and graphics program as standard and an additional User-Port.

Atari 7800

USA, 1984

Units sold:	Unknown
Number of games:	60
Game storage:	Cartridge
Games developed until:	1992

★ ★ ✯

First person shooter on 8-Bits: Atari's Alien Brigade borrowed its mechanics and weapons from Operation Wolf by Taito.

In terms of sprites and animation, Atari games played in the same league as the NES: Basketbrawl (1988).

Following the showiness of the Super System 5200, Atari turned in another direction with its second go at a VCS successor: The 7800 was small, uncomplicated and compatible with all VCS carts. The case was taken from the Japanese Atari 2800, while the CPU was based on the proven 6502 processor, the heart of all 8-Bit Ataris. The new graphics chip `Maria´ could display more colours and sprites than other consoles. Unfortunately, Atari leaned back on the VCS' '70s sound technology instead of using the four-channel `Pokey´ chip from the Atari 5200.

The test release of the Atari 7800 went by totally unnoticed amidst the market crash. Then, Time Warner sold the company to Commodore founder Jack Tramiel, whose interest was for computers but not for toys. For two years, he allowed Atari to sit on the 7800, until Nintendo's success roused him. To grab a share of the console market, Atari

delivered the old 7800 unit across the world and developed new software. A colourful mix of arcade and computer conversions was the result, including flight simulations **Ace of Aces** and **Tomcat F-16**, the British Nebulus port **Tower Toppler** and puzzle game **Jinks** from Germany. There were good arcade conversions too, although by the end of the '80s they didn't impress too many people anymore: **Ms. Pac-Man**, **Galaga** and **Dig Dug** by Namco, **Mario Bros**, **Joust** and Capcom's **Commando**. Some games like **Xevious** used the second fire button of the 7800 controller.

Atari's half-hearted marketing approach stood no chance against Nintendo and Sega, especially since the similar, but incompatible Atari XE Game System was being advertised at the same time. In 1991, the production of the 7800 ceased.

Late 7800 games like Title Match ProWrestling came from the Activision runaways Absolute Entertainment.

Ms. Pac-Man made
7800 owners drool
for another go.

POWER

PAUSE

ATARI

7800

SELECT

RESET

The 7800 sold either with two ProLine sticks
or, across Europe, with simple joypads.

Variants and successors

Atari 7800	1984	A few thousand 7800 consoles were shipped in the US during the first marketing attempt. The rare original version had an expansion slot that should have connected to a Laser Disc player for instance, but was never used.
Atari 7800	1986	Apart from the missing expansion slot, the mass-market version was identical to the first series. European machines contained **Asteroids** inside the ROM. Some PAL variants were shipped with joypads instead of sticks; the French model featured a RGB output via Peritel (SCART).

Amstrad CPC 464

GB, 1984

Units sold:	2.5 Million
Number of games:	1,200
Game storage:	Tape, Disk, Cartridge
Games developed until:	1992

★ ★ ★ ★

In Germany the C64 rival was marketed by Schneider.

Neither British company Amstrad, nor its German partner Schneider had experience in developing and marketing micro computers when they entered the booming market in 1984. Both companies were specialists at creating affordable audio-visual electronics and made the most of this knowledge in the development of the CPC 464. The low budget computer was shipped with a Z80 CPU, integrated Datasette and either monochrome or colour monitor. Both configurations were affordable and suitable for beginners. The longish housing with typewriter keys and separate space, number and direction keys came with a speaker, stereo output and volume control. The power supply for the whole system was located inside the monitor.

For £230 or £330 respectively, 200,000 units were sold in the first 15 months according to Amstrad, establishing the CPC as an alternative to the Spectrum and C64. But the CPC could not match the success and endurance of these two competitors. As the machine did not have any outstanding technical features, very few exclusive games appeared, and the vast majority of titles were simply conversions from other platforms. Thanks to its success, the CPC 464 and disk version CPC 664, were blessed with games from diverse developers such as Infocom and Ultimate (today known as Rare), Psion, Activision, Gremlin, Hewson, Sensible Software and Reflections. Releases included ports of **Sim City**, **Lemmings**, **Star Glider**, **Nebulus**, **Elite**, Sid Meier's masterpieces **Pirates!** and **Silent Service**, as well as sound conversions of prominent Japanese and American arcade games like **Bomb Jack**, **Contra** and **Rainbow Islands**.

The inexpensive CPC computers were particularly popular in southern Europe. Towards the end of the '80s, French and Spanish programmers were pushing the limits of the hardware and – as opposed to their British counterparts –

In England and Spain, the CPC looked funky with special keys in red, green and blue.

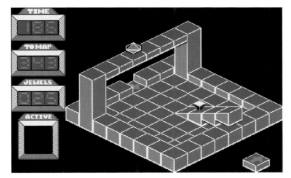

At first, British developers supported 'their' Amstrad computer (Spindizzy, 1986), later …

… the scene shifted to southern Europe: Get Dexter is an early CPC action adventure from France.

even developed games exclusively for the CPC. Some of the most original software stemmed from companies who never reached influential positions in the international C64 and Amiga markets: Loriciel, Infogrames, Cryo, Tomahawk, Ocean France, Titus, Topo and Dinamic. In 1988, Spanish developer Opera Soft released a conversion of Umberto Eco's successful book 'The Name of the Rose'. The isometric view of the cathedral in **La Abadia Del Crimen** brought the medieval thriller to gothic action adventure life.

Outside Spain the two graphically improved hardware successors, CPC 464+ and 664+, and the game console GX were dead ducks on the Amiga and Atari ST dominated market. In the early '90s, both Amstrad and Schneider dropped the hardware family in favour of CP/M and DOS compatible PCs.

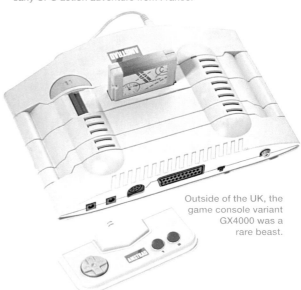

Outside of the UK, the game console variant GX4000 was a rare beast.

Variants and successors

CPC 464	1984	'The complete home computer' was equipped with a Datasette and shipped with a 12-inch colour or green monitor, featured 64 K of RAM and, like all successors, the tried and tested AY-3-8912 chip for sound generation. RS232 interface was optionally available for £50.
CPC 664	1984	The 664 was the 464's successor, featuring an identical chipset and similar, but grey housing with a rather unusual 3" disk drive instead of the tape. It sold for £340 (including green monitor) and £450 (colour) and was dropped quickly in favor of the CPC 6128.
CPC 6128	1985	A new version for semi-professional users, which came in a smaller housing and with 128 K – double the memory of older CPCs. It shipped with BASIC, Amdos and CP/M Plus.
CPC 464+	1987	A new 64 K version in a white case, with improved graphics (4,096 colours, 64 sprites, scrolling and split-screen), integrated tape deck, cartridge port, connectors for digital and analogue joysticks as well as a light gun port. The 464+ lacked the internal operating system and only works with a BASIC or game cartridge inserted.
CPC 6128+	1987	Similar case to the 464+ but with 128 K of memory and equipped with a 3" floppy disk drive instead of the Datasette.
GX4000	1990	Videogame console with 128 K RAM based on the +technology. The stylish housing without keyboard or drive featured two joystick ports, an analogue controller port, RF and even RGB output. The thirty GX games released by Ocean, Gremlin and French companies Titus, Loriciel and Infogrames came on 128 K and 512 K cartridges.

The 16-Bit era

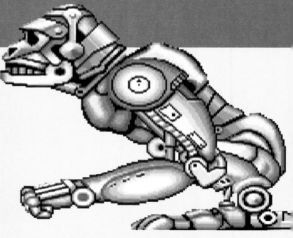

Late bitmap games became graphically explicit: Namco's Splatterhouse features an unlicensed Jason, while Capcom's acrobatic Strider battled Soviet robots in the Cold War.

The crash had seen the demise of videogame consoles and in 1985 the scene consequently shifted towards real computers – initially to the C64, and then to the mighty 16-Bit beasts. The Atari ST, the Amiga and the Mac were powered by the Motorola CPU 68000, while IBM chose Microsoft and Intel to brew up a standard for Personal Computers.

State of the Art processors, specialized custom chips, more memory: The evolution shift C64 to Amiga improved the visual and audio experience in particular, but entering new gameplay territory with the 16-Bit hardware proved difficult. Many games from the 16-Bit era were developed simultaneously for 8-Bit computers or were simply conversions of older Apple II, Atari or C64 concepts. American publishers in particular preferred to play it safely, issuing the third, fourth or fifth episodes of **King's Quest** or **Ultima**.

When designing action games for home computers, developers would often seek inspiration from arcade games. Games by Yu Suzuki (Sega), Tokuro Fujiwara and Yoshiki Okamoto (Capcom), Konami, Taito and Namco were converted by western companies to the new machines and provided the ideas

and benchmarks for American, British and German programmers. Thus, Irem's scrolling **R-Type** influenced countless shoot 'em ups, like **Wonderboy** by Sega did for the jump'n run genre.

Every once in a while, Atari succeeded with an arcade hit: In 1983 and 1985 with the 3D vector games **Star Wars** and **Empire Strikes Back**, and **Marble Madness**, in 1989 with **Hard Drivin'**, the first polygon and force feedback simulation game. Most of the coin-ops operated with one or more 68000 processors. In Japan, arcade games like **Afterburner** and **Rainbow Islands** reached home consoles

Rainbow Islands
(Taito, 1987)

1

by the end of the '80s: The PC-Engine, which teamed an 8-Bit CPU with 16-Bit graphics, and the Mega Drive which used the MC68000 CPU (and old Z80 for support) were the first of a new generation of consoles.

The most popular games machine of the era however, wasn't coin-op, Amiga or Mega Drive, but a cheap and technically limited 8-Bit hardware. The Famicom, launched in 1983 in Japan, had finally arrived on western shores and became surprisingly successful as the Nintendo Entertainment System (NES), enabling a surreptitious comeback for videogames that couldn't have been predicted. Children and families, rather than hardcore gamers, were the main target group for this grey machine.

The other platform to corner the global games market looked equally dull and inconsiderable: With EGA and VGA graphics, sound card and hard-drive, the `IBM-compatible´ DOS PC began chipping away at the Amiga and Atari scene – first in the US, then later in Europe. The CD-ROM and multimedia revolution (see page 84) had to start without Atari and Commodore.

In 1988, Namco modelled the F1 circus with vectors and polygons – four years prior to Sega's Virtua Racing.

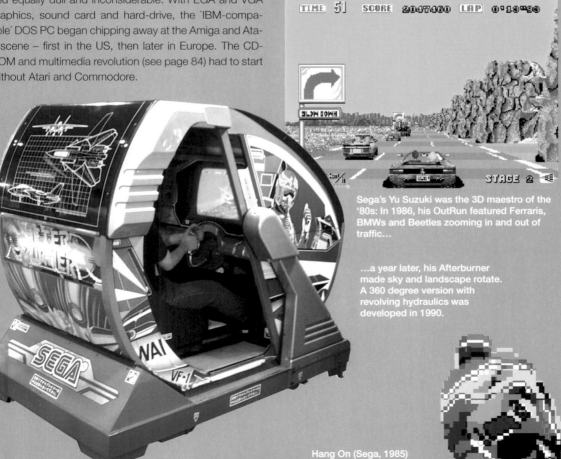

Sega's Yu Suzuki was the 3D maestro of the '80s: In 1986, his OutRun featured Ferraris, BMWs and Beetles zooming in and out of traffic…

…a year later, his Afterburner made sky and landscape rotate. A 360 degree version with revolving hydraulics was developed in 1990.

Hang On (Sega, 1985)

IBM PC/AT

USA, 1984

Units sold:	Many
Number of games:	3,000
Game storage:	Disk
Games developed until:	1992

★ ★ ★ ★ ◡

The IBM PC separated keyboard from central unit and held – thanks to 1 MB RAM, hard-drive and floppy – enough memory for complex games.

IBM, the world's biggest computer manufacturer, took some time to make the transition from the mainframe to the domestic market: It wasn't until 1981, the inaugural year of the 'Personal Computer´, that it finally made the leap.

While IBM's original PC was well received, its successor, the PC Jr. flopped, mainly due to a low quality keyboard. IBM returned its attention to serious hardware, presenting the hard-drive equipped eXtended technology PC/XT in 1983 and a year later the PC/AT, which featured an Intel 286 16-Bit processor. The AT achieved what the Jr. didn't: Within a few years, it became the most popular games platform.

Software for all IBM PCs came from Microsoft, whose Disk Operating System (DOS) replaced older competing system software. When Compaq and others joined the standard, Microsoft's partnership with Intel made it the driving force behind PC development. The term `IBM compatible´ remained popular right into the '90s, although in fact, the definition MS-DOS compatible would have been correct.

At the same time as the CPU, the graphics capabilities were enhanced: After monochrome Hercules and four-colour CGA cards, EGA became the de facto standard, displaying 16 colours from a palette of 64, and as an alternative to mono chirps, sound cards were fitted to the PC.

American insiders were the first to smell the roses: *'In late 1983 (a year after the release of the IBM PC) we were somewhat disappointed that the PC entertainment market fell far short of the predictions'* wrote Russell Sipe in his Computer Gaming World magazine (CGW). *'Then in a dramatic move, IBM reacted to the underwhelming response from the public by revamping the Jr. into one of the best buys in computerdom ... replaced the keyboard with a real one, expanded to a basic 128 K configuration ... The third parties were translating more and more of their titles and we began to see significant games that were exclusively IBM. The era of IBM gaming has arrived'.*

LucasArts lent a human face, humour and emotion to the 320 x 200 pixel EGA resolution: The Secret of Monkey Island (1990).

The first PC games were monochrome, later four-coloured: Flight Simulator II (1982).

Sierra put its bets on EGA 16-colour graphics in King's Quest (1983) and...

...subjected colours to 'dithering' in the fourth part (1988).

Not quite. Because Atari, Apple and Commodore stood in the way of the multi-vendor avalanche of DOS compatibles, the breakthrough took longer than expected. CGW strategy expert M. Evan Brooks quoted Microprose and SSI, the two biggest developers of simulations and RPGs, in May 1987. Both saw the IBM *'as an area of expansion'*, but were still sceptical due to *'poor graphics'*.

At the end of the '80s, the 286/386 CPU platform with its EGA and VGA graphics finally equalled the Amiga and Atari ST, reaching acceptance as the third major platform in the European game market. But it was Germany, rather than the previous micro stronghold, England, that became the dominant market for the DOS powerhouses, and their first-class 3D simulations, RPGs and adventures.

The 286 generation had reached its limits with the tailor-made **Falcon AT** flight simulator by Spectrum Holobyte and the pixel-cinematic **Monkey Island**. The dramatic, but also extremely funny, in-depth, but user-friendly pirate romp was written, created and realized by LucasArts in old EGA resolution as well as in splendid 256 colour VGA mode.

The early '90s saw DOS move forward into the multimedia age; computers with 486 CPUs replaced the AT. More and more games were released on 3.5" disks and ran under Windows. 'Whatever the PC has, we've had it for ages,' mocked Amiga and ST users, but had to eat their words when they saw Windows becoming popular with game developers. The integration of CD-ROM went smoothly on the PC, while Atari and Commodore failed at multimedia. By 1995, both competitors had disappeared from the market.

The PC Jr. was the only IBM micro with a port for game cartridges (1983). Nobody liked its faulty infrared keyboard.

Variants and successors

IBM PC	1981	The first IBM computer for the private household was a desktop separated into three parts (keyboard, monitor, central unit), which featured the 8-Bit CPU Intel 8088, a minimum of 64 K RAM and a disk drive.
IBM PC/XT	1983	The internally very similar successor was mostly shipped with the 16-Bit-CPU 8086. It had a hard-drive, a maximum of 1 MB memory and additional expansion card slots. With Hercules, CGA and – from 1985 on – EGA graphics it stayed on duty until the end of the '80s.
IBM PC Jr.	1983	A hobby and living room PC with 64 K RAM (128 K in 1984), EGA graphics (640x200 pixels in two, 160x200 in 16 colours), integrated sound chip SN 76496N, 5.25" floppy, two cartridge ports and an analogue joystick. Initially sold for $1,300, this micro was the target platform for Sierra's first animated adventure King's Quest.
IBM PC/AT	1984	The Advanced Technology successor to the XT sported Intel's 80286 CPU, a 20 MB hard-drive and the new 1.2 MB floppy as standard. It held a maximum of 16 MB RAM, although DOS only supported 1 MB. In the early '90s, a 12 to 16 MHz clocked AT with EGA or VGA graphics, Adlib or SoundBlaster card was standard for games. The first PC with a 32-Bit CPU was delivered by Compaq, not IBM in 1986: The power of the Deskpro 386 was tapped by '90s games like Wing Commander by Chris Roberts.

Apple built the aesthete's dream-machine.
The Mac's graphical user interface sparked off a cult and spawned
a unique scene of entertainment software.

Apple Macintosh

USA, 1984

Units sold:	22 Million
Number of games:	300
Game storage:	Disk, CD
Games developed until:	1993

★ ★ ★ ◢

Apple Mac taught urban management: Smog, traffic jams and natural disaster vs. the mayor of Sim City (1989).

The early authoring system HyperCard was used by artists to design interactive novels: The Manhole by Cyan.

Following the Apple III and Lisa failures, Steve Jobs started 1984 with stunning advertising. In its TV spot the new Apple Macintosh promised to free the world from the claws of a totalitarian force (ie. IBM): '*On January 1984 24th, … you'll see why 1984 won't be like 1984.*' The dark, short film is legendary, just like the hardware, which was announced but not shown at the time: With mouse control and graphical user interface (GUI), a 16-Bit CPU by Motorola and Sony's small 3.5" disk for data storage, the Mac was a successful implementation of the vision of the 'two Steves', Apple founders Jobs and Wozniak.

Apple packed the new technology into a smart case: Computer, drive and monitor were combined in a cube with only mouse and mini-keyboard separated. The micro cutie was designed with creative users in mind and retailed for a bold $2,500 in its 128 K version; the 512 K 'Fat Mac' sold for a hefty $3,200. In contrast to the Apple II, it seemed to be useless as a game machine: Graphics were high-res but grey, while sound chirped in mono. This changed with the $4,000 Mac II in 1987, which was upgradeable to revolutionary graphics in 16 million colours.

The Mac leapt to the forefront of graphics and desktop publishing, but games wise it remained an outsider. Innovative originals emerged for the Mac instead of conversions: Adventures inspired by the GUI and controlled via mouse and menu panels (**Deja vu**, **Uninvited**) and user-friendly

Because the hardware and software relies on the one-button mouse, there was no need for a keyboard. Still, the first Macs were shipped with a small one; the keypad, shown to the far right, was a cute add-on.

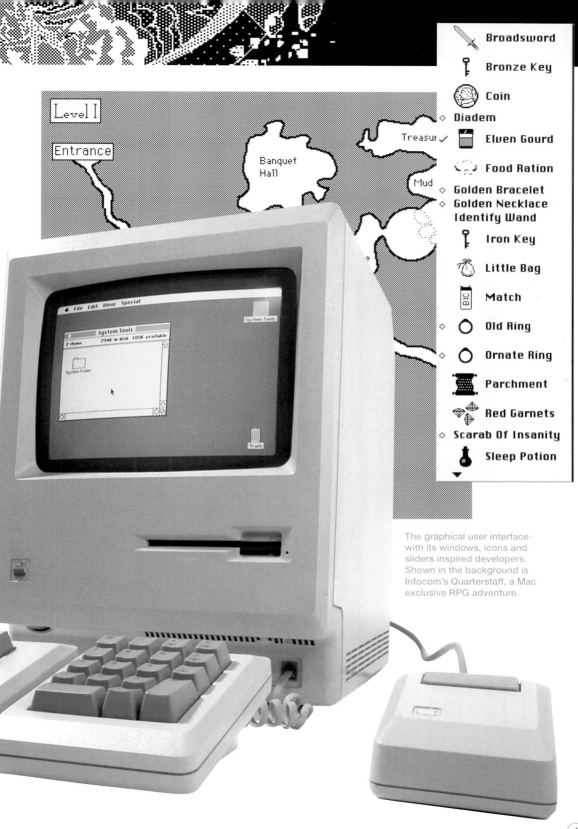

Level I

Entrance

Banquet
Hall

Treasur ✓

Mud

⚔️ Broadsword
🗝️ Bronze Key
🪙 Coin
◇ Diadem
🥤 Elven Gourd
🍽️ Food Ration
◇ Golden Bracelet
◇ Golden Necklace
　 Identify Wand
🗝️ Iron Key
👝 Little Bag
BIC Match
◇ ⭕ Old Ring
◇ ⭕ Ornate Ring
📜 Parchment
💎 Red Garnets
◇ Scarab Of Insanity
🧴 Sleep Potion
▼

🍎 File Edit View Special

System Tools

System Tools

2 items   294K in disk 105K available

System Folder

Trash

The graphical user interface ·
with its windows, icons and
sliders inspired developers.
Shown in the background is
Infocom's Quarterstaff, a Mac
exclusive RPG adventure.

strategy games like **Balance of Power** by ex-Atari designer Chris Crawford. Customers were fed addictive puzzles (**Shanghai**, **Ishido**) and edutainment instead of action. The educational game **Fool's Errand** was award-winning; contrasting with the infamy of the graphically explicit jump 'n' run **Dark Castle**. Some of the early network games were originally developed and released for the Mac too.

In 1989, Will Wright wrote his masterpiece **Sim City** whilst the Miller brothers made their debut with the Lewis-Carroll experiment **The Manhole**. Four years later, Rand and Robyn created the most successful Mac game, enticing punters to the CD-ROM age with **Myst**.

The Mac LC opened Apple's product range to the low-end sector: In Europe, the affordable machine was nicknamed 'pizza-box' because of its flat case.

This room is being redecorated
I must ask you not to come in

A good part of the last generation of MC68000 based games were multimedia adventures on Hybrid-CDs: The Japanese Gadget (1993) played on both, Mac and PC.

The entry level SE kept the cubic design with integrated monochrome monitor; it had an internal hard-drive as well as a new keyboard and mouse.

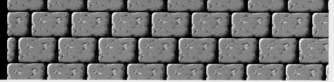

Macintosh variants and successors

Macintosh	1984	The first Mac appeared as a cube (computer, 9" monitor and disk drive in one unit weighing 7.5 kg) with single-button mouse and mini-keyboard. The 128 K model (January) was followed by the 512 K 'Fat Mac' (released in Japan as DynaMac, featuring Kana and Kanji fonts) and from April 1986 on, by the 512 Ke with 800 K disk drive and larger ROM.
Macintosh Plus	1986	The Plus had 1 MB as standard, upgradeable to 4 MB, a larger keyboard with numerical pad as well as SCSI bus on the rear panel, paving the way for the Mac peripheral market.
Macintosh II	1987	With the 16Mhz MC68020 CPU and Maths co-processor (FPU), configured with 8 MB and equipped with a graphics card, the Mac II was the perfect graphics workstation and capable of outputting to several monitors at once. It was beaten only by the $8,000 IIx in 1988 with its 68030 CPU, FPU, a maximum of 128 MB, internal 40 to 80 MB hard-drive and one or two 1.4 MB Floppy drives ('SuperDrives'). The IIFx from 1990 is a Unix variant for US authorities and saw Apple crashing through the $10,000 barrier.
Macintosh SE	1987	In contrast to the powerful II, the SE was kept in cube design with integrated b/w monitor. It was as expandable as the Plus, and boasted an internal hard-drive and the Apple Desktop Bus (ADB), which daisy chained up to 16 peripherals. The minimum configuration was 1 MB and 20 MB HD, the maximum 4 and 40 respectively. In 1989, the SE/30 with IIx technology appeared in the same case, just like the SE FDHD with a 40 MB hard-drive and one or two SuperDrives.
Macintosh IIc	1989	Boasting a slimmer case, standard SuperDrive and two ADB ports, the cx was released in March equipped with IIx technology. The ci came six months later with an accelerated CPU (25 MHz), 24-Bit graphics and 1 MB VRAM. An even slimmer case was used for the IIsi with 68030/20 CPU and 1 MB RAM. At the end of 1992, Apple released the IIvi (16 MHz) and IIvx (68030/32, FPU) for the first time in larger cases, in preparation for the CD-ROM. It was the predecessor to the Performa 600.
Macintosh Portable	1989	The first Macintosh for mobile users was based on the old 16 MHz 68000 CPU and was expandable to 8 MB. The light for the active display was initially available as a construction kit only, after 1991 it was on-board. Weighing 7 kilograms and selling for $6,500, it didn't meet with success and was replaced by the improved PowerBook in 1991, designed in co-operation with Sony.
Macintosh LC	1990	In abandoning the FPU and expansion slot, Apple managed to create a series of elegant introductory models in a slim case. LC stands for Low Cost: The first (68020/16, 2 MB RAM) was replaced by the $1240 LCII (68030/16, 4 MB) in 1992. In 1993, the series came to an end with the LCIII (68030/25, FPU), arriving at the low-end brand of Performas.
Macintosh Classic	1990	With a modified SE, the cube had its retro-comeback. Located at the low-end of the price range, the 68030/16 CPU machine was somewhat less powerful than the Classic II released in 1992. A year later, the first Color Classic appeared with LCII technology and an optional FPU.
Macintosh Quadra	1991	Apple's first tower represented the high-end alternative to the LC and replaced the IIx as a DTP workstation. The Quadra 700 and the more expandable Quadra 900 appeared in 1991, the 950 with 33 instead of 24 MHz 68040 CPU in May of the following year, the cheaper mini-tower 800 in early 1993. From that year on, the name Quadra was used for cheaper models in desktop cases (Centris). The last Quadras were shipped as Performas.
Macintosh Centris	1993	Short-lived mid-price range from Apple. Together with the 680LC40/20-equipped Centris 610, came this FPU-accelerated, 25 MHz-clocked 650 in a higher case than the IIvx. In October, the 610 and 650 replaced both computers. The planned Centris 660av was released as the Quadra 660av.
Macintosh Performa	1993	The introductory range replaced the LC model name and comprised of low-performance desktops (such as the Performa 400 to 430, also known as the LC II, Performa 475 and 476, also known as the Quadra 605) as well as Performas in complete cases (computer, 14"-CRT, Floppy and CD drive): Performa 520 (LC 520, 1993), Performa 575 to 578 (LC 575, 1994), Performa 580CD and 588CD (LC 580). Other Perfomas were low end like the Classic II (Performa 200), Color Classic (Performa 250) and the Japan-only Color Classic II with 33MHz (Performa 275). From 1995, LC computers with PowerPC CPU carried the Performa tag.

Atari ST

USA, 1985

Units sold:	6 Million
Number of games:	1,000
Game storage:	Disk
Games developed until:	1994

★ ★ ★ ★ ★

Musicians and DTP artists bought their Atari ST with the 12" monitor SM 146 and got a small, but crisp picture.

In 1984, while devising its 16-Bit computer range, Atari invested in the Amiga company, owned by ex-employee Jay Miner. However, a bullish negotiating-style drove the hardware team to competitor Commodore, which promptly swallowed Amiga and released a computer of the same name simultaneously to the Atari ST.

Miner's graphics chips were missing from the ST, but other than that it was similar to the Amiga: Both machines used a Motorola 68000 CPU, 3.5" disks and a mouse as input device, and both enticed punters with a graphical user interface. GEM was the name given to Atari's GUI with its

small drive and drawer symbols accompanied by the `Tramiel Operating System´ (TOS). The Atari ST was cheaper than other 16-Bit machines and was supported by many games manufacturers. 1987 turned out to be its most successful year: In the US, the real-time RPG **Dungeon Master** was released, along with Dan `Choplifter´ Gorlins' **Typhoon Thompson** and **Midi Maze** which networked 16 computers anticipating the deathmatches of the '90s. After that, the scene shifted to Europe. Prominent programmers like the Bitmap Brothers (**Speedball, Cadaver**), Eric Chahi (**Another World**), the adventure specialists Magnetic Scrolls as well as 3D pioneers Paul Woakes (**Damocles**) and Jez

French adventure artists dropped 8-Bit in favor of the ST: Future Wars by newcomers Delphine.

San (**Starglider**) supported the platform right into the '90s. Germany was another stronghold for Atari, where Thalion developed mainly for the ST, releasing huge RPGs (**Dragonflight**) and fast action games (**Wings of Death**).

By 1990, the Amiga overtook the Atari as a graphics and games machine, but due to its MIDI port, the ST remained the first choice for professional musicians. Similarly, small DTP offices used it as an affordable alternative to Macs. The final variant was the 68030-driven Falcon in 1992.

New wine in old bottles: The last ST compatible was called Falcon and was audio-visually more powerful than its predecessors, though it wasn't a success.

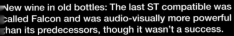

Dungeon Master was a revolution. If you didn't own an ST, you had to wait ages for a conversion of this realtime expedition.

Variants and successors

520ST	1985	The 512 K ST first shipped with a monochrome monitor, an external power supply as well as TOS on disk. It was replaced by the 260ST and 520ST+ (1 MB) and was also available as STm (with TV modulator) and STf (internal floppy drive).
260ST	1986	This short-lived 520ST twin (also with 512 K, external floppy) was shipped only in Europe.
1040ST	1986	A 1 MB computer with TOS in ROM and internal power supply. An `m´ in the name stands for TV modulator; `f´ for a sideward floppy drive.
Mega ST	1987	A desktop PC with separate keyboard, integrated floppy, up to 4 MB memory as standard and two new chips for graphics acceleration. Professional add-ons were hard-drive and removable media with up to 60 MB as well as a DTP-suitable 19" monitor.
1040STe	1989	The 520ST successor was enhanced in terms of graphics (4,096 colour palette, hardware scrolling, Blitter) and memory, shipping with 1 to 4 MB, in the UK and France along with 512 MB RAM as 520STE. Apart from two ordinary 9-pin ports Atari used its own 12-pin controller ports.
STacy	1989	The laptop with monochrome LCD, mini-trackball, 4 MB RAM and 40 MB hard-drive was replaced in the early '90s by a lighter, just as unsuccessful ST-Book (no LCD backlight, no floppy).
Atari TT	1990	A compatible successor with new 68030 CPU (2 MB RAM, up to 8 MB on top of the TT's RAM) and better graphic modes: 320x480 in 256 of 4096 colours, 640x480 in 16 colours and a monochrome mode in 1280x960 pixels. It was replaced by the Falcon.
Mega STe	1991	Mega-ST successor with separate keyboard, a CPU clocked at 16 MHz, cache and an optional co-processor.
Falcon	1992	A keyboard computer with integrated floppy, 68030 CPU as well as a programmable DSP, 4 to 14 MB RAM and a graphics resolution of 640x480 pixels in 16-Bit colours.

Commodore Amiga

USA, 1985

As the C64's successor, the Commodore Amiga was the most popular game micro of the late '80s and at the same time, the last internationally successful home computer. When the A1200 marked the final episode in the Amiga story in 1992, Atari, Sinclair and others had long been vanquished and gamers played with Microsoft and Intel technology.

Before that, Motorola's 68000 processor was seen as the best consumer CPU around. A stripped-down variant could be found inside the Sinclair QL in 1984, while the full-blown 16-Bit version formed the heart of the Apple Mac. Competitors roared their engines, desperate not to miss the 16-Bit transition. Hence, Atari held back their 8-Bit development, and Commodore did the same. Both companies chose the new Motorola chip as CPU and both had in mind a multimedia machine with a graphical interface (GUI) designed for creative users and gamers. Atari turned to its ex-designer Jay Miner, whose company Amiga was busy developing a 68000 based games

The A500 bestseller was an integrated computer with a disk drive in its side.

Units sold:	More than 5 Million
Number of games:	1,500
Game storage:	Disk, CD
Games developed until:	1996
★★★★✦	

The first and prettiest Amiga had a keyboard that slid underneath the main case.

computer. Atari supported Amiga financially and sought to receive the 16-Bit technology in return.

So by a close call, the Amiga hardware nearly landed not with Commodore, but with its archrival. However, during negotiations, Atari put the Amiga team under pressure, which played into Commodore's hands. On August 13th 1984, Atari filed a lawsuit against the technology's supplier, and two days later Commodore announced its takeover of Amiga. Whilst Atari had to ship its 520 ST without the intricate video chips, Commodore unveiled its extraordinary graphic and sound marvel Amiga 1000 in July 1985, thanks to Jay Miner and team.

Based on his experience with the Atari 800 project, the Amiga designer invented two custom chips to help the main processor: Agnus and Denise. The computer had no text mode anymore, but sported 4,096 colours and bitmap modes up to a resolution of 640x512 pixels. Other than LoRes (64 colours), the Amiga supported a `Hold and Modify´ mode (HAM) which displayed digital pictures in near photo realistic quality. Additionally, the graphics chips produced either standard TV interlace pictures or could bring a double-interlace resolution to the screen (albeit with considerable flickering).

After 1990, the best games hailed from Europe: Lotus II had long-distance view, link-mode and engine reverb in tunnels.

Early games by US developer Cinemaware (Defender of the Crown), mesmerised with breathtaking graphics, stereo...

...sound and Hollywood drama. The TV Sports events (shown here: Basketball, 1989) were announced by a bitmap-moderator.

Some Lemmings fell alone, but most died by the dozen (Psynosis 1990).

8-Bit concepts were ported to the Amiga too: Lords of Chaos, an early master piece by the Gollop brothers.

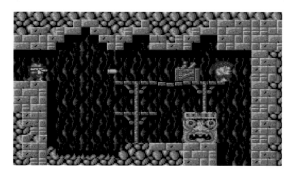

Avoiding traps and nasties in ancient ruins: Core's Rick Dangerous was Lara's 2D daddy.

A 'Blitter' chip speeded up the calculation and rendering of lines, shapes, vectors and polygons. The Amiga was capable of displaying two independent, layered bitmap screens ('dual playfields') and sprites. Hobby and professional videographers loved the 'Genlock' feature that synchronized the screen output to an external video signal.

As an office computer, the 16-Bit machine wasn't taken seriously, but the Amiga's biggest asset was being a strong games machine. After a slow start, it began establishing itself against the Atari ST, with the result that more and more companies supported the powerful Commodore.

In the States, Electronic Arts was an early Amiga partner, releasing games and also the **Deluxe Paint** program used by many developers as a professional tool to design sprites and background images. In the UK, Psygnosis focussed their R&D on the Amiga, moving away from the ST.

Interactive Movies made Cinemaware famous: Graphically bombastic strategy and adventure games like **Defender of the Crown, Rocket Ranger** and the **TV Sports** series were tailored to suit the 16-Bit architecture. These games were far better evidence of

The 600 failed due to lack of dissociation and add-on incompatibility with the A500. As the smallest Amiga, it was practical for anyone who was into playing games, not into coding.

British participation in 16-Bit culture spawned original concepts: Populous presented a gripping idea (you play a God) with innovative graphics.

Primarily used for video and image processing, the 2000 (picture), 3000 and 4000 models spread among creative users. A minimum of 1 MB RAM, second floppy drive and hard-drive turned the work-stations into cumbersome, yet able game terminals.

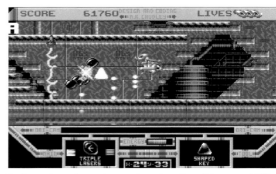

the audiovisual advantages the Amiga had to offer than the 8-Bit ports of **Archon, Ultima** and **Bard's Tale.**

In 1987, Commodore expanded the range with the A2000 workstation and the A500 entry-level Amiga. By 1990, the compact A500 home computer (CPU, keyboard and drive were inside the case) became the most successful Amiga and ultimately the Number 1 in Europe. Now England provided the best Amiga games: Masterpieces like **Populous, Lemmings** or **Lotus 2** implemented excellent two-payer modes. France, Germany and Scandinavia developed commercially successful Amiga originals too, such as **Turrican, Battle Isle, The Settlers** and the **Pinball** series by Sweden's Digital Illusions.

While European programmers reached the hardware's limits, Commodore USA had already been on the retreat since 1988. DOS PCs edged other home and personal computers off the market and the 68000 development shifted to the Mega Drive console. A new Amiga generation with AGA chipset kept the Amiga scene alive until the mid '90s, but neither improved graphics, nor the integration of a CD-ROM drive could save the range. Intel computers as well as Sega and Nintendo consoles took over the 16-Bit market. The CD 32 console proved to be dead on arrival and put an end to the Amiga history in 1993. On 19th April 1994, Commodore filed for liquidation, and the Amiga brand was bought by German computer manufacturer Escom but not followed up with new models. When Escom bit the dust in 1997, Amiga ended up with Gateway and turned into an independent software producer without any relation to its glorious hardware past.

Sadly underestimated, even in spite of cool intro and killer samples: The Killing Game Show.

Served up at the start of German development: Great Courts by Blue Byte (later bought by Ubisoft).

Prior to Lemmings, David Jones wrote an inhumanly tough shoot 'em up for two players: Blood Money.

Back then unpopular, today very rare is the CDTV, which was treated to suitably black peripherals.
Not all Amiga software ran on this multimedia console – its Kickstart 1.3 operating system was out of date the day it shipped.

Commodore Amiga variants and successors

Amiga 1000	**1985**	The first Amiga was the most elegant model, and had a separate, slim keyboard that fitted underneath the main unit. It retailed for $1,500 at launch, contained 256 K RAM and the signatures of the design team inside.
Amiga 500	**1987**	Keyboard and disk drive in one case: The successful home computer variant of the semi-professional Amiga 1000 was shipped with 512 K RAM and expanded by most users to one meg. The practical Amiga was superseded by the hardware flops A500+ (1991) and A600.
Amiga 2000	**1987**	Owing to a German design, the workstation featured 1 MB RAM, with loads of card slots and bays for hard-drive and disk drives. Thanks to Genlock, the machine, and its separate keyboard, was popular with video professionals and graphic artists and enhanced to become the low-cost workstation Video Toaster. As such it was used way until the late '90s.
Amiga 3000	**1990**	A 32-Bit update with 68030 CPU (16 or 25 MHz), 2 MB RAM, SCSI bus and a new OS (Workbench 2), also available as the 3000T in a tower case. Other than its implementation inside the 3D arcade games by Virtuality (e.g. Dactyl Nightmare, 1991), the A3000 made no impact on the games scene.
Amiga CDTV	**1990**	Failed CD-ROM and multimedia console in a black, keyboard-less case. The CDTV (launch price: $699) was made compatible with disk games via an external drive, and thanks to a separately available mouse and keyboard, it could be transformed into a computer. Other than some interactive movies there were few custom made games, only aurally enhanced ports of older disk titles. The best CDTV title was the Sim City conversion from 1991.
Amiga 600	**1992**	The small successor to the A500 home computer was reduced in price several times after its introduction and soon bargained. The keyboard lacked a number pad, but it was the first Amiga to have a PCMCIA port.
Amiga 4000	**1992**	Thanks to the 68040 CPU the A4000 is a true 32-Bit computer. Its AGA chipset could display 256 colours from a palette of 16.7 million as well as up to 256,000 colours simultaneously in `HAM-8´ mode. For the first time, an IDE drive was included instead of SCSI.
Amiga 1200	**1992**	The second Amiga with AGA chipset, launched in December as the A4000's little brother. It was affordable and reasonably successful in Europe. The CPU was 68020, memory was 2 MB. A PCMCIA port was onboard.
CD 32	**1993**	Commodore's second attempt at a CD-ROM console was this time focused on games and featured the AGA chipset and the Akkiko graphics accelerator. In spite of clear market positioning, it was just as unsuccessful as the CDTV. In the face of the PlayStation debut, the unattractive looking machine found no niche, although in the UK, conversions and a handful of CD originals appeared, such as Liberation by Tony Crowther.

Enterprise

GB, 1985

Units sold:	250,000
Number of games:	50
Game storage:	Tape, Disk
Games developed until:	1986

★ ┛

British manufacturer Intelligent Systems (IS) proclaimed its Enterprise as the ultimate computer: A racy beast with 64 K or 128 K RAM, great graphics, stereo sound and built-in joystick. For two years, IS (inventor of the **Cyrus Chess** simulation and several chess computers) developed, tweaked and tuned to take the final step on the ladder of British 8-Bit micros.

At the time, each month brought forth a new computer and the press reacted impatiently to the numerous delays that beset the launch. *'Don't call me Elan, Flan or Samurai – just call me very late'* laughed the April 1984 issue of Your Computer, mocking the almost monthly name changes by David Levy, Robert Madge and their team, which ruined the initial hype.

Neither May 1984, nor September saw the launch of the computer. The Enterprise was shipped in early 1985, a difficult time given competition from Amstrad and MSX and even the 16-Bit Amiga and Atari ST machines. The street price of £170 for the Enterprise 64 and a hefty £230 for the 128 K model were lower than a BBC B or a colour Amstrad, but more expensive than a Spectrum or MSX.

The Enterprise landed, but most of the promised add-ons were missing – no 4 MB memory expansion, no 3.5" double floppy and almost no software. When the Enterprise was scrapped a year after launch, the 100 promised programs were nowhere to be seen. Instead there were just a couple of straight and soulless ports by US Gold, Elite and Mastertronic, mostly on tape, rarely on disk.

The first idea was *'to produce … a Spectrum with a better keyboard and interfaces'* said the inventors in January 1984. They managed Spectrum-compatibility at least: A Spectrum emulator provided the machine with an acceptable selection of games. But the 672x512 pixel high resolution and the 256 colours available to the Enterprise remained untapped.

A port of Cyrus Chess was the only first-party game Intelligent Systems did for their Enterprise micro.

Beast without software: The cartridge port of the Enterprise took on more memory or a Speccy emulator, but no games. A floppy drive was released as an add-on for the port on the other side.

Acorn unleashed raw computing power, but outside the universities no one used a `Reduced Instruction Set Computer´. It took another 10 years before RISC technology established itself on a large scale.

Acorn Archimedes

GB, 1987

Units sold:	500,000
Number of games:	150
Game storage:	Disk
Games developed until:	1995

★ ★ ★ ★ ★

Zarch was David Braben's killer application for the Archie – a fast and furious shoot 'em up dream with polygons, particles and physics.

It was the prime time of home computing: C64 and Amiga ruled, very few played on DOS. In the UK a million punters used machines by Acorn. Their BBC B was the standard format at British schools and universities.

Despite this unique market position, Acorn fell into difficulties. At first Olivetti backed Acorn; later the Italians took over the company. Whilst founder Hermann Hauser joined the Italian group's management, his `Acorn RISC Machines´ division (ARM) unveiled the successor to the BBC. The new 'Reduced Instruction Set' CPU of the Archimedes calculated faster than conventional chips, which struggled with complex instructions.

Today, there's RISC technology inside every PlayStation and Game Boy, but in 1987, the ARM chip was revolutionary and without competition. The Archimedes was twice as fast as the Amiga, generated graphics in 640 x 512 pixels,

featured a 4,096 colour palette, and prefigured a polygonal future with fast 3D animation. Most users utilized the power for scientific simulations. Retailing for £1,000 without monitor the hardware was too expensive for the common gamer.

And so, the `Archie´ slid into an even more elitist corner than its forefather. Only technically versatile BBC programmers like David Braben and Nick Pelling had the guts to code on the RISC PC. The best original game was Braben's **Zarch**, a flat shaded 3D update to Defender. Krisalis supplied prominent ports: **Lemmings**, **SimCity** and **Speedball**.

In 1990, Acorn let its CPU division go, the `A´ now stood for `Advanced´. With initial support from Apple and VLSI, ARM became the leading manufacturer of cheap, power-saving CPUs. After Apple's Newton, ARM delivered chips for 3DO, WinCE handhelds and mobile phones. Ultimately, the technology was used by Nintendo and built into the GBA.

Variants and Successors

A300	1987	The first `Archies´ (A305 with 512 K RAM and A310 with 1 MB) were desktop computers with 3.5" floppy and separate keyboard. Internally the ARM2 CPU was supported by chips for graphics (VIDC), memory (MEMC) and ports (IOC). The A440 (1989) was an enhanced version with 4 MB, four expansion ports and hard-drive. It was replaced in 1989 by the A410/1, A420/1 and – with an improved MEMC – A440/1.
A3000	1989	The keyboard computer with sideward floppy and 1 MB RAM looks a little bit like an Amiga 500. It was somewhat faster than the desktop predecessors, but most ports were stripped away.
A540	1990	No game could tap the power of this mighty Archie with 33MHz ARM3 processor, 4 to 16 MB RAM and 120 MB hard-drive. The Unix variant appeared as the R260.
A5000	1991	The penultimate generation contained an ARM3 chip clocked at 25, later 33 MHz. It had a 1.6 MB floppy, hard-drive and VGA output in a taller case. Also available as the A4 laptop.
A3010	1992	The last low-end approach of the Archimedes is the only model to feature a joystick port (network port I in the variant A3020) and an ARM250 CPU, with its 7.2 MIPS, positioned between the power of the ARM 2 and 3.

NEC PC-Engine

Japan, 1987

Units sold:	7 Million
Number of games:	650
Game storage:	Card, CD
Games developed until:	1996
★ ★ ★ ★ ★	

Rectangular, not much bigger than a handheld and with a slim slot instead of a fat cartridge flap: The PC-Engine was an achievement of diminishing electronics. Even 15 years after its launch, it still appears modern and practical. Games came on thin HuCards – to date the smallest media for stationary hardware.

The joint development by chip manufacturer NEC and games producer Hudson marked the transfer from the 8-Bit age to the 16-Bit era. Released in 1987 in Japan, the

PC-Engine, with its 6502-related processor and 16-Bit custom graphics chip, stood between the best selling NES and the highly anticipated Mega Drive and Super Nintendo consoles. Although it was based on a CPU similar to that used by the Apple II, NES and C64, the PC-Engine hardware was totally superior graphically and acoustically. Tapped to the full potential by experienced programmers, the PC-Engine even left Amiga computers behind in comparison. In 1987 and beyond, the machine was second to none.

The very first PC-Engine was square, white and tiny. A CD-ROM drive similar in design was added just a few months after its release.

Konami's characters came late to the PC-Engine, but when they did, it was something special: Dracula X (1993).

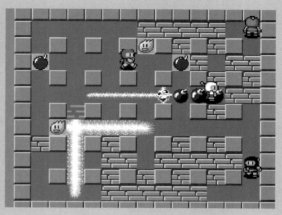

Give me five: Bomberman tournaments required the multi-player adapter and a lot of pads (1990).

Pixel-perfect coin-op conversions of **R-Type** and **Galaga 88** proved to Japanese gamers (and a band of western import freaks), that NEC and Hudson had created a milestone – unfortunately, it also became clear very soon that nobody was thinking of a release in Europe. A US version named Turbo Grafx 16 arrived late and came under fire from Sega and Nintendo. The outcome was that outside of Japan, the PC-Engine was subject to obscurity.

In Japan however, sensational events unfolded. As early as 1988 NEC shipped an add-on CD-ROM drive, beating the competition by several years. Although there were only a small number of noteworthy discs before 1990 (Capcom's **Fighting Street**, Hudson's **Monster Lair** and two episodes of the **Ys** RPG series), after 1992 all publishers moved to the new medium. The ultra flat HuCards with a maximum of 20 Mbit (on average only 4-8 Mbit) became defunct and Konami, despite its late

Does the little witch below look somehow familiar to you? Maybe you've met her in later games by Magical Chase developer Quest, in Ogre Battle or in Final Fantasy Tactics.

The ultimate machine for
2D gaming: Duo Engine.

PC-Engine commitment (1991), also jumped onto the CD-ROM bandwagon. The company breathed new life into the PC-Engine scene and enriched the already exceptional shoot 'em up assortment (**Tiger Heli, Soldier Blade, Super Star Soldier, Super Darius** and **Helfire**) with conversions of its own arcade hits. The classic **Nemesis** was followed and exceeded by the flaming inferno of **Gradius** and the amusing **Parodius.** Konami later bestowed fans with games from other genres like Hideo Kojima's cyber adventure **Snatcher** and the sumptuous action adventure **Dracula X,** which

Epic storyline and voluptuous manga graphics polished the space strategy game Super Schwarzschild 2 (1992).

After R-Type set the pace, many space shooters were released. Despite the old hardware, Aero Blasters played and scrolled better on PC-Engine, than it did on Mega Drive.

116

Hudson's vertically scrolling shoot 'em ups like Final Soldier (1991) got gamers hooked with weapon upgrades.

The black US Turbo Grafx was compatible with Japanese variants' CDs, but not with the HuCards.

in turn paved way for the brilliant PlayStation Castlevania. With its dozen games Konami became the second important software supplier in the last years of the PC-Engine's lifespan – right after Hudson, which pumped out some 100 cards and CDs between 1987 and 1996.

The biggest commercial successes were Hudson's huge CD-ROM RPGs. The Japanese `All Catalog 1993´, a bible for PC-Engine gamers, recommends the Kabuki odyssey **Far East of Eden** as the best release, just edging out the **Dragonslayer** series. Action, RPGs and

strategy titles, polished with more and more fantastic anime sequences were accompanied by excellent sports titles including the Baseball series **Power League**, Human's **Firepro Wrestling** and **Final Match** – for a long time the benchmark tennis game.

Until the mid '90s, NEC released five `System Cards´ as well as regular hardware and case updates to enhance and modernize the PC-Engine. The two portable GT and LT versions are regarded as the most attractive PC-Engine variants, but quickly drained battery life – a fact

Around 1990, PC-Engine consoles were looking strange: This spaceship had a card slot right below its cockpit window.

that was generally disregarded thanks to excellent colour displays and a huge software library. Other variants differ in minor details from the first Engine. Two `Arcade Cards´ (Pro and Duo) expanded the memory of the console and initiated a series of successful beat 'em up conversions. Martial arts novices could afford to miss the Arcade Card but there was another add-on that was a must-have for every Engine fan: In 1990, the five player adapter launched **Bomberman's** multiplayer career, turning video games into party fun and sociable events.

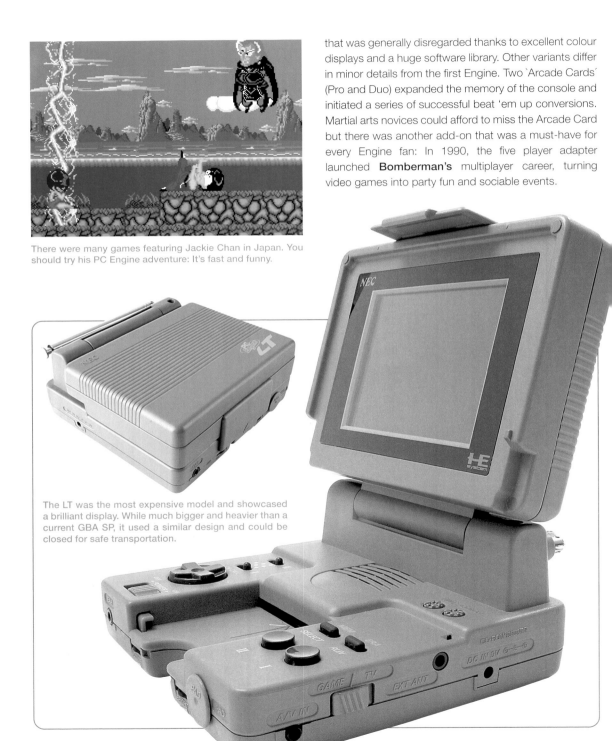

There were many games featuring Jackie Chan in Japan. You should try his PC Engine adventure: It's fast and funny.

The LT was the most expensive model and showcased a brilliant display. While much bigger and heavier than a current GBA SP, it used a similar design and could be closed for safe transportation.

Mobile gamers paid for top technology and a wonderful display with high battery consumption, weight and size. The GT won't fit in your pocket.

PC-Engine variants and successors

PC-Engine	**1987**	The white, compact initial model retailed for 24,800 yen. Regrettably, it has only one joypad port.
PC-Engine CD-ROM 2	**1988**	The additional CD-ROM drive was similar in size and design to the console, but retailed for 57,300 yen – twice as expensive as the base machine.
Turbo Grafx 16	**1989**	The American version of the PC-Engine came in a considerably larger black case and with a modified joypad port and is not HuCard-compatible with Japanese machines.
PC-Engine Shuttle	**1989**	Lower cost (18,800 yen) PC-Engine successor in a futuristic, rounded and larger case. In contrast to all other Engine pads, the Shuttle controller was not angular but featured two small horns.
SuperGrafx	**1989**	This exotic upgrade of the PC-Engine retailed for 39,800 yen. The machine in its ugly science fiction case had more RAM and better graphics hardware, but was supported by only five dedicated SuperGrafx games. The rare cards' crystal cases were shipped within cardboard sleeves; they do not run on any other PC-Engine. 1941 and Ghouls 'n Ghosts are regarded as two of the best arcade conversions.
PC-Engine CoreGrafx	**1989**	Successor to the white PC-Engine retailed for 24,800 yen and came in similar dimensions, but with a grey/blue case and a slightly modified controller.
PC-Engine GT	**1990**	The most expensive version at arrival (44,800 yen), this was a black, LCD equipped handheld without CD-ROM support but with a link port. Sold in Japan and as the Turbo Express in the US. Brilliant display but also high battery consumption required gamers to play using rechargeable batteries and power supply. See picture above.
PC-Engine CoreGrafx II	**1991**	Price reduced to 19,800 yen, second CoreGrafx variant that came with Super CD-ROM 2 software installed.
PC-Engine Super CD-ROM 2	**1991**	CD-ROM 2 successor in CoreGrafx II colours, retailed for 39,800 yen.
PC-Engine Duo	**1991**	For 59,800 yen the most practical PC-Engine (console and top loader CD-ROM in a new black case), this sought-after '90s games machine ran CDs from any country, but either American or Japanese HuCards. Bomberman was hidden in the operating system.
PC-Engine LT	**1991**	The most expensive and exclusive PC-Engine at 100,000 yen: A mobile variant with folding 5 inch display, integrated direction pad and fire buttons. Gaming fun in mini laptop design, just a little bigger than the first Engine.
PC-Engine Duo-R	**1993**	Cheaper Duo Engine in a slightly modified white case, retailed for 39,800 yen.
LD-ROM 2	**1993**	An add-on module for 39,000 yen, that turned the Laser Disc player Pioneer CLD-A100 into a games console. LD-ROM 2 enhanced players are compatible with all PC-Engine games and about ten special Laser Disc titles. The joypad was black and lettered gold, the typical colours of consumer electronics.
PC-Engine Duo-RX	**1994**	Reduced price (29,800 yen) Duo Engine in a slightly modified white case and with a revised six button joypad.

Games manufacturers used CD-ROM capacity for cute cut-scenes: Ranma 1/2 by NCS.

Sharp X68000

Japan, 1987

Units sold:	Unknown
Number of games:	200
Game storage:	Disk
Games developed until:	1994

★ ★ ★ ★

The battle of home micros was nearing its end. In the US, Atari was knocked for six, in Japan, Sharp lost out to other platforms. The MZ was no longer of relevance, the hobby series X1 eclipsed by NEC and Fujitsu. To replace those oldies, Sharp once more cooperated with software-manufacturer Hudson in the design of a 16-Bit computer.

The first X68000 retailed for 370,000 yen and packed substantial power in an imposing case-design. Next to an RGB monitor, stood two slim mini-towers with AV and controller ports and volume control embedded in their bases. Computer and components were completely black, although Sharp later shipped grey versions. Sharp utilised a Motorola 68000 CPU, a chip that was already employed in ST, Mac and Amiga computers for some years. Sharp's

68000 however, was clocked faster. In terms of sound and graphics, the Sharp computer was also better than its western relatives: With a maximum resolution of 768 x 512 pixels and a palette of 65,536 colours, up to 128 sprites, parallax scrolling and a Yamaha synthesizer, Sharp was leaning towards the state of the art in arcade technology. No other console or computer could compete with this kind of raw power.

Bitmap objects were rotated and scaled effortlessly by the X68000, making faithful conversions of Sega hits **Afterburner** and **Space Harrier** a piece of cake. Optimized 2D action (**Parodius, Final Fight**) and, of course, a bulk of fantasy RPGs and adventures were released. Apart from arcade hits by Konami, Capcom and SNK, original games

The second series was grey and had a CPU-upgrade. As always AV- and controller-ports were found at the mini-tower's front.

Märchen Maze was a weird Alice in Wonderland interpretation by Namco. As some games were harmless and cute...

...others were sexy: Shangrlia 2 mixed Langrisser strategy with softcore pictures. For adults only.

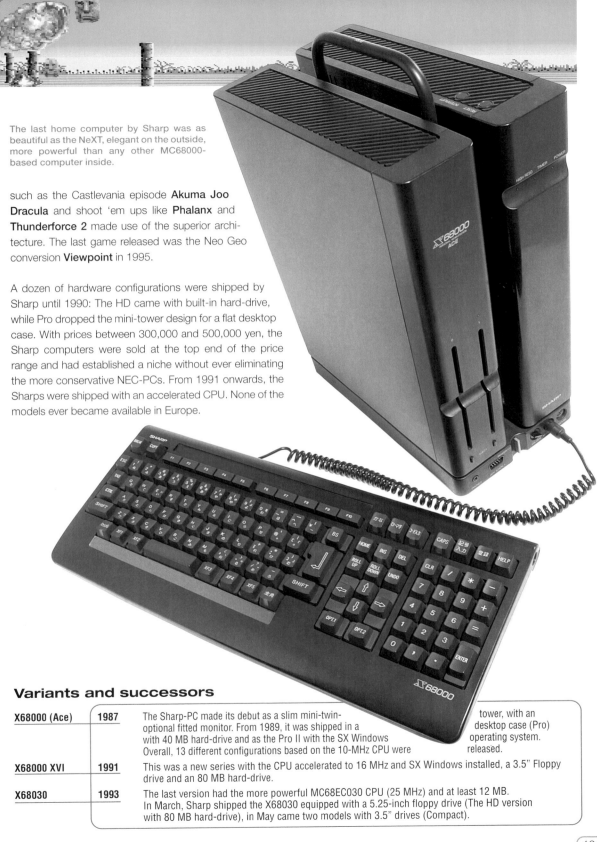

The last home computer by Sharp was as beautiful as the NeXT, elegant on the outside, more powerful than any other MC68000-based computer inside.

such as the Castlevania episode **Akuma Joo Dracula** and shoot 'em ups like **Phalanx** and **Thunderforce 2** made use of the superior architecture. The last game released was the Neo Geo conversion **Viewpoint** in 1995.

A dozen of hardware configurations were shipped by Sharp until 1990: The HD came with built-in hard-drive, while Pro dropped the mini-tower design for a flat desktop case. With prices between 300,000 and 500,000 yen, the Sharp computers were sold at the top end of the price range and had established a niche without ever eliminating the more conservative NEC-PCs. From 1991 onwards, the Sharps were shipped with an accelerated CPU. None of the models ever became available in Europe.

Variants and successors

X68000 (Ace)	1987	The Sharp-PC made its debut as a slim mini-twin-tower, with an optional fitted monitor. From 1989, it was shipped in a desktop case (Pro) with 40 MB hard-drive and as the Pro II with the SX Windows operating system. Overall, 13 different configurations based on the 10-MHz CPU were released.
X68000 XVI	1991	This was a new series with the CPU accelerated to 16 MHz and SX Windows installed, a 3.5" Floppy drive and an 80 MB hard-drive.
X68030	1993	The last version had the more powerful MC68EC030 CPU (25 MHz) and at least 12 MB. In March, Sharp shipped the X68030 equipped with a 5.25-inch floppy drive (The HD version with 80 MB hard-drive), in May came two models with 3.5" drives (Compact).

Trendsetter Sega commenced the age of 16-Bit consoles, becoming popular in western markets. Supporting the console were almost 1,000 games, add-ons for all purposes and tastes, as well as several upgrades.

Sega Mega Drive

Japan, 1988

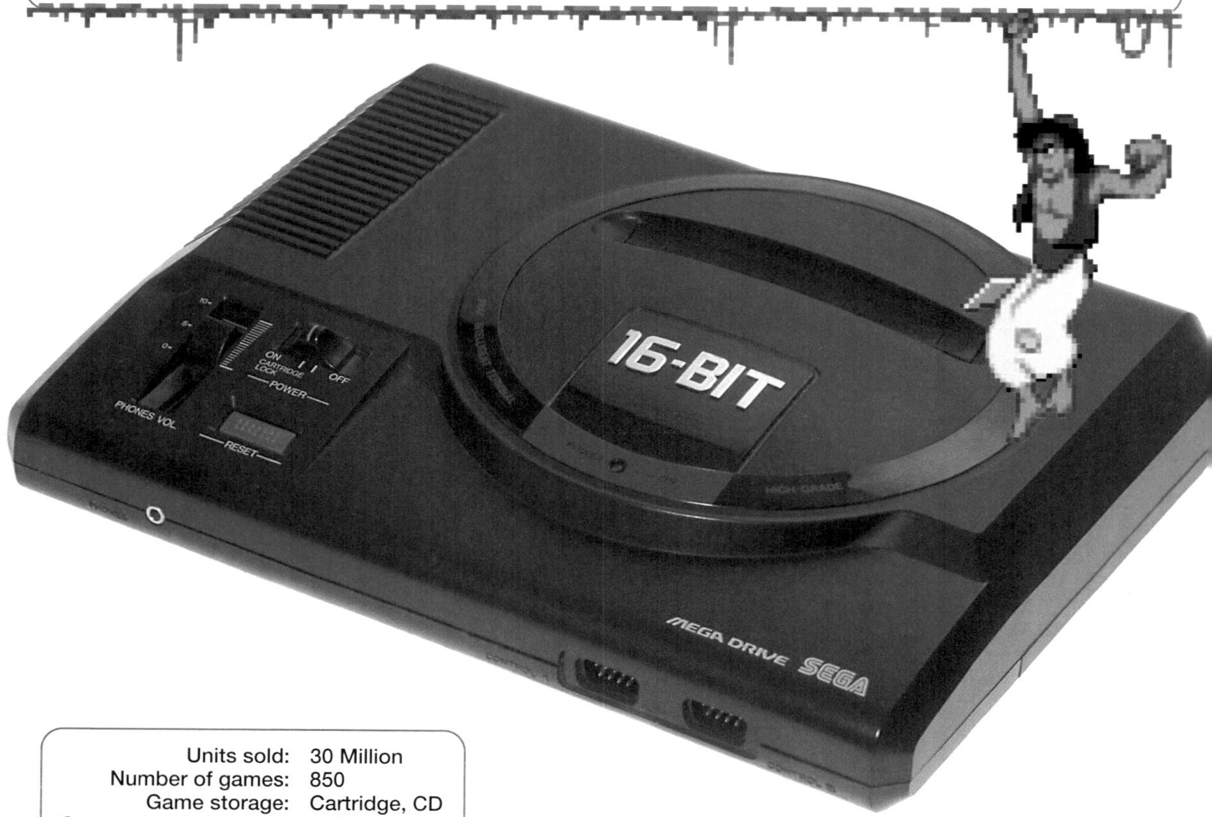

Units sold:	30 Million
Number of games:	850
Game storage:	Cartridge, CD
Games developed until:	1997

★★★★★

Japanese games manufacturer Sega had always come in second – producing accomplished technology and brilliant arcade and console games, but lacking the worldwide success of Nintendo. In joining the 16-Bit fray, Sega finally sought to capture the market from its rival: As the successor to the Master System, the Mega Drive was released in Japan in 1988, arriving in Europe two years later.

American and European gamers welcomed the new hardware: The console was technically similar to the successful Amiga and ST home computers, but graphically superior and thanks to proven and well documented chips, pretty easy to code for.

Early releases like **Altered Beast** had good visuals, but were a let-down gameplay-wise. Thereafter new cartridges went to prove both the hardware's capabilities, as well as the creativity and talent of Sega's developers: The RPG **Phantasy Star II**, the Capcom conversion **Ghouls 'n Ghosts** and – a year after the launch – the excellent action skirmish **Revenge of Shinobi**. But in spite of Sega's internal development teams programming full steam ahead, the large third-

The peaceful dolphin Ecco was brought to life by Novotrade in Hungary, later known as Appaloosa.

Sega itself created the best cartridges: Advanced Military Commander even supported the Mega Drive modem.

This is excellent vertical action: Musha Aleste was coded by Compile for Sega and published in late 1990.

parties held back in order to avoid complications with Nintendo. Square, Enix and Konami ignored Sega; Capcom preferred to sell licences instead of developing and publishing Sega software under its own logo.

In the west, the machine was much more welcome, as developers thirsted for an alternative to Nintendo's licence-dictatorship. At first, Atari ST and Amiga games were converted, followed by original Mega Drive game concepts. In the UK Virgin supported Sega with games and hardware distribution, in the US Electronic Arts immediately stood by Sega. Nearly all EA Sports series started out on the Mega Drive, while computer-hits like **Populous**, **Budokan** and **Starflight** were converted, the action-adventure **Immortal** even with enhanced graphics. From 1992 on, the Mega Drive became the most popular platform amongst western developers.

Sega countered the introduction of the Super Nintendo with a CD-ROM upgrade: The Mega CD introduced a second 68000 chip, and was placed under the actual console, merging with it to become more powerful than any hardware. However, as few Mega Drive users bought the upgrade, the market remained too small to attract a

Mickey Mouse was charming as one of the first licensed Mega Drive heroes: Castle of Illusion (1990).

To fight Nintendo, Sega invested heavily in internal game development (picture: Story of Thor) and...

...manufactured the flat Mega Drive 2 (sparing minor details like the volume control) as well as a cheaper Mega CD device.

Core proved their competence and squeezed the most out of the complicated Mega CD setup: Thunderhawk

major commitment by the software companies; developers rarely utilized the CD capacity or the power of the second CPU. Just a few months after release (12.12.1991 in Japan), the CD system was perceived to be dead whilst Nintendo's new cartridge machine the Super Famicom replaced the market-leading NES.

In the west, Sega closed in on their arch-rival selling 12 million consoles before the end of 1993 in the US alone, where

Unreliable ports, area-coded lock out and dependence on a second mains outlet limited the Mega CD's use. The picture shows the Japanese, first variant; the Mega CD II was shipped world wide in a new look.

A glimpse into the future: The polygon background in Silpheed streamed from CD. Smaller vehicles were rendered in realtime.

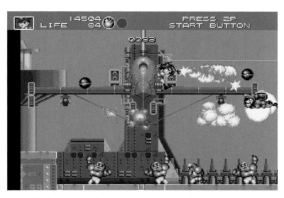

In 1993, Japanese developer Treasure unleashed a late sprite- and pixel-feast starring the Gunstar Heroes.

the console was released as the Genesis, and where the industry veteran Tom Kalinske was in charge. According to US magazine 'Wired', Sega's market share of 45% overtook Nintendo's 44%; in Europe as many as 66% of gamers played with the Mega Drive. With **Sonic the Hedgehog**, Sega provided their console with a mascot that was more modern and swaggering than Mario. Now, Acclaim and Konami, previously exclusive Nintendo partners, joined Sega's bandwagon.

'Sega's Plan for World Domination' declared Wired as it put the blue hedgehog on its cover and quoted EA's Bing Gordon: *'The Genesis has an older custom base than Nintendo. And that's the growth market for the back half of the '90s.'*

Gordon was eventually to be proved right, but it wasn't Sega that tapped into this adult market of gamers, but Sony. Following the introduction of the Mega CD, the Sonic-

With adapters for the cart port, the Mega Drive played both, past and future: The Master System Converter for 8-Bit cartridges and cards was released 1992 ...

... four years later, the 32X add-on with its RISC chips appeared. It required its own power supply and had only 40 games.

Avoiding any additional cables the Mega Jet was a combination of pad and console, designed for in-flight use.

In America, the Mega Drive was more successful than in Japan. The screenshot shows US hero Vectorman from 1995.

empire fell apart. Projects such as virtual reality glasses were stopped, and a hardware update, the 32X, was released but failed.

The combination of Mega Drive, Mega CD and 32X made use of two 16-Bit CPUs, two RISC processors and various supporting chips. At least, in theory. Three power-supplies were required; for both players and developers, the set-up was far too complicated.

With the announcement of the Saturn, Sega itself began digging the grave for the hardware. At the same time, the industry awaited Sony's 32-Bit entry. In 1995, the cartridge market collapsed and Sega's heyday in the west receded.

The Multimega was a portable combination of Mega Drive and CD – available only in the western market.

Mega Drive variants and successors

Mega Drive	1988	Sega's first 16-Bit console was shipped world wide in a similar case, but branded Genesis in the US. Including the Altered Beast cartridge it initially retailed for 21,000 yen and $189 respectively. It was later bundled with Sonic the Hedgehog.
Terradrive	1991	Retailing for 148,000 yen this black desktop PC had a Mega Drive built in and hence came with two CPUs (80286, 68000) as well as a Z80A for support, up to 2.5 MB RAM, disk- and hard-drive, additional graphics and sound memory as well as connectors for monitor and TV. The European model was built and sold by Amstrad.
Mega CD	1991	The CD-ROM drive expanded the Mega Drive with a second 68000 CPU, which was clocked nearly twice as fast as the console's processor. The add-on sold 2 million units world wide and saw the release of around 80 original games and about the same amount of conversions. The initial retail price in Japan was 49,800 yen.
JVC Wondermega	1992	The combination of Mega Drive and Mega CD was sold from April on by JVC for 82,800 yen. Audio controls, Karaoke- and Midi ports made the Wondermega a well-equipped music and games console. The mascot Wonderdog was created by English company Core, the Wondermega however was never released in Europe.
Mega Drive 2	1993	World wide case update in combination with a price reduction to 12,800 yen: The second Mega Drive is rounder and smaller than the predecessor but apart from missing headphone jack and volume control technically identical. The Mega CD also got new clothing, turned into a top loading device and shipped as the Mega CD 2 in July 1993.
JVC Wondermega 2	1993	The externally revised Wondermega successor was sold for 59,800 yen by JVC (starting July) and was shipped with Midi port and a wireless infrared 6-button controller.
Pioneer MegaLD	1993	The Control Pack was available as an add-on for Pioneer's Laser Active disc player. It was pushed into a special slot and contained the complete Mega Drive hardware (chips, joypad and cartridge ports) making the disc player compatible with Sega games as well as interactive Laser Discs like Taito's 3D ride Pyramid Patrol.
Mega Jet	1994	This combo consisted of a Mega Drive and 6-button controller (port for second joypad included) and was devised for use on board the JAL and sold in Japan only (starting price: 15,000 yen). With an LC display, the compact system could have been a handheld.
Multimega	1994	CD Drive, cartridge port and two CPUs in a Discman-like case: The most powerful and beautiful Mega Drive was available in limited numbers in the west only. The name used in the US was Genesis CDX.
Aiwa CSD-GM1	1994	Retailing for 45,000, this ghetto blaster with integrated Mega Drive ran cartridges, Mega- and Audio-CDs as well as CD-G discs and was sold as a Karaoke machine in Japan only.
32X	1994	This hardware add-on topped the Mega Drive with two Hitachi SH2 RISC processors, 2 Mbit of main- and video memory respectively, as well as new sound and graphics chips. Sold for 16,800 yen it multiplied the Mega Drive's power, yet only 40 cartridges and CDs supported it.
Nomad	1995	Console, joypad and LCD combined. The only true handheld version of the Mega Drive was sold in the US and box-moved just shortly after release. Today, it's a collector's item.
Genesis 3	1998	The last Mega Drive was marketed by American distributor Majesco as a very compact cartridge console including the 6-button joypad.

The end of the '80s marked the Game Boy's introduction. Thanks to robust technology, simple usability, low battery consumption and software support from across the globe, the grey handheld became the most successful console. Ever.

Nintendo Game Boy

Japan, 1989

Units sold:	120 Million
Number of games:	1,200
Game storage:	Cartridge
Games developed until:	2002

★ ★ ★ ★ ★ ★

Each Game Boy came with Tetris: Russian software on Japanese hardware formed a dream team of the '90s.

The Game Boy was treated to exclusive Final Fantasy and Dragon Quest games.

Many US titles were ported, like Marble Madness (above). Right: Four Player Adapter.

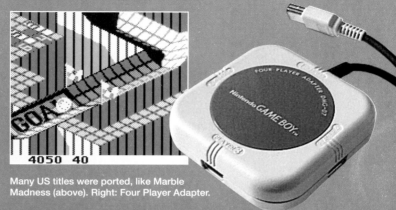

With the 8-Bit NES, Nintendo spearheaded the videogame comeback. But its biggest coup was the portable Game Boy, five years later. While Atari and Sega colour handhelds were both in progress, Nintendo made the most of the opportunity, shipping a simple black and white unit onto the market. Instead of showing off with technical gimmicks, the Game Boy relied on its clear design and simple control elements. It was a handheld for everyone, not just hardcore gamers.

The hardware, designed by Game & Watch inventor Gunpei Yokoi, was backed by optimal software: Each Game Boy included a Tetris cartridge and a two-player link cable – killer applications for the gaming scene of the early '90s, leaving the competition without a chance. Battery-hogging, cumbersome opponents Lynx and Game Gear sold slowly (and were soon dropped by their manufacturers) while the Game Boy travelled across the globe and became synonymous with Nintendo's market leadership. Japanese firms Capcom, Konami, Square,

Taito and Sony but also western publishers released software – original concepts and also conversions of prominent computer games. It took until 1995 and several hundred cartridges for the public to begin speculating about a new – this time colour – handheld by Nintendo. But instead of a hardware successor, Nintendo played a surprise trump card: The RPG Pocket Monsters, developed by Nintendo's (at the time unknown) partner Game Freak.

'Search, collect and love 'em' is the maxim behind an amazing entertainment success story of the '90s. Game Freak grabbed recognizable RPG elements (hit-points, experience levels, turn-based battles) but abandoned the typical 'Dungeons & Dragons' style milieu. Instead of orc, troll and giant spider, Game Freak boss Satoshi Tajiri brought fantastic hybrid-races to the screen, a mix of animal and manga characters, sometimes bizarre, sometimes cute. The original **Pokémon** sold more than six million copies in Japan alone, followed by calendars,

Some of the best games were made by Capcom and Konami, who gave Mega Man and Castlevania Game Boy exclusive updates.

A smaller case and the Pokémon craze gave the Game Boy scene a strong push in the mid '90s.

Towards the end of the hardware's life cycle, Wario, Link and other Nintendo characters returned in full colour.

trading cards, comics and TV serial, figures, cups and an Nintendo 64 version that gave the PlayStation competitor a needed boost.

Suddenly, due to the success of **Pokémon** and the hardware update Game Boy Color (1998), the world once again went crazy for the handheld. From Acclaim to Eidos, Infogrames, Ubi Soft and Konami right up to THQ, Electronic Arts and Mattel – all produced Game Boy games.

Apart from the many rehashes and clever original concepts, it was surprising to see the quality of later PC and PlayStation conversions: Instead of making a quick buck from soulless,

rushed appearances of Lara, **Rayman** and Solid Snake, developers devised new gameplay to fit the Game Boy's specific capabilities.

The relatively minor effort required for Game Boy development helped small teams and software nations step into the industry. The big players hired studios in Spain, Denmark, Sweden, Morocco and Malaysia to develop their handheld titles. And Nintendo was just as surprised as its competitors by the Game Boy revival. Because of **Pokémon**, the release of a hardware successor was delayed. Instead, Nintendo connected its evergreen to the Nintendo 64 and shipped unusual add-ons like a funny camera and printer.

In 1999, the Camelot team behind Shining Force created the brilliant Mario Golf.

The last colour games had great graphics and animation: Rayman 2 (2000).

In 1997, Nintendo gave the Game Boy another push and released a photo camera and printer.

This Game Boy with backlight is rare even in Japan. Shown on its screen is Kid Dracula by Konami.

In 2001, twelve years after the launch of the Game Boy, Nintendo finally revealed the much awaited 32-Bit update at a trade show in Japan. Despite new technology, the `Advance´ was completely backward compatible, meaning that even after its release, games for the old Game Boy were still published. The last batch of 8-Bit games was shipped in 2002 in Japan and 2003 in the west.

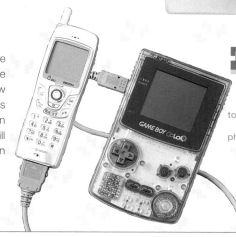

In January 2001, Nintendo took the Game Boy into the mobile phone network; the `Mobile System´ connection was shut down in December 2002.

Game Boy variants and successors

Game Boy	1989	The first Game Boy in a bare grey white case was shipped with Tetris and a link cable. Later red, blue, yellow and green, white, black and translucent versions were released. Display resolution was 144x160 pixels.
Super Game Boy	1994	...made the Super Nintendo run Game Boy games: The SGB adapter was plugged into the cartridge port of the console, added colour to monochrome games and borders (which could be defined with simple drawing tools) to utilise the TV resolution. The SGB improved some games' sound and music; the Game Boy remake of Space Invaders contains a mode that can only be played on the SGB. An update was released in 1996 as `Super Game Boy 2´; it had a link cable port (unlike its predecessor) and was available bundled with Pokémon Blue or Red.
Game Boy Pocket	1996	A Game Boy update in a smaller case replaced the first series and came in colour variants, including silver, gold and translucent versions. For Toyota, All Nippon Airline and games magazine Famitsu, Nintendo produced rare special versions. Coinciding with an N64 competition, Imagineer released a luminously coloured Game Boy.
Game Boy Color	1998	56 Colours instead of 4 grey scales: Larger and heavier than the Game Boy Pocket, the handheld added colour to older cartridges but also ran new colour games with up to 32 Mbit capacity (instead of 0.25 to 4 Mbit). With the `Mobile System´ cable, the Game Boy Color became compatible with the Japanese mobile phone net.work.
Game Boy Light	1998	This version came with a background light for the LCD, for 6,800 yen just before the debut of Game Boy Color in Japan. Sized 80x135x29 mm, it was larger, but 190 g lighter than other versions and was available in gold and silver only. Two batteries powered the handheld to give 12 hours of backlight, 20 hours in regular mode.

Atari Lynx

USA, 1989

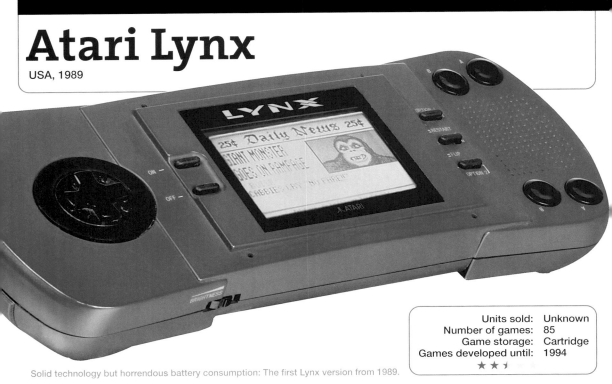

Units sold:	Unknown
Number of games:	85
Game storage:	Cartridge
Games developed until:	1994

★ ★ ✦

Solid technology but horrendous battery consumption: The first Lynx version from 1989.

Epyx was an industry veteran, founded in 1978 by Jim Connelley and Jon Freeman as Automated Simulations for developing computer role-playing games. In the early '80s, Epyx swallowed Starpath, the developer of the VCS Supercharger. The know-how gathered from this takeover went into action hits like Summer Games, Breakdance and Impossible Mission and gave Epyx confidence. After software, the company was aiming to market its own hardware and contacted Dave Needle and RJ Mical. Together, the two well-known personalities from the

Amiga development team devised a portable games machine.

Epyx brought Needle and Mical on board, pushed the `Handy´ project forward to a releasable state and sold it to Atari in 1988. The name of the machine was changed to Lynx, the price dropped to $200 – still twice as expensive as the Game Boy. And that's basically the most interesting part of the story: As usual, Atari lacked both marketing muscle and the faith of retailers and developers. By the

Unlike US games (shown here: Hard Drivin' from 1991), ...

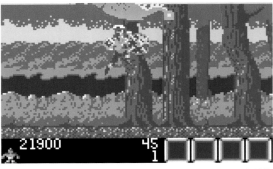

... Japanese concepts seldom played on the Lynx: Rygar (1990).

end of the '80s, Nintendo also reached market leadership in the States. Ironically, the Lynx's technical merit turned out to be its downfall: The colour display consumed six batteries in four hours. Nintendo avoided this by using simple technology and a monochrome display. The Game Boy was more economical, smaller and lighter than the Lynx. And it ran Tetris.

The Lynx could not attract ingenious game concepts or third-parties. Only Atari delivered games before 1994. The only Lynx original worth of note stems from old Epyx days: Chuck Sommerville's 1989 cute puzzle game **Chip's Challenge** was developed exclusively for the Lynx and was highly addictive. Interesting, but not as playable were 'ComLynx' network games: **Slime World** featured a romp with up to eight explorers while four players conducted aerial dogfights in **Warbirds**. A conversion of Centipede that used the screen vertically was never released.

The Atari fan base kept the Lynx alive: Harry Dodgson sold his **Lynx Othello** from the States and presented the unreleased Eye of the Beholder AD&D game. In Germany, Bastian Schick and Matthias Domin program-med tools, games and demos. The company Songbird even released new Lynx carts and can be found at http://songbird.atari.net.

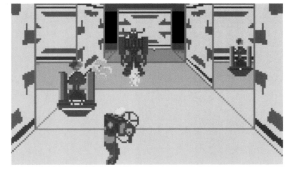
A portable arcade: Atari converted 30 coin-ops to the Lynx, eg. Klax, Joust, Rampage and the 3D shoot 'em up Xybots.

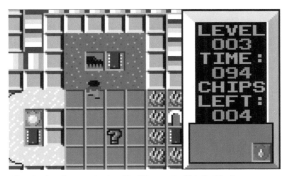
Like the hardware, the terrific 2D puzzle Chip's Challenge was developed by Epyx (and later ported to micros by US Gold).

What's that nerd looking at? Chip was the biggest talent among the Lynx heroes.

Shanghai, shown on the display of the second Lynx model (right), was an addictive puzzle, designed in the US, not in Asia.

The successor

Atari Lynx II	1991	The Lynx II came in a new case, was a little smaller and lighter than the predecessor. Battery consumption was reduced: During a game pause, it was possible to switch off the display. An LED blinked whenever the batteries were low, the headphone output was stereo (unlike that of its predecessor). A limited version was released in collaboration with Marlboro: The red machine with a white logo of the cigarette brand was sold several hundred times for promotion (together with a `Marlboro Go!´ game and a Marlboro bag). Like the Coke variant of the Sega Game Gear, this is a rare collector's item.

Fujitsu FM Towns

Japan, 1989

Units sold:	Unknown
Number of games:	400
Game storage:	CD, Disk
Games developed until:	1996

★ ★ ★ ★

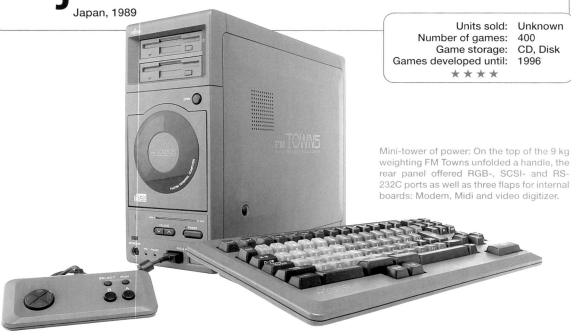

Mini-tower of power: On the top of the 9 kg weighting FM Towns unfolded a handle, the rear panel offered RGB-, SCSI- and RS-232C ports as well as three flaps for internal boards: Modem, Midi and video digitizer.

In the west, the home computer era was nearing its end; Commodore and Atari were making way for the supremacy of DOS and Intel. In Japan, the war of the systems was not yet over: Fujitsu and Sharp were battling NEC PCs with their own sets of standards.

Fujitsu replaced its 8-Bit series FM-7 with a super computer to bridge the gap between high tech office and virtual playground. The FM Towns combined PC functionality with Macintosh creativity, was based on Intel's high-end CPU 80386DX and incorporated its own, non-Microsoft-compatible operating system. The standard resolution of the deluxe computer was 640x480 pixels in 256 colours drawn from a 24-Bit palette ('True Color') and – to rival Sharp's X68000 – exhaustive bitmap graphics capabilities with multi layer parallax scrolling and more than 1,000 sprites.

Externally, the CD-ROM drive dominated the grey mini tower. Fujitsu decided to use the 'hyper-medium'

CD as standard long before PCs and Macs did. Beneath the CD flap sat two floppy drives and the multimedia controls: Volume, microphone and headphone jacks as well as ports for keyboard, mouse and joypad. The joypad, a grey clone of the Famicom pad, was included with each computer.

The technical might and user-friendliness instantly made the FM Towns the hottest personal computer available. Even in the west, computer experts and game developers raised their heads in interest. Although the FM Towns, like Sharp's X68000, failed to end the dominance of NEC's PC-98s, it was well supported with games and creativity software. Japanese simulations (**A-Train, The Tower**), arcade conversions (**Tiger Heli, Splatterhouse**) and erotic fantasy RPGs (**Princess Maker, Rance IV**) were accompanied by conversions of western VGA games: **Wing Commander** and **Falcon 3.0, Alone in the Dark, Monkey Island** and **King's Quest V**. As CDi and CDTV failed to take off and multimedia was still pretty unexplored

Genocide 2
(Zoom, 1993)

Gamers and collectors sought after the white, first edition of the top loader console and the second grey-blue variant with a more powerful CPU.

territory to Microsoft, progressive American, British and French developers got their hands on FM Towns to experiment with CD-ROM.

Fujitsu itself was the driving force behind most releases and had a sharp eye for influential software. LucasArts' early online community **Habitat** was enhanced by Fujitsu scientists and survived into the '90s.

Three years after the computer came the console variant Marty, much anticipated by gamers, but commercially without success. The CD-ROM machine was deployed some 18 months before the PlayStation in Japan only. Thanks to a 3.5" floppy drive and PCMCIA slot, the Marty was compatible with FM Towns computer games.

Because of its technical capabilities, FM Towns became the target platform for early 3D and CD experiments by Liverpool-based Psygnosis (Scavenger 4, 1993).

Variants and successors

FM Towns	1989	Computers of the first series were grey mini towers with keyboard, mouse and joypad, with either one (Model 1F) or two floppies (2F). At the end of 1989, the hard-drive equipped variants 1H and 2H were launched and sold until 1992, then replaced by 40H and 80H with 40 MB and 80 MB hard disks respectively.
FM-Towns II	1991	The same case as its predecessor but shipped with V2.1 operating system. The CX20 had two floppies, the CX40 an additional 40 MB hard drive. It was replaced by the desktop model HR, the last grey cased FM Towns computer, 1992.
FM-Towns II (UX)	1992	All-in-one system with SX CPU: Like early Mac computers, the unit itself, a 10" Trinitron tube and speakers formed a compact tabletop. Only keyboard, mouse and joypad were separate. Beneath the CD-ROM front loader sat a pair of disk drives. UX20 and UX40 came with internal hard-drives.
FM Towns Marty	1993	The first console variant with 16MHz 386 CPU, 1 MB RAM and 640 K VRAM, came in a white case and with a colour-fitting joypad; a successor with yellow logo and button, using the better CPU, was introduced 1994 as Marty Model 2. Brand and platform were also used by the navigation computer Car Marty; with the CD-ROM missing, roadmaps and other data were loaded via PCMCIA.
FM Towns II MX, MA, ME	1993	Revision in a white case: The MA and ME were based on the i486SX with 8 K cache, 25 or 33 MHz. The high-end model MX used an i486DX2/66 and a double speed CD-ROM. Apart from that, MX and MA were identical: 4 MB memory (expandable to 28), 1 MB VideoRAM, a maximum resolution of 1024x768 pixels in 256 colours as well as two floppy drives and a hard-drive. The ME came with half the memory and had graphics resolutions of 320x240 in 32,000 colours and 640x480 with 256 colours. Four card slots made all models easily expandable, ME and MA were upgradeable with a 486DX2 chip ('Overdrive Processor'). They came bundled with joypad or microphone.
FM Towns II Fresh	1994	The 'all in one' successor in a modified case with external, sideward speakers had the i486/33 CPU, 6 MB RAM, 170 MB hard-drive, 'Overdrive' expandability, Towns OS, MS DOS and Windows. It was replaced 1995 by the Fresh E and Fresh ET and the FM Towns II Model MF with 4 Mbyte RAM.
FMV-Towns	1995	With the new model name, Fujitsu sold Pentium equipped computers running Win95, which were compatible to old Towns OS programs and games.

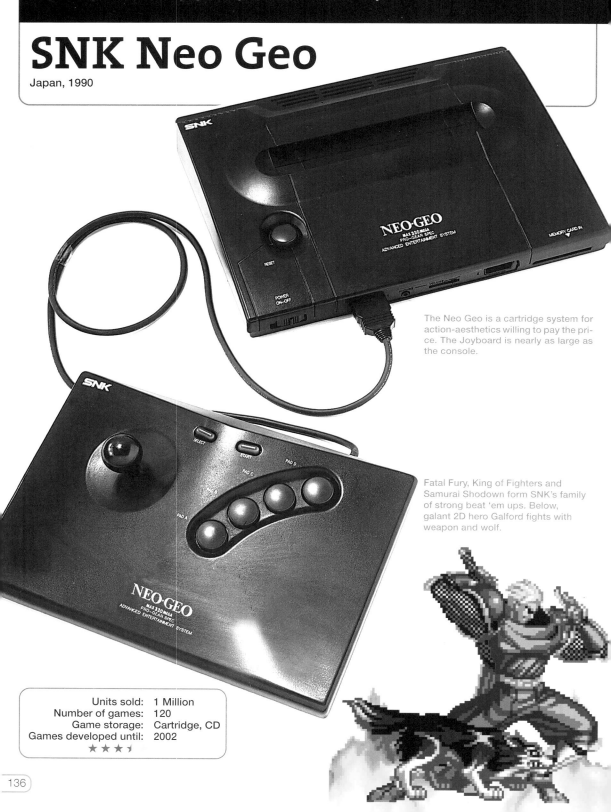

Arcade feeling in the living room. The Neo Geo and its massive cartridges were a dream come true for those dedicated to action. The deluxe console remained an outsider, despite a loyal fan base carrying their system into the 21st century.

SNK Neo Geo

Japan, 1990

The Neo Geo is a cartridge system for action-aesthetics willing to pay the price. The Joyboard is nearly as large as the console.

Fatal Fury, King of Fighters and Samurai Shodown form SNK's family of strong beat 'em ups. Below, galant 2D hero Galford fights with weapon and wolf.

Units sold:	1 Million
Number of games:	120
Game storage:	Cartridge, CD
Games developed until:	2002

★ ★ ★ ✦

Throughout the '80s, coin operated arcade games were the benchmark for graphics, sound and speed. Home conversions were stripped down, rarely meeting the standard set by coin-ops and by the time they did, it was long after their release in the arcades. In 1990, the Japanese company SNK broke this rule by developing the Multi Video System (MVS) which appeared as both an arcade game format and a console for home use. The price of 58,000 yen ($600 outside of Japan) for the hardware and up to 32,000 yen for a cartridge made the Neo Geo the most expensive video game.

The shaft for the huge Megashock cartridges dominated the flat housing, to which two joyboards could be connected. The deluxe controllers carried a heavy-duty stick and four large fire buttons. They were designed for action and intended to be placed down on a strong and level surface – not held like joypads. Apart from the golden lettering, the Neo Geo was sleek and minimalist in appearance. The front featured a power switch and controller ports as well as a headphone socket with volume control, to the right of this was a neat inlet for the novel memory card. Using this storage device, players could save high-scores and game positions, and exchange them between consoles and arcade machines. The memory card was an ingenious invention; later to be adopted and improved by Sony for the mass-market PlayStation.

The first Neo Geo games were conventional, yet technically better and faster than titles for any other platform. The shoot 'em up **Nam 1975**, the sports spectacular **Baseballstars Professional** and the fantasy game **Magician Lord**, developed by SNK's partner Alpha-Denshi (ADK), were followed by 21 cartridges before the end of 1991. Early cartridges had a capacity of up to 50 Mbits,

four times as much as Nintendo or Sega games. The Street Fighter clone **Fatal Fury** laid the foundation for the Neo Geo's reputation as the best console for beat 'em ups. The horizontal scrolling shoot 'em up **Last Resort** (1992), with its huge biomechanical monsters and R-Type inspired gameplay, transformed the Neo Geo into a dream machine for 2D shoot 'em ups.

The first memory card

With the second beat 'em up series **Art of Fighting**, SNK broke the 100 Mbit barrier and for the first time, gave beat 'em up fans 'zooming', which saw the sprites of approaching players become bigger.

But this tough action came with an equally hard-hitting price tag: The home console was a peripheral success, backed by loyal fans and supported by the success of the arcade version MVS. Exclusive games for home use were not released, but still, home versions were identical to the MVS variants and technically better than respective PlayStation or other 32-Bit console conversions. As the cartridges were four to five times more expensive than Sony games, SNK released a Neo Geo with CD drive instead of a cartridge slot in 1994. Nearly all games were ported to this cheaper platform and re-released at a more competitive price. The CD games were identical to the cartridge versions but suffered from loading times.

In 1995 the Neo Geo reached the peak of its popularity. Among the 20 games developed and published that year were titles by Technos (**Double Dragon**), Video System (**Sonic Wings 3**), Hudson, Takara and Sunsoft.

Vertical shoot 'em ups such as ADK's Alpha Mission 2 in 1991 were...

...followed by horizontal scrolling games inspired by Irem: Last Resort, 1992.

King of Fighters: Nearly half of all Neo Geo games are beat 'em up updates.

Metal Slug explodes in a maximum of on-screen sprite action: Metal Slug X, 1999.

Likewise, plenty of ROM was poured into **Metal Slug**, a series of militaristic jump 'n' shoots which became SNK's strongest brand, and the third instalment shipped on a 700 Mbit cart. But the cult series could not save SNK from demise – the era of 2D was over. The lack of success achieved by both the MVS sequel Hyper Neo Geo 64 (which featured a 64-bit RISC CPU and nearly 200MB RAM) and the hand-held Neo Geo Pocket as well as the decline of the arcades eventually led to a takeover by Korean investors.

Today the most popular Neo Geo brands are systematically updated and ported to other systems by the new company SNK Playmore, while other activities (Neo Geo hardware among) were closed or buried for good.

After 1996, support from third-party developers slowly dried out but widespread arcade distribution kept the Neo Geo alive even after 3D graphics became mainstream.

As the Neo Geo was not suited for polygon rendering, developers had pushed 2D sprite animation and scrolling to the limit by the end of the '90s. Shoot 'em ups such as Aicom's massive 305 Mbit **Pulstar** and countless beat 'em ups on cartridges carrying more than 200 Mbit of data were Neo Geo's speciality. SNK concentrated its head-to-head fighting experience into the release of **King of Fighters** in 1994, gathering all the heroes and villains of the SNK series in one majestic bout. The smooth and detailed animation of this all-star tournament appeared as 196, 250, 362, 460 and 680 Mbit carts – and ultimately as 892 Mbit episode **King of Fighters 2001**.

Die-hard Neo Geo fans don't waste their time waiting for a CD to load and sniff at later hardware variants: They play with Megashock carts or – even better – MVS arcade cabinets only.

Neo Geo variants and successors

Neo Geo	1990	The original model shipped with a huge joyboard. In Japan it was sold with red fire buttons for a short time.
Neo Geo CD	1994	This lower-cost, CD-only console was available in two versions, as a top- or a front-loader. Only the front-loading version came with a joyboard, the other with a simple gamepad instead.
Neo Geo CDZ	1995	Apart from a changed housing and faster CD drive, the CDZ was otherwise unimproved – and loading times remained too slow.
Hyper Neo Geo 64	1997	The completely redesigned 64-Bit-RISC successor was not compatible with the 16-Bit MVS or original Neo Geo and never released for home use. The technically powerful, yet unsuccessful arcade architecture saw seven games released, including polygon updates of Samurai Spirits and Fatal Fury.

Sega Game Gear

Japan, 1990

Units sold:	3 Million
Number of games:	300
Game storage:	Cartridge
Games developed until:	1996

★ ★ ★

With its first handheld hardware, Sega overtook the Game Boy: The Game Gear boasted 32 colours and a backlit display at a time when Game Boy visuals were still grey.

Beneath the black housing rested the technology of Sega's Master System. The number of colours was increased, but the resolution slightly reduced to 160x146 pixels. A compulsory add-on was the 'Master Gear Converter' which could run Master System cartridges on the handheld. In addition, Sega sold display lens, an external battery pack and a TV tuner with AV input: In theory, it is possible to use the Game Gear as a portable monitor for stationary consoles like Saturn or Dreamcast.

While Sega initially delivered classics like **Space Harrier** and **Wonderboy**, the Game Gear later benefited from the Mega Drive's success and reaped conversions of **Ecco**, **Lunar** and **Shining Force**. From 1993, western licensees took over: Acclaim published **NBA Jam, Terminator 2, Robocop** and **Mortal Kombat,** Electronic Arts released **FIFA** and **John Madden** games; and the British company Codemasters converted its **Micro Machines**. Sega's answer to Nintendo's Super Mario Kart was two exclusive and network-capable **Sonic Drift 3D** racers. Finally, at the end of 1996, **G-Sonic** and **Virtua Fighter Mini** appeared – at 8 Mbit, the biggest Game Gear cartridges.

Apart from the connector for the power supply, the handheld also featured a headphone jack with volume control, a foldaway stand and a port for linking a second Game Gear.

Please feed it with six batteries: Sega Game Gear

Variants and successors

Game Gear	1990	Following the dark Game Gear (19,800 yen), the mid-'90s saw multiple colour variants released for 13,800 yen in Japan, including red and blue, and (from 1995) 'Character Pack' bundles priced at 15,800 yen – coloured consoles including one game.
Game Gear White	1991	The white Game Gear priced at 34,800 yen, was manufactured in limited numbers (only 10,000 units were ever sold) and released with a matching TV tuner and a carrying-case.
Coca Cola	1994	The rare Game Gear version in design and colours of the famous soft drink brand was released with the Coca Cola Kid cartridge.
Kids Gear	1996	The final model in Virtua Fighter-Anime look, in greys and one distinctive colour and with blue buttons. It was bundled with VF Mini and only released in Japan for 14,800 yen.

Super Nintendo

Japan, 1990

The grinning asteroid points to the secret passageway into sector Y and Z: Starfox (1993).

With the Super Famicom, Nintendo dared to release a grey toy. The only elements of colour are the logo and four fire buttons.

Units sold:	50 Million
Number of games:	2,000
Game storage:	Cartridge
Games developed until:	2000

★ ★ ★ ★ ★

At the end of the '80s, nearly 40 million NES consoles were sold and each week a few hundred thousand units rolled out of the factory. Nintendo was in no hurry with the next generation. While Sega and NEC were planning for a future of CD and 16-Bits, the market leader calmly prepared the platform successor and finally brought the 'Super Famicom' to shops at the end of 1990 – three years behind PC-Engine, 25 months after the Mega Drive. It took another year for its release in Europe: For British, French and German fans, the end of the 8-Bit era came in summer 1992.

The Mode 7 graphics technique zoomed and rotated the court in NCAA Basketball, developed in 1992 by Sculptured USA.

The 16 Mbit in Street Fighter 2 were used for furry heroes, smooth animations and idyllic backgrounds.

Nintendo's cool plan worked out: At home in Japan, the Super Famicom immediately overtook the Mega Drive. The best game developers Konami, Capcom and Square stood by Nintendo, but as usual, the market leader didn't rely solely on third-party support, and delayed the launch until there were enough self-developed titles ready: **Super Mario World** was an update of the most popular video game of the '80s, while sci-fi racing game **F-Zero** gave an outlook on the 3D future. With the kind of gameplay, originality and audiovisual fine-tuning found in **Super Mario World**, many insiders suspected that the game was not tailored to suit the machine, but the other way round: The hardware was built around Shigeru Miyamoto's game.

On the outside, the machine stood out from other game consoles with its ordinary look – it did without a cool black, or funky colours. A light tone, rounded corners and big buttons were all more reminiscent of Bang & Olufsen than of Sony. The unit looked original and modern, but at the same time robust and childproof. The only colour spots were the logo and the four fire buttons of the joypad, which, for the first time, featured two shoulder buttons located on the sides of the pad.

Technically, the Super Nintendo was not really better than its competitors, the Mega Drive and PC-Engine. While Sega used a pure 16-Bit CPU with the 68000, Nintendo implemented a successor to the old 6502 chip: A 65816 clocked at a conservative 3.58 MHz. On the other hand, the Super Nintendo had the better graphics architecture and a powerful sound chip. Sega melodies croakily whinged, Nintendo games played a full orchestral soundtrack. The acoustics chip was developed by a Sony team under Ken Kutaragi. Some time later, Sony perfected the chip for its own PlayStation.

The trump card against the Mega Drive turned out to be the `Mode 7´ graphics. Rotation, zooming and shrinking of playfields made for simple yet convincing three-dimensional effects, featuring bitmaps instead of polygons: **F-Zero** and **Pilotwings** were two early examples of this pseudo-3D. Later, the first-class Mode 7 race **Mario Kart** laid the foundation for the genre of multiplayer fun racing games.

Nintendo enhanced those rudimentary 3D capabilities with special chips that were included in game cartridges, widening the gap to the Mega Drive even more. As early as

The modem shipped by X-Band for Japanese and American consoles enabled online duels. It was revolutionary but unsuccessful.

This adapter made Game Boy software run on Super NES. Shown here is the version for US consoles.

1990, the Digital Signal Processor DSP-1 in **Pilotwings** accelerated bitmap zooms and rotations, and later Nintendo engaged Argonaut, a British pioneer of 3D computer games. Jez `Starglider´ San and his team invented the SuperFX chip for Nintendo, a RISC processor specialising in vector manipulation that was capable of moving and flat shading 100 polygons per second. The FX game **Starfox** was developed in cooperation between Shigeru Miyamoto and Argonaut. Japanese drama and British tech know-how made for a science-fiction masterpiece, although it sold comparatively slowly due to its unconventional blocky graphics style. The 3D shoot 'em up and nine further polygon games remained outsiders in Nintendo's circus of cute sprites.

Most Super Nintendo expansions were never released in the west. `Satellaview´ turned the Super Famicom into a mini-tower for

There's no better fun racing game: Mario Kart still justifies a Super NES as a secondary console.

broadband downloads in 1995. This expansion, sized and designed to fit the base machine, was slid underneath the console, and received updates of **F-Zero** and charming **Zelda** via satellite, which were then saved on 1 Mbit Flash Cards the size of a Game Boy cartridge.

A CD-ROM drive was planned but never realised. As the only console manufacturer, Nintendo stayed true to the expensive yet in many ways advantageous ROM cartridges. Step by step, Nintendo expanded the size of its games until Capcom was allowed to use a 16 Mbit cart for **Street Fighter 2**. The investment in a fat ROM paid off: The graphically fantastic arcade conversion was one of the biggest Super Nintendo successes. Square's **Final Fantasy V** used 8 Mbit, the 1994 sequel swallowed even more: 24 Mbit. For **Mario RPG**, the crowning combination of Miyamoto's universe and Final Fantasy, Nintendo sported a 32 Mbit cartridge. Although the game sold some 1.5 million copies in Japan, Square and Nintendo parted after that.

Western games were not as original or well done as those by Konami and Capcom, Enix and Square. Movie and TV licences made Acclaim the strongest partner in the US, but only a few of the Hollywood games were as thrilling as **Alien 3**, which was programmed by Probe in 1993. Australian developer Beam created a recommendable **Shadowrun** conversion and a **Mechwarrior** game that allowed the player to let rip against zooming Mode 7 robots, while Nintendo's foothold in the Britain was Rare, a company

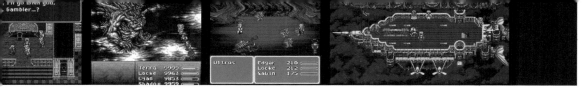

Battle and game scenes from Final Fantasy VI (1994).

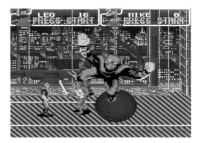

Major third-party Konami included The Teenage Mutant Ninja Turtles in their catalogue, one of its few 'alien' licences.

The Kong family was reborn on SGI computers. Animals and backgrounds were rendered, not hand drawn.

Strategy and fantasy gems like Fire Emblem (1994) were not localized by Nintendo for the west.

founded in the early '80s and now bought by Nintendo. Their Super NES debut was **Donkey Kong Country**. The monkey race's characters and animations were modelled in 3D, rendered by SGI hardware and then turned into 2D sprites. The prerendered animations were not as flexible as the real-time rendering of later 32-Bit consoles but looked a lot better – the games community smiled at Gouraud shaded monkey bellies in 8x16 pixels.

Despite the 700 games published in the west, many PAL gamers only saw the tip of the iceberg. In Japan, hundreds of additional strategy, RPG and adventure titles, as well as Pachinko and tabletop simulations were released. Many of them were not sold regularly but as a Satellite download. Finally, half way through 2000, Nintendo stopped the Satellaview service.

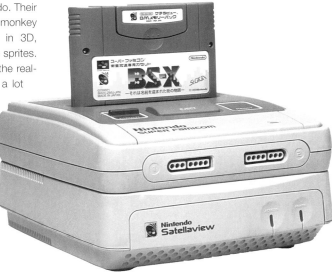

Japanese Nintendo gamers received their programs via satellite. The BS-X adapter contained a small flash cartridge.

Super Nintendo variants and successors

Super Famicom	1990	The original model was released in Japan retailing for 9,800 yen, in the UK two years later as the Super Nintendo for £150. The European variant is only compatible with NTSC games via an adapter or an internal modification.
Sharp Famicom Televi SF-1	1990	A TV with cartridge port on its top was released in November 1990 and retailed for 128,000 yen. In the west, the unusual 21" apparatus was on display at the ECTS show in London but never commercially released. Apparently, there's a smaller version with a 14" tube.
Super NES	1991	The US variant came in a rectangular case with a purple slider. Its joypad dropped the four signal colours of the original logo too, bearing indigo buttons instead. The cartridges are square and too large for the cart slot of European or Japanese machines.
Super Famicom Jr.	1998	Smaller hardware, price-reduced to 7,800 yen. After Japan, it was also sold in USA.

Strange vehicles were zooming and rotating in F-Zero.

Goodbye to bitmapped heroes and 2D landscapes: 32-Bit processors, CD-ROM and real-time 3D animation elevated computer and videogames to the next level.

Rendered crazy

Interactive cinema: Wing Commander was a 3D space opera with traditional handcrafted graphics, which spawned a whole series of episodes.

Early first person shooters weren't real 3D simulations, but `cheated´ to give the appearance of height and depth. Dark Forces by LucasArts was first to feature underpasses and bridges.

A revolution had cast its shadow over the computer and videogame industry. Compared to the massive leap to the 32-Bit age, the move from 8- to 16-Bit hardware some years earlier was small. Two divergent technologies – CD-ROM and real-time 3D – fashioned virtual worlds and fostered whole new gaming experiences.

CD-ROM is merely a storage medium. It's not particularly fast, it's not re-writable, but it is inexpensive and large; a CD-ROM carries up to 400 times more data than a floppy and was hence wholeheartedly welcomed by (for the most part)

American adventure game developers. In the early '90s, Sierra and others shipped their seminal VGA games on four, six or even eight floppy disks in heavy boxes. A single CD on the other hand, could carry all the required data, including 32-Bit sound and music and for the first time, even films in MPEG-1 quality (Full Motion Video, FMV).

In the west, Philips and Commodore produced CD-ROM consoles; in Japan, NEC and Fujitsu did. It quickly became evident that most software developers had no idea what exactly to do with the large storage capacity. The promised

Fast, technical and flat shaded: Virtua Racing by Sega (1992).

Moving chaos in real-time: Command & Conquer, Westwood, 1995.

multimedia experiences (educational programs and interactive comics, music clips and interactive movies) weren't too exciting, and games on CD played no better than their disk counterparts or cartridge versions, simply beefed up with music and movie clips instead. Indeed the lack of inspiration saw old Laser Disc games republished on CD-ROM.

At a fraction of the price of a 2 MByte cartridge, the 600 MByte disc still became the standard storage medium for games. Only Nintendo stuck to solid-state cartridges.

While the CD was important for economics, the mass production of RISC processors and the advances in 3D animation gave videogames a much needed creative and technical push. Yu Suzuki started the new generation of onscreen action in 1992 with **Virtua Racing**, in which the racing circuit and vehicles were no longer frame-animated like cartoons, but modelled in 3D and rendered in real-time by Sega's new arcade hardware. The company's Model 1 board moved and shaded 180,000 polygons (each representing the side or part of an object) per second, which looked more abstract than conventional sprite and bitmap games. Real-time 3D hadn't the level of detail of 2D graphics, but made more realistic movements possible and added dimension: In a polygon word, you could see and move behind things.

A year later, Yu Suzuki's **Virtua Fighter** proved that the animation of human bodies was also possible with polygons. In cooperation with American arms supplier Lockheed-Martin, Sega enhanced its 3D board to Model 2. Two 32-Bit RISC processors moved several hundred thousand polygons, shaded and clothed them with detailed bitmap textures.

Disappointing all Sega and Nintendo fans, Sid Meier (wearing a toga) preferred to design computer games only: Civilization.

Namco saw the potential of 3D graphics early, as did Sony, who gave the planned PlayStation a 32-Bit CPU and a Geometry Transfer Engine (GTE). The PlayStation launch was accompanied by a conversion of Namco's arcade game **Ridge Racer** – an event that marked the end of cute 2D sprites, and flat and linear animation. From then on the industry revolved around vectors, polygons, textures and perspective corrections.

Myst and **Virtua Fighter** marked the two poles of 3D development. On the one hand, games like **Myst** used prerendered effects for landscapes (in a quality done real-time ten years later) and saved these on CD as movies or digital pictures. Games like this needed memory, not processor power. On the other hand, titles like **Virtua Fighter** or **X-Wing** by LucasArts rendered 3D graphics in real-time and didn't bother with CD storage space.

Static, dreamy, finely textured and Gouraud shaded: Myst by Brøderbund (1993).

Philips CD-i

Holland, 1991

Units sold:	1 Million
Number of games:	90
Game storage:	CD
Games developed until:	1999

★ ★

Rubbish on CD: Both Zelda games by Philips were behind the times.

Complex MPEG1 adventures like 7th Guest appeared towards the ...

... end of the CD-i life-span, just like Namco's simple Pac-Attack.

The era of digital entertainment began as Dutch electronics manufacturer Philips presented its first CD player in 1979. Together with Sony, Philips laid out the specifications for CD-ROM, Video-CD and various other formats and wrote them down in `Books´. In 1988, the `CD Interactive´, in short CD-i, was invented as a combination of standards.

Sony and Philips defined the CD-i within the Green Book and included Red Book (Audio-CD) and Yellow Book (CD-ROM) functionality: The playback machines were compatible not only with CD-i discs but also with music, picture and photo CDs.

Boasting more than 500 MB storage capacity for video and CD-quality sound, Philip's announcement sent waves through the industry. But before the device finally went on sale, it was no longer in the lead: NEC and Fujitsu, Commodore and Sega were already competing with their own CD-ROM formats.

In the following years, Philips spent time positioning the multimedia player, which was advertised as an edutainment machine for the family, games console or movie player, depending on the need. For movies, CD-i required a digital movie cartridge: The must-have extra for the expansion port on the back made the machine compatible with Video-CDs (MPEG1, the predecessor of the DVD movie format).

The first multimedia console: CD-i 210.

Stripped of the FT display, infrared receiver and RGB output, the cheap CD-i 450 appeared in 1994, looking much like a games console.

For gamers, the CD-i was a disappointment. The planned alliance with Nintendo didn't come to pass and licenses like **Zelda** were downgraded to little children's games, although Laser Disc oldies from the arcade were converted: Thanks to MPEG1, the CD-i ran near-authentic home versions of **Dragon's Lair** and **Space Ace.**

Despite some historically relevant remakes, the games palette lacked a clear pattern. Ambitious projects like **The 7th Guest, Voyeur** and **Burn: Cycle** joined the games library in the mid '90s but by then gamers had already lost interest in the console.

One deterrent was the combo of joypad and infrared remote that was included with the CD-i. The inaccurate controller was replaced with a Touchpad later – the Logitech manufactured four button pad could be mounted with a short stick. Alternative controllers were a pistol, mouse, trackball (shown below) and the Roller Controller for small kids.

Many of the CDs were interactive movies, not proper games: Escape from Cyber City was based on a japanese TV anime...

...while Voyeur was developed from scratch by an American design team. The soft erotic content was for adults only.

An `ethno-fiction saga´: Inca by French developer Coktel (1992).

Philips held on surprisingly long to the unsuccessful hardware and even at the end of 1995, it presented new variants like a TV with integrated CD-i, a CD-i component in mini tower format and a PC card.

The last attempt to save the hardware into the future was a 14.4 Kbps modem released in England and the Benelux countries. In 1999, production of the hardware – now only professionally used for sales and training purposes – was stopped.

The late CD-i 470 was designed to fit as a component for Philips' own Hifi racks and systems.

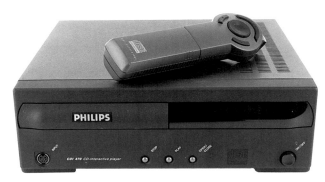

CD-i variants and successors

First series: From 1991

CD-i 205	The first CD-i player for the mass-market sold in 1992 for nearly £500; outside Europe it was called 910. Like all variants it featured Motorola chips and OS-9, a legendary multitasking and multi-user operation system first used in Tandy's Color Computer (1980), later ported on Japanese micros Fujitsu FM-7 and Sharp X68000.
CD-i 210	The successor to the CD-i 205 is internally identical but within a slightly modified case: Smaller front loader, fewer control elements.
CD-i 220	The deluxe version of the CD-i 210 based on Philips' Matchline series of consumer electronics and had more controls, better FTD display and a door for the CD front loader. Later models even had optical out for digital audio.
CD-i 310	This exotic portable had a sideward 3.5" disk drive but no display. The docking station 9124 made it compatible with digital video.
CD-i 360	Truly portable CD-i with integrated, flip-up LCD. The docking station 9124 made it DV compatible.
CD-i 350	Low-cost successor of the portable CD-i 360 with Sharp instead of Philips LCD, 740x240 instead of 756x556 pixel resolution. A DV cartridge could only be used with the docking station.
Sony IVO-V10	Very rare, portable `Intelligent Discman´ from Sony, not compatible with the DV cartridge. Available both with and without LCD; the successor IVO-V11 solved some compatibility issues with other CD-i machines.

Second series: From 1994

CD-i 370	The portable CD-i was no longer produced by Marantz but by Goldstar and marketed by the Korean firm as the GPI 1200 without the 5.6" LCD or as the GPI 1000. It had 32 K NV-RAM, S-video output and serial port. Thanks to the new 68241 CPU which contained the MPEG decoder the CD-i 370 is compatible with digital movies and more compact than other CD-i handhelds. Display resolution: 720x234 pixel.
CD-i 450	Cheap game console look-a-like in a grey case without FTD display and infrared receiver. The DV expansion port was left to the CD top loader on the machine's top. Goldstar marketed similar machines GDI 750 and GDI 1000. The most common model.
CD-i 470	CD-i component for 26cm mini HiFi systems, with or without DV decoder, depending on the series. For commercial use and schools, also available as the CD-i 490 with an MPEG1 decoder and 32 KB NV-RAM as standard; in Germany also spotted as the Grundig CD-i 110E.
CD-i 740	The deluxe variant (black LD player look, metallic feet) featured RS232 and two controller ports as well as a digital audio output for the `Sony/Philips Digital Interface Format´ or S/PDIF.
CD-i 660	Portable CD-i with 4" flap-down LCD, two controllers and RS232 port.
Philips FW 380i	Rare audio mini tower (amplifier, tuner, cassette deck, speakers) with integrated CD-i and Digital Video component. Comes with a wired, not infrared remote.
Philips 21TCD-i 30/ CD-i 130	A TV with integrated CD-i player and MPEG1 decoder: The drive is hidden behind a flap on the top of the machine.
Others	Several professional machines for educational and development purposes with integrated disk drive, more RAM and new ports. The last pro units were the CD-i 660 (with integrated DV decoder) and CD-i 670 with control for a DVD player and ZIP disk support.

Watara Supervision

Taiwan, 1991

Units sold:	Unknown
Number of games:	40
Game storage:	Cartridge
Games developed until:	1992

★

Its size and the trick with the joint made the difference between the Supervision and its Nintendo inspiration.

Units wearing the the logo of Hartung Spiele Berlin were dark grey and had a red control disc and blue buttons.

Gamers know China, Hong Kong and Taiwan as specialists for reproducing hardware and software (rather than creating them from the scratch) and as a wellspring of Atari and Nintendo cartridges of questionable originality. Outside of Japan, three kinds of far eastern games can be categorized: Illegal copies, licensed replicas and – representing the grey area in between – the plagiarised products that imitate the idea or concept of the original without violating its copyright.

The Supervision grabbed its chance on the world market as an example of this third category. The two-step swivelling display was its major difference to the Game Boy. Upon second glance, it copied every element of the million selling original: To the left a contrast slider and power connector, on the front a headphone socket, to the right the volume control and a cover for the two-player link (a 9 pin port, á la Atari). The CPU was a variant of the stone-age 6502 chip.

The Supervision was about 25% larger than the first Game Boy (and hence nearly twice as big as later handhelds). The 160x160 pixel display and stereo sound were the strongest selling points. Instead of Tetris, the handheld shipped with the Breakout clone **Crystball.** Several case variants were available from Audiosonic, Hartung and Quickshot, which were thrown onto the market without any major advertising.

Of the 60 promised cartridges, only half made it to stores. Most were worn-out concepts: **Galaxy Fighter** and **Tasac 2010** were conventional horizontal shoot 'em ups; **Eagle Plan** copied Sega's Afterburner; and **Hash Blocks** was inspired by Tetris. The most avid Supervision developer was Thin Chen, also known as Sachen, a Taiwanese company notorious for unlicensed Nintendo games. This is how the Supervision's **Pyramid** and **Penguin Hideout** made it to the NES without Nintendo's `Seal of Quality´ in 1989.

Variants and successors

Watara Supervision	More widely available than the version without swivel-display (marketed in Europe as the Audiosonic GB-2000 for example) was the Supervision with a two point joint in the middle, which was used to change the angle of the 6x6cm LCD (Hartung, Quickshot, Audiosonic GB-1000). The screen and controls were larger than the Game Boy's; while the GB-2000 had a conventional control pad, the joint variant featured a rhombus-shaped direction pad.
Magnum Supervision	The reduced size, Game Boy styled version was available and advertised in green, yellow, and grey. Gameplan has not seen or tried this variant yet.

Atari tried a final comeback with 64-Bit architecture and fast 3D graphics.
But dubious marketing, weak distribution and a general distrust toward Atari
left the cartridge-based Jaguar without a chance in a market dominated by the Japanese.

Atari Jaguar
USA, 1993

After considerable corporate restructuring and a series of hardware failures, Atari was no longer a major force in the video game industry. With his company close to collapse, Sam Tramiel combined his American and European know-how to initiate a last comeback attempt. His Jaguar was cartridge-based, like all Nintendo platforms, built by IBM and used a concept by British developers Martin Brennan and John Mathieson of Flare Technologies, who had already invented but not manufactured a multi-processor video game machine in 1986. Their dream was to be realised by joining Atari.

Just like earlier Atari consoles, the Jaguar made use of a powerful, but complicated architecture. The console's CPU was an off-the-shelf 68000 from Motorola, but two custom chips handled most of the work. 'Tom', with three processors, took care of 3D, sprites and FX and contained a 26.6 MHz clocked 32-Bit GPU (26.6 MIPS), a 64-Bit 'Object Processor' and a 64-Bit Blitter, whose job was to improve 3D animation with Gouraud-Shading and Z-Buffering. The second custom chip, 'Jerry', coupled sound and I/O functions and contained a DSP with similar architecture and power to the GPU.

The last Atari hardware relied on games from the old world. The British-developed Cybermorph was included with the console.

The hardware was more powerful than the SNES and Mega Drive and positioned at the low price point of $250 including the Jaguar-exclusive game **Cybermorph**. The release date was well chosen – with 16-Bit drawing its last breath, both the industry and the consumers awaited the next generation of hardware. In spite of this, Atari failed: It lacked marketing muscle and Japanese third-party support – Konami, Namco et al. displayed no interest in making Jaguar games. Western developers didn't push the Jaguar architecture, choosing to keep effort and risk at a minimum. Most games were ported from the Amiga and Mega Drive, frequently unoptimised. The Jaguar's vast possibilities remained untapped.

Atari announced 3D glasses (made by British VR-manufacturer Virtuality) but never started production.

The joypad is nearly as large as the Jaguar, which is topped by the additional CD drive in this picture.

After that, it took some time until noteworthy, original games were released: Rayman from France and…

…the tactical mech battle game Iron Soldier by German Atari veteran Mark Rosocha.

Atari's page-long wish lists of 'available soon' software eventually ended in a puny games selection with few highlights. Apart from boring conversions, three excellent examples of graphics and gameplay appeared that became well known outside the Atari scene: The jump 'n' run **Rayman**, the mech battle game **Iron Soldier** and Jeff Minter's **Tempest 2000**.

Other games such as the potential killer application **Alien vs. Predator** looked outdated and clumsy compared to PC or PlayStation titles, while 3D driving games **Atari Karts**, **Chequered Flag** and **Club Drive** were deemed ridiculous in the face of titles such as Ridge Racer.

By the time an external Jaguar CD-ROM drive was ready to ship, it was too late; the announced add-on for movie playback was consequently buried. Atari and those who bought the CD-ROM expansion hoped it would bring the Jaguar up to par with the competition, but instead of the expected CD flood, only a few games appeared, like fusty conversions of **Dragon's Lair** and **Myst**.

Other Tramiel add-on promises were either never kept (3D glasses, speech modem) or only marginally fulfilled: Atari shipped the two-player adapter (Jag-Link) to dealers, which was supported by John Carmack's **Doom** conversion, but buried the previously presented 'Cat Box' for connecting 32 Jaguar consoles. Cat Box and later the Scat Box were sold by smaller dealers in limited numbers, as were linkable games **Air Cars** and **Battlesphere**, released five years late in 2000.

Units sold:	250,000
Number of games:	65
Game storage:	Cartridge, CD
Games developed until:	1997
★ ★ ✦	

With the arrival of CD-ROM and the vision of a worldwide standard,
Electronic Arts founder Trip Hawkins attempted to blur the boundaries between game and media industry.
Instead of building hardware, his new company merely sold the specs to international licensees.

3DO Interactive Multiplayer

USA, 1993

In 1990, Electronic Arts was already the largest video game publisher in the western hemisphere; its founder, Trip Hawkins (who learned marketing at Apple), heralded as the industry visionary. EA produced both computer and console games and initially backed Sega, not Nintendo – until the Mega Drive market took a dive. To avoid similar platform risks in the future, Hawkins changed his strategy and aimed at an ambitious goal – the creation of a global game and multimedia format, that could break the dominance of Japanese manufacturers. He chose the CD-ROM as the inexpensive storage medium for his 'Interactive Multiplayer'.

Hawkins stepped down from his CEO position at EA, founded the 3DO company and quickly landed a series of illustrious investors: electronics conglomerate Matsushita, US telco AT&T, and media groups Time Warner and MCA backed the concept of an Interactive Multiplayer. The machine was developed by the New Technology Group (NTG), led by legendary Amiga co-designers Dave Needle

US developer Crystal Dynamics delivered the first games and later provided a talking mascot for the 3DO: Gex (1995).

and RJ Mical; later NTG became 3DO's in house R&D studio. Its design for the 3DO hinted at things to come from Sega and Sony: A 32-Bit CPU by British RISC pioneer ARM supported by two graphics processors, allowing sprite-similar 'Cel' effects and according to the manufacturer, was capable of rendering 64 million pixels per second. The Multiplayer didn't boast the floating point calculation and

Units sold:	1.5 Million
Number of games:	200
Game storage:	CD
Games developed until:	1996

★ ★ ★

Warhammer in 3D: Space Hulk by Electronic Arts, 1995.

For 3DO all EA brands were improved, some new-born: After the next gen FIFA ...

... came the first part of the Need for Speed series of racing games.

Campaigning with Wagner, Grieg and Rimsky-Korsakov in Dolby Surround: Return Fire.

polygon power of PlayStation and Saturn which appeared a year later, but already posessed most of their other features. The 3DO supported graphics and sound decompression, warps, transparency, anti-aliasing and texture mapping. Apart from game CDs, it also played audio and Photo CDs.

In October 1993, Matsushita subsidiary Panasonic released the first Multiplayer – a black machine majestically resting on rounded pillars. Power and eject buttons were found to the left and right of the disc tray; a red LED displayed the status. Apart from a sideward shaft for the delayed MPEG cart, all connectors were located on the back: AV jacks, S-video output and a second expansion port. Unlike other consoles, the 3DO only had one joypad port; more controllers were 'daisy chained'. The USB-like concept scared off developers, making multiplayer games rare. More seriously, the machine suffered from its high price (three times as expensive as a Nintendo), unclear market positioning and a weak software line-up during its first year. Most developers had no experience with the new storage medium and converted dated interactive movies (**Dragon's Lair, Night Trap**) and

Amiga games (**Battlechess, Out of this World**) on CD, instead of pushing the hardware to its limits with original concepts. Only EA became really involved, bringing its famous Mega Drive sports games to new 32-Bit heights. The company stayed faithful to 3DO until the end – with an outstanding port of space opera **Wing Commander 3**, an updated **Road Rash** and the first **Need for Speed** racing.

By the time Goldstar and Sanyo brought out their own 3DO models, and Panasonic's cheaper FZ 10 arrived on the market, it was too late. Any faith left among customers was scattered by the announcement of the successor 'Bulldog': The prototype shown in 1995 had a Power-PC CPU, ten coprocessors and a 64-Bit bus; it never went into production. In 1995, development was abandoned and the Bulldog technology sold to Panasonic.

In Europe, the Goldstar 32 was released before Panasonic's original model.

Hardware variants and successors

Panasonic FZ-1 3DO	1993	The first model, with CD front loader, RF and composite video output, stereo and S-video jacks as well as two expansion ports, was released in North America, Japan and England. Launch price including the racing game Crash 'n Burn: $700.
Sanyo Try 3DO	1994	Selling at 54.800 yen in Japan only, this was the second licensed 3DO. It had a flatter case and a tiny cover for the controller port.
Goldstar System 32	1994	The Korean company was the third hardware licensee and released the 3DO in new clothes in the USA ($399) and in Europe, where it appeared a month before the Panasonic version. A successor with a more simple top loader case (GDO 203P) was presented but never shipped.
Panasonic FZ-10 3DO	1994	The second Panasonic model, with reduced chipset and cheaper top loader instead of CD front loader. It was slimmer and cheaper than the massive original. The new operating system featured a memory manager for the internal Save RAM. It was released in Europe in 1995.
Creative Labs 3DO Blaster	1995	ISA card for the PC contained all components of the console (even the 32 K Save-RAM, excluding the CD-ROM drive) and was shipped with a joypad. It only worked with CD-ROM drives made by Creative.

Sega Saturn

Japan, 1994

Units sold:	10 Million
Number of games:	1,200
Game storage:	CD
Games developed until:	2000

★ ★ ★ ★ ♪

In the mid '90s, things weren't going well anymore for Sega. The video game industry's number two was not sure how to repeat its Mega Drive success. Expensive add-ons like the Mega-CD and 32X made gamers weary, and at the same time Sega's bold online and broadband plans for the Mega Drive vanished into thin air.

The introduction of the Sega Saturn in November 1994 cleared the fog: The Mega Drive was dead and was to be replaced by a CD console that was not compatible with its predecessor or its expansions. Two SH2 chips formed the heart of the new hardware: The CPUs were early 32-Bit RISC processors from Hitachi's SuperH series, an

architecture which later ended up in WinCE handhelds and Dreamcast. Some Mega Drive and 32X relics could also be found on the Saturn board. With two CPUs, two video chips and a Yamaha synthesizer, it was well specced but also pretty complicated.

The Saturn shipped one month ahead of the PlayStation but messed up its lead with **Virtua Fighter**. The game played well, was fast and sported real-time 3D but lacked textures. In December, Ridge Racer overtook the blocky fighters and in 1995 Toshinden appeared with smooth shaded figures and translucent clothing – the PlayStation graphics looked almost a generation ahead.

In Japan, the first Saturn model was a grey beast with black and blue buttons.

SHUN   JEFFRY
27 ᵈᵉ
STAGE 3   1'57"0

In later episodes, the Virtua Fighters were dressed in textures, just like PlayStation heroes.

To make system expansion easy, Sega derived the cartridge port from the Mega Drive. Graphically intensive conversions were released as a CD/cartridge combo.

Sega got back on its 3D feet (later 3D games were textured), but the platform's reputation was damaged for some time to come. The Saturn was perceived as a 2D machine; gamers who preferred 3D had to opt for the PlayStation. To be fair, the Saturn combined the best of both worlds – realistic polygon battles and classic hand-drawn 2D adventures. It just lacked the big names and heroes of Nintendo, Sony and their third-parties. The

Saturn was the last bastion for smaller independent companies, who outdid themselves in Japan.

There, more than five and a half million machines were sold, as many as in the US and europe together. Exclusive developers like Red (**Sakura Taisen**), Game Arts (**Lunar the Silverstar**, **Gun Griffon**), Tecnosoft (**Thunderforce**) and NCS (**Langrisser**) as well as SNK and Capcom's beat 'em

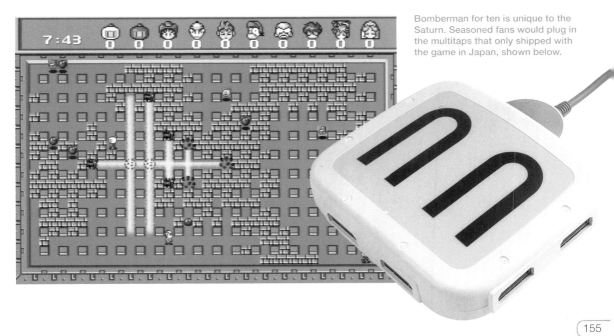

7:43

Bomberman for ten is unique to the Saturn. Seasoned fans would plug in the multitaps that only shipped with the game in Japan, shown below.

Inside the 'Net Keyboard' box, Sega surfers found a start CD for Habitat, the first graphical online community. Developed by LucasArts in 1986, it was enhanced by Fujitsu in 1990.

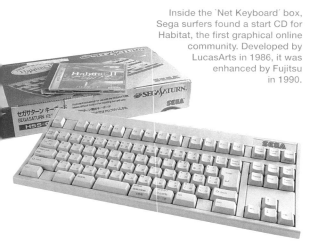

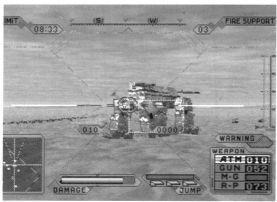

Gun Griffon was a feast for hardware geeks. The mech battle supported MPEG cart, Link connection and the Twin Stick.

ups established the fan base. Mainly intended for 2D beat 'em ups, a ROM expansion appeared in Japan, and in 1996, a RAM cartridge, helping to make arcade hits like **King of Fighters** look better and move smoother than on the PlayStation. Other coin-ops were ported 1:1: From 1994 to 1998 Sega, Tecmo, Sunsoft and Raizing developed 24 games for the STV board, which was architecturally nearly identical to the Saturn home console.

In the west, nobody cared any longer. Sony had started a marketing and price frenzy that took Sega's breath away. The few loyal studios turned their backs on Sega. Core for instance, developed the **Tomb Raider** sequel for PlayStation only. Every now and again, American software

companies would convert a game to the Saturn – but largely they simply ignored it.

The fact that Sega released half a dozen clever controllers or that it bundled an analogue pad with Yuji Naka's **Nights** (1996) and that it released an MPEG-1 cartridge or Photo CD software wasn't helping. The initial positioning as a multimedia console and all-rounder failed just like the internet application offensive with its two year delay. Only a few Japanese network games (including **Habitat II**) supported modem and keyboard. Japanese 2D and beat 'em up fans kept the Saturn alive until 2000, the same year Capcom released the last Saturn game: The arcade conversion **Final Fight Revenge.**

After collaborating with French comic artists, the internal Sega team responsible for Panzer Dragoon was promoted and renamed to Smilebit studio (above). To the left a Langrisser princess by Satoshi Urushihara.

Sega changed the joypad design and the hardware's colour for western markets, but didn't touch connections and ports of the Saturn.

Saturn variants and successors

Sega Saturn	1994	The grey original retailed for 44,800 yen, just four weeks prior to the PlayStation. After some price reductions, it was replaced by a milky white version in 2000 (which retailed for 20,000 yen). In the west it was always black.
V-Saturn	1994	Built under licence in a slightly different case by JVC, released in Japan for 44,800 yen; not available in Europe.
Hi-Saturn	1995	The Hitachi version with a slightly different case sold for 64,800 yen and was both Photo and Video CD compatible. In Japan, the system was also used as an info-terminal and sold as a navigation system with 4-inch monitor for 150,000 yen.
Skeleton Saturn	1998	With a price tag of 20,000 yen, and limited to a run of 30,000, this was the cheapest Saturn so far. The case was grey toned, translucent and allowed a glimpse at the technical insides.
Saturn Derbysta	1999	To celebrate the release of the horse race game Derby Stallion, Sega sold the last Saturn version in a blue, translucent case and retailed it like the first Skeleton Saturn for 20,000 yen, available in Japan only.

Sony PlayStation

Japan, 1994

Units sold:	101 Million
Number of games:	3,000
Game storage:	CD
Games developed until:	2004

★ ★ ★ ★ ★

The Ridge Racer series introduced breakneck speed drifts. Shown here is Type 4 (1998),

With some helping hands from Hollywood, an all-
star team of Square designers turned Japanese
fiction into survival horror: Parasite Eve (1998)

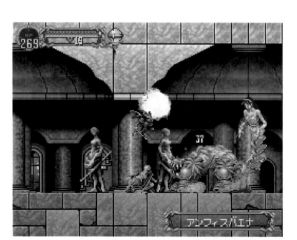

Konami entombed gothic horror inside a multi-level 2D crypt:
Castlevania X (1997), called Symphony of the Night in Europe.

Capcom shocked the world with a new kind of adventure,
3D suspense and splatter: Resident Evil spawned a genre.

Nintendo's market leadership seemed carved in stone when Sony announced that it was entering the console business. Like others, the Walkman inventors believed that the time had come for a new hardware generation. Sega tweaked at its Saturn, Panasonic started the 3DO production, and NEC unveiled a 32-Bit successor to the PC-Engine. All manufacturers believed in 3D and CD. To most insiders, there seemed little room in the hard-fought market for console debutant Sony's hardware.

Thirteen months after announcement, the PlayStation stood in dealers' showcases and with it, the sensational **Ridge Racer** by Namco. The new console was '*the mouthwatering machine of the future*', recalls Steven Poole years later in his book on the art of video games, Trigger Happy, and adds: '*just because of the unprecedented speed and solidity of ... Ridge Racer.*' The launch title underlined Sony's hardware talents: Fast 3D animation in real-time. The rendered and realistically shaded polygon worlds stood out from Nintendo's handcrafted 2D visuals and made for a new gaming experience.

At the end of 1995 and a few weeks after the launch in the USA and in Europe, three million PlayStations had already been sold, and demand was increasing. By the time Nintendo brought its own 3D machine to maturity, Sony had long conquered the market.

Ironically, the PlayStation resulted from a collaboration with Nintendo: Sony's engineer Ken Kutaragi developed a powerful sound chip for the Super Nintendo, before going on to devise a Nintendo CD-ROM as well as a console with both cartridge and CD ports. Then, Nintendo bullied Sony away and their common plans were buried. Insulted, Sony president Norio Ohga decided not to withdraw from the business. Hence, Kutaragi was allowed to continue work on a CD game machine – not with Nintendo, but against it.

Kutaragi's team was inspired by competitors: The joypads were a clever enhancement of the classic Super NES controllers, while the idea of a small and exchangeable

Sony attracted hobby programmers with the dark Net Yaroze console, its PC connectivity and its development tools.

Another 2D epic turned 3D, as Square designed the Final Fantasy episodes 7 to 9 for PlayStation only.

After training her first moves on Sega hardware, beauty Lara Croft was hired by Sony and tied through exclusivity contracts.

storage unit (Memory Card) was borrowed from Neo Geo manufacturer SNK. When Nintendo presented a Rumble Pak for its Nintendo 64 controller, Sony too released a Dual-Shock pad with rumble functionality and analogue stick.

Sony Computer Entertainment's (SCE) new licensing model brought in renowned game developers. First came Namco. The arcade developer and inventor of Pac-Man shared Sony's belief in a 3D future and supported the hardware launch with its perfect **Ridge Racer** conversion, and in 1995, produced the first million selling PlayStation game, **Tekken**. The result of the battle of consoles was confirmed when Square, developer of **Final Fantasy**, decided to join Sony, releasing the next RPG episodes exclusively for PlayStation and not for Sega or Nintendo, thus grabbing a million die-hard customers in Japan alone.

SCE took over British developer Psygnosis (famous for Lemmings) to help plough through the western market, a spectacular coup that shook the scene. The European launch title **wipEout** (high-speed sci-fi action with a techno soundtrack) unleashed a cult and formed the basis of success in the west, leading SCE to invest in more studios. In 1999, it was promoted to an independent group that reported directly to Sony's top management without having to go via Sony Music. Ken Kutaragi was put in charge of the business. His strategy of marketing the PlayStation as a games machine and not as a multimedia all-rounder like the 3DO or Saturn was successful: The PlayStation couldn't run video or Photo CDs, and Sony provided no modem or exchangeable storage device. Instead of expanding into related areas, SCE optimised and reduced the cost of the hardware. The analogue Dual-Shock controller, which

The Pocket Station was available in Japan only.

LOADING

Only the first PlayStation model had all of the ports. With each revision, more connections on the back were stripped away.

The separately available flip-up LCD was a major selling point for Sony's tiny PSOne, the last of its 32-Bit range.

replaced the standard joypad worldwide and the super Memory Card `Pocket Station´ (only launched in Japan) were the highlights of Sony's sparse peripheral strategy. Success was based on the quality and quantity of PlayStation software. After Nintendo scared away many developers with their rigid refusal to look to the CD, the PlayStation became the cradle of life for new genres and characters. Capcom's **Resident Evil** initiated survival horror, Konami's **Metal Gear Solid** brought stealth into the game, and Sony's car simulation **Gran Turismo** set new standards in racing realism and complexity. The best western PlayStation games were made in the UK: After Core's **Tomb Raider**, came the hit series **Driver**, **GTA** and **Colin McRae Rally**.

Orbital: Well-known techno acts delivered beats for WipEout.

PlayStation variants and successors

PlayStation	1994	The 1000 series retailed for 39,800 yen. The model 3000 update was sold for 29,800 yen from July 1995 onwards. To celebrate the release of Tekken 2, Sony shipped the SCPH-3500 with two pads and a Memory Card for 29,800 yen under the name `Fighting Box´.
PlayStation (5000 series)	1996	Internally optimised successor without a standalone S-video output. The price was reduced to 19,800 yen. To use Namco's GunCon, a special AV adapter (SCPH-1160) was required.
Net Yaroze	1997	With its PC port and software, this black PlayStation was programmable and sold directly from Sony. Unlike other variants, it runs NTSC and PAL CDs (but not self burned discs).
PlayStation, white	1997	This rare variant for the Asian export market contains an MPEG1 decoder and is thus Video CD compatible.
PlayStation (7000 series)	1998	Internally reorganised and cheaper PlayStation that lacked both the S-video and the composite port. The launch price of 18,000 yen included a Dual-Shock pad for the first time. In the States, the price was reduced to $129, in the UK to £99.
PlayStation (9000 series)	1999	The last variant in the old case also lacked the wide expansion port. From all of the original interfaces on the back, only the Mini AV and Link ports remained.
PSone	2000	New, much smaller case with a minimum of connections which retailed for £79. The only variant that had no link port. Instead, the tiny console can be connected to a separately available flip-up LCD monitor.

Announced as `Iron Man´ this late PC-Engine successor turned out to be a dead duck in a market full of 3D hardware, as NEC lacked any confidence to go head to head against Sony and Nintendo.

NEC PC-FX

Japan, 1994

Units sold:	400,000
Number of games:	80
Game storage:	CD
Games developed until:	1998

★ ♪ ☆ ☆ ☆

NEC and Hudson had a surprise success in Japan with the 8-Bit PC-Engine (and early pioneering work during the CD era) so fans were hoping for a treat with the mystery successor. In 1991, the first pictures of a hardware called `Iron Man´ surfaced, Hudson showed demos of fast polygon graphics. But NEC was in no rush to produce the system and a launch on western shores was never mentioned. The company wanted to avoid crossing joypads with newcomer Sony.

Thus, by the time the PC-FX appeared, the mighty prototype had transformed into a rather more reserved CD-based console inside a stern looking mini-tower case. Instead of the raw 3D power witnessed in earlier demos, NEC decided to go for 2D bitmap capabilities, 16.7 million colours and Motion JPEG compression. Instead of polygon games, the machine sported mainly FMV, Anime, and still-frame adventure titles.

The memory of its legendary predecessor was trampled on by the soulless failure of the PC-FX. Most users kept the three expansion port flaps (front, rear and top) closed. As add-ons, only a `Backup Memory Pack´ (BMP) for saving games and a SCSI port were available, the latter transforming the console into little more than an external CD-ROM drive for a PC.

Nonetheless, NEC, Hudson as well as Micro Cabin, Riverhill and other companies that NEC had onboard since the PC-Engine heyday, released games. But renowned publishers like Konami, Capcom or Namco

on the other hand, who even gave the 3DO a try, stayed away from NEC's multimedia machine. The FX had to live without decent action games and was buried under a pile of adventures and RPGs (controlled with the optional mouse): **Farland Story, Graduation, Lunatic Dawn, Angelique** and as the single US-designed game **Return to Zork**. The best titles were **Langrisser FX**, an improved conversion of the strategy classic with extra CD sound and Anime FMV and the erotic PC-98 port **Dragon Knight 4**. Even today, both are price-stable collectors' items.

Variant

PC-FXGA
The PC-FX was also stripped down and released as a `game accelerator board´ for Japanese computers. Two versions exist: One for the C-Slot of the dominant NEC PC-98 series and a second as ISA card for DOS computers. Both came with two ports for the PC-FX joypads. The cards showed NEC's strategic direction, turning away from the console market. PowerVR, their next game hardware, was developed in cooperation with British company Videologic instead of Hudson. This 3D accelerator was shipped as one of the first 3D graphics cards in Europe, later improved to PowerVR2 and integrated in the Dreamcast.

Nintendo Virtual Boy

Japan, 1995

Units sold:	1 Million
Number of games:	22
Game storage:	Cartridge
Games developed until:	1995

★ ☆ ☆ ☆ ☆

The volumetric effect was achieved by displaying offset pictures for each eye and much parallax scrolling.

Encompassing the user within a virtual world of 3D graphics was the holy grail of the multimedia and consumer electronics industries throughout the '90s. Everything about Virtual Reality was en vogue, and speculative pictures of cumbersome 'Head Mounted Displays' saturated the media. Console manufacturers who had already toyed with this idea in the early '80s were inspired to restart their research on affordable stereoscopic graphics.

Market leader Nintendo gave stereo graphics priority over CD hardware. With American display technology and a 32-Bit chip by NEC, Game Boy inventor Gunpei Yokoi led the development of a dual screen device – one for each eye.

Yokoi specialised in the creation of mobile toys and innovative consoles but his last design for Nintendo was ill-

Frontal body blow! Virtual Boy sessions resulted in headache and neck pain (Teleroboxer, 1995).

fated: Cost-saving measures resulted in the lack of a colour display (all games appeared in red on a black background) and due to safety concerns and the weight of the device, the Virtual Boy was immobile. Unlike other VR glasses, the Virtual Boy needed to sit on a firm base or a table.

Although the 3D impression created by the stationary glasses was good, using it over long periods placed significant strain on the user's eyes, neck and back. Consequently, the system was subject to criticism and mockery as soon as it was launched. Sales were disastrous. In anticipation of the release of the N64, Nintendo had no patience for its cyber-hardware und granted it little room at Nintendo's own Shoshinkai show in Autumn 1995. After a handful of games, both Nintendo and third-party developers Atlus, Kemco and Hudson stopped creating further software. The European release was initially set back, then cancelled altogether. By the time the Virtual Boy was being sold for under $100, Gunpei Yokoi had already left his long-time employer.

Nintendo 64

Japan, 1996

Units sold:	35 Million
Number of games:	400
Game storage:	Cartridge, 64DD
Games developed until:	2001

★ ★ ★ ★ ♪

The launch of the PlayStation hit the market-leader Nintendo right between the eyes. Suddenly, 2D graphics seemed antiquated, the world played with polygons, textures and real-time shadows. Whilst Sony had already sold its first ten million consoles, Nintendo's very own 3D hardware `Project Reality' was delayed until summer 1996. Thus, the console hit Stateside shelves in September; Europe had to wait even longer until March 1997. Although the console became quite popular in the west, it could never catch up with Sony.

The fact that Nintendo stuck with ROM cartridges as a storage medium caused much debate. PlayStation games came on inexpensively manufactured CDs, while Nintendo burdened its partners with a copy-protected, yet expensive technology. Because its cartridges commonly held between 12 or 16 MB, Nintendo lost the support of those third-parties who needed more storage space, such as RPG developers Square and Enix. Nintendo was eager to point out the lack of loading times but this couldn't stop the CD revolution. N64 developers were left with little memory for textures and music; compression techniques were used to make the most out of the available space.

The N64 was the fruit of a collaboration between Nintendo and Silicon Graphics (SGI), which was, at the time, the leader and prime mover of the 3D industry. SGI's multimedia double-team of 4300i CPU and `Reality Immersion Engine' co-processor designed specifically for Nintendo, rendered 32-Bit pixels (16.7 million colours plus an 8-Bit alpha channel), wrapped perspective-corrected textures on polygons and removed graphics chunks and sawtooth distortion with tri-linear mipmapping and anti-aliasing.

The N64 came in a world-wide identical case. It had four joypad ports and a flapped slot for memory expansion.

In Japan, there were some crazy controllers and add-ons: This Bio-Sensor was worn on the earlobe. It could 'sense' your excitement.

NINTENDO64 NUB-A-BIO-JPN

バイオ
センサー

©1998 SETA CORPORATION
MADE IN JAPAN
Seta Licensed by NINTENDO

The microphone was released across the globe for a casual chat with Pokémon Pikachu.

The Z Buffer too made the N64 more advanced than the PlayStation. For its memory Nintendo used fast Rambus-DRAM, five years ahead of the PC market. Nintendo brought down the price of cutting edge hardware to consumer level. Retailing for 25,000 yen or $250, the console was cheaper then Sony's and Sega's CD-ROM machines.

The excellent 3D debut **Mario 64** was the launch title for the console and laid the foundation for the 360° adventure genre. In the US, Acclaim released **Turok**, a first person shoot 'em up – expanding the title to a popular franchise over the next years. Both technically and in terms of gameplay, cartridges by British Nintendo subsidiary Rare stood at the development forefront: Its James Bond licence **Golden Eye** was a tough action game for adults. Between 1996 and 2001, Rare blessed the N64 with exceptional jump 'n' runs (**Banjo-Kazooie, Conker's Bad Fur Day**), driving games and shoot 'em ups (**Diddy Kong Racing, Jet Force Gemini, Perfect Dark**), but none of these titles could ever match the cult status of the 007 first person shooter.

Mastering soaked races with 3D thumb stick and shoulder buttons. An inserted Rumble Pak let you feel every wave.

Not a machine for the core gamer, but for the whole family: Most games for the Nintendo 64 could be played by four.

Games by Japanese and western Nintendo studios were the pick of the bunch: 1997 saw Starfox's reflection on alien oceans, a season later 1080° stirred up lots of powder snow. For Rare's anti-hero Conker, it rained cats and dogs: Bad Fur Day, 2001.

In 1998, Nintendo doubled the N64's memory to 8 MB: The Expansion Pak was stuck in the provided slot, was smaller and less complicated than Sega's unfortunate 32X adapter and much easier to market. Apart from games that used the additional memory for a 640 x 480 pixel resolution (**Turok 2** and **Rogue Squadron** by Factor 5), some releases ran with the expansion only, such as **Majora's Mask**, the sequel to Miyamoto's ingenious **Legend of Zelda: Ocarina of Time**,

selling seven million copies. In 1999, Rare's **Donkey Kong** 64 was bundled with the RAM pack.

While the N64 managed to establish itself in the west, back home in Japan it remained a niche machine, making its appearance in the sales charts only thanks to Nintendo's own games. An attempt to upgrade the machine with a rewritable medium was a technically progressive, yet half-

The Japanese 64DD expansion was ambitious but without success; pictured here with a 'Smoke Black' console.

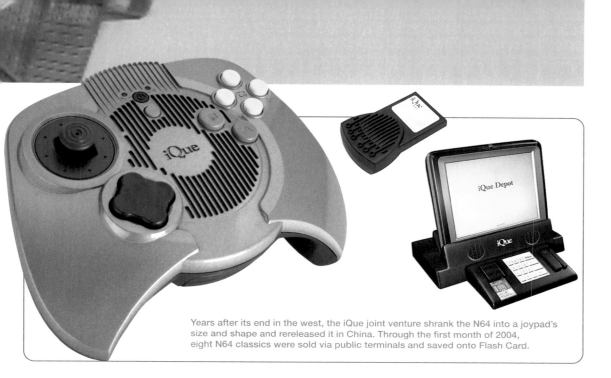

Years after its end in the west, the iQue joint venture shrank the N64 into a joypad's
size and shape and rereleased it in China. Through the first month of 2004,
eight N64 classics were sold via public terminals and saved onto Flash Card.

hearted concept: The 64DD drive was shipped in early 2000 together with mouse, modem and internet browser and stored 256 MB of data onto media similar to Zip. This all-round solution made large games possible, as well as editors and creativity programs like **Mario Artist**, but quickly lagged behind due to a small user base. Planned projects such as Zelda 64 were released on a cartridge instead of a 64DD disk and on western shores the 64DD was never available. On 28 February 2002 Nintendo pulled the plug on the 64DD in Japan. In comparison with NES, Game Boy and Super NES, the lifespan of Nintendo's last cartridge-based console was short. When Sega's Dreamcast appeared in 1998, followed by Sony's PlayStation 2 in 2000, the N64 was deemed totally outdated.

In Japan, the last carts **Derby Stallion** and **Bomberman** were released in August and December 2001 respectively. **Tony Hawk's 3** skated in as the final US cartridge in 2002.

Nintendo 64 variants and successors

Various case variants	Until 2001	In all three territories (Japan, USA and Europe), Nintendo marketed the N64 in a black, and later, coloured or translucent case. Consoles were bundled with Mario 64 or as the `Pokémon Stadium Battleset´ with two controllers, Transfer Pack, game book and a trading card ($146). Five translucent variants (violet, green, orange, blue and red) and `Smoke Black´ were sold with one pad for $100. There's also a `golden´ model; in the States, the N64 was sold with the Episode One racing game (Star Wars Edition) or in the unusual half-transparent `jungle´ case, bundled with Donkey Kong. The most unusual Japanese variant was a half-black/half-orange coloured version and the `Clear Black´ console for 64DD users only.
Pikachu Edition	2003	The final variation had not only its colour changed (to blue and yellow) but its appearance too: The Pikachu Edition boasted a Pokéball and the famous Pokémon hero as reliefs on the case – Pikachu's left foot operated as a reset button.
iQue	2003	Specifically for the huge Chinese market, Nintendo minimised the console and threw it into an all-for-one case with USB and Flash Card port, roughly the size and shape of a normal N64 joypad. Classic Nintendo software like **Mario 64, Yoshi's Story** and **Waverace** were sold for €5 each and played from Flash card instead of cartridge. Loading stations with a connection to a Nintendo server were found in retail shops.

Bandai Atmark (Pippin)

Japan/USA, 1996

Units sold:	40,000
Number of games:	15
Game storage:	CD
Games developed until:	1997
★	

A miniature trackball rested in the centre of Atmark's stylish controller; on its back, it featured shoulder buttons. Sadly, there were no games to recommend for Bandai's console.

During the '70s and '80s, Apple excelled as the prime mover in the digital industry. In the '90s, it fell behind. The idea of a networking multimedia console came pretty late – in previous years, Commodore, Philips, Sega and 3DO already got burned with multi purpose set-top boxes.

The Pippin was based on the PowerPC CPU, invented 1994 by IBM, Motorola and Apple to combat Intel's Pentium, it came with 5 MB RAM, VGA and S-video outputs. With neat specs and modern I/O ports, it had a slight technical edge over earlier multimedia attempts, but aside from that, it seemed about as useless as CDTV and 3DO: No one had any idea what a stripped down PC should be good for.

Even Apple failed to see any virtue in its own concept and sold Pippin specs to licensees instead of building its own console. It was offered to all, but only the Japanese toy and TV corporation Bandai could be persuaded to become a hardware manufacturer. Its newly founded Digital Entertainment division produced and marketed the hardware and the majority of the software.

Only children had some fun with Atmark and primitive games like SD Ultraman.

The machine was called Atmark and shipped in a white case with an external 33.6k modem and joypad; a small quantity of black consoles were sold in the US. Technically, the Atmark was designed to work worldwide: Like a PC, the CD-ROM console was compatible with the European 240V mains while the composite and S-video outputs could be toggled between PAL and NTSC TV standards.

That would have been practical if there had been better software available than the 40 dull edutainment and multimedia discs and roughly a dozen games (half of them Mac ports). Foolishly, the Atmark was technically similar, but not compatible with the Macintosh computer: while Pippin software like **Gundam**, **Ultraman** and the port of **Nobunaga's Ambition Returns** ran on the Mac, Mac games didn't work on Pippin. Thus games had to be adapted which, due to the meagre distribution of Pippin, turned out to be too much hassle for the software companies.

In 1998, Bandai shut down its Digital Entertainment division. The costly hardware flop had nearly ruined the company. Just prior to a proposed merger with Sega, Bandai managed to compensate for its heavy losses with the virtual pet Tamagotchi, a multi-million selling LCD accessory that became a worldwide craze at the end of the last millennium.

Tiger Game.Com

USA, 1997

Units sold:	Unknown
Number of games:	20
Game storage:	Cartridge
Games developed until:	1999

★ ★ ★ ★ ★

Introduced in 1978, Randy Rissman and Roger Shiffman used their Tiger brand to market cheap TVs, soon moving on to electronic toys and LCD handhelds. Ten years after publishing a dozen Atari cartridges under the Tigervision label, the US company followed Nintendo's example and produced their most expensive and ambitious product, the portable Game.Com.

To go up against the Game Boy, Tiger put the emphasis on technical innovation and increased value. Calendar, calculator and address book were built in; the applications and a **Solitaire** game were controlled using the touchscreen and a plastic stylus. The handheld had its second cartridge slot specifically for the optional internet cartridge with text browser and mail program. This software came with an adapter, which connected the Game.Com to a conventional 14.4k modem.

The hardware release was backed by TV game show conversions (**Jeopardy, Wheel of Fortune**) as well as movie and arcade licences such as **Jurassic Park 2, Batman & Robin, Duke Nukem 3D** and the **Mortal Kombat Trilogy**. Third-parties ignored the hopeless Game Boy

competitor; Tiger however acquired the rights to the Sega games **Sonic, Indy 500** and **Virtua Fighter**.

Tiger had no muscle for an effective third-party program or a much-needed marketing offensive. A year after the Game.Com launch, the company was swallowed by rival Hasbro which also assimilated Parker, Milton Bradley and all Atari rights in quick succession. The Game.Com (and plans for a European release) received a second chance from its new parent company, who supported the modernised Game.Com Pocket with titles from its own portfolio. Presented at US trade shows, but later quietly shelved, were conversions of Castlevania and Metal Gear Solid. Of all the dedicated projects for the Game.Com comeback, only **Resident Evil 2** made it to the shelves, where it was bargained next to the $30 Game.Com Pocket.

The first Game.Com displayed grey tones only. A colour version, stripped of stylus and touchscreen (below), was released later.

Variants and successors

Game.Com	1997	Like Nintendo, Tiger employed a CPU by Sharp. The colourless case and the LCD screen (200 x 160 pixels, 4 grey scales) are considerably larger than the Game Boy's. The touchscreen stylus is embedded in the console's front.
Game.Com Pocket	1998	The shrunken successor came in the translucent, coloured style of early iMac computers, with only one cartridge slot and using two instead of four batteries. The colour variants were: A translucent green, blue, red and violet with a `silver´ bracket around the display. Around 1999, a model with a backlight LCD (Pocket Pro Light) was released in a small, grey case.

The 21st century:
Caught in the net of gaming.

Half way through the '90s, the hysteria surrounding the internet had reached its zenith: Everything had been networked, everybody was surfing and chatting. Sega and Nintendo's promises of gamers connecting to the net were to be fulfilled in the coming century, while PC users already stood at the forefront of this development – both locally (LAN) or worldwide via the Internet.

Veterans of the US role-playing game scene were the first to get things moving in the new computer game era: The academic Multi User Dungeon of the '80s turned into 'Massively Multiplayer Online Roleplaying Games' (MMORPGs), habitat to thousands of players. In 1997, Richard Garriott, inventor of the Ultima games, relocated his fictive continent Britannia to the net. It was a parallel world with its own laws and social structure. Players fought, traded and flirted – even marriages and funerals took place in **Ultima Online**. A part of the development team later created a similarly successful MMORPG for Sony Music called **Everquest**, before turning Star Wars into an online adventure.

The second major impulse came from first person shooters: An action genre that reduces the hero pretty much to his arms and the calibre of his weapon. Already earlier games like **Doom** (which was banned for its violent content in Germany) contained multiplayer modes that lured eight, 16 or even more combatants into the arena. Based on the game mechanics of Doom was **Half-Life** in 1998. This action adventure became famous for its dramatic solo mode but it also gave the multiplayer scene a strong push. First, a deathmatch modification appeared, then, American fan Minh Le released a Half-Life mod that set assault teams in tactical

First person shooters run via the internet and within local LAN parties. Between four and four thousand gamers can join in. If you aren't playing, you keep wondering: Is this paramilitary training or just a digital form of 'Cowboys and Indians'?

<AFK>Delikat
<MakroLegenD>
<Hellboys>

The last battle for western RPG developers? After many European and American companies buried their online visions due to high R&D and maintenance costs, Asian companies took over. Facing the World of Warcraft, shown here and released by net gaming pioneer Blizzard at the end of 2004, stands the competition of dozens of Koreans MMO games, which are already played by millions in the far east.

Snapper).

Handhelds with Palm or WinCE operating systems provide a platform for games by hobbyists and professional developers. Jeff Minter and John Romero are coding games, as do Sega, EA and Infogrames/Atari. Shown left is the Palm OS version of Sim City.

skirmishes with terrorists. **Counter-Strike** was available as a free download from 1999 and is today seen as one of the most famous and notorious games ever. First person shooters, as well as racing and strategy games, are played via the internet or at LAN parties – players often carry their computers for miles to join the battle.

In Japan, things were (as always) treated a wee bit smaller. Within two years, the iMode mobile phone service helped the Japanese NTT group to overtake AOL as the world's biggest internet provider. Incidentally, the first generation – ´Browsersphones´ with monochrome graphics displays – was replaced with colour Java mobiles in 2001. The most popular iMode applications? Not information services, but games.

Early iMode games (1999) were mail or HTML based adventures and social simulations, while later Java games could be downloaded from the internet to stay in the mobile's memory as ´iApplis´. Namco, Konami and Taito, Sega, Capcom and Hudson, all Japanese game companies were

Telephone or games console? The second iMode generation (iAppli) and its competitor J-Phone turned mobiles into pocket computers with CPU, colour graphics and multi-channel sound. Via GPRS and UMTS the data phones load diminished classics by Capcom, Hudson or Namco right into your pocket.

keen to join iMode and (since 2001) J-Phone, the Japanese subsidiary of Vodafone. As Java games are technically about on a par with 8-Bit micros, classic brands like **Pac-Man**, **Scramble** and **Ghosts'n Goblins** were once again the biz. In 2003, Vodafone started the engines of a mobile **Ridge Racer**, in 2004 Square converted **Final Fantasy** and distributed the iMode exclusive episode **Before Crisis** for the UMTS phones by NEC, Panasonic, Sharp & Co. Reaching from **Lode Runner** to **Tenchu**, from **Wizardry** to **Arc the Lad**, the mobile revival of old arcade, Nintendo and PlayStation action shows one thing: Great games never die.

Sega Dreamcast

Japan, 1998

カーシュナ家の密売買を摘発しました。

Fantastic strategy RPGs were released in Japan only: 100 Swords by Smilebit (2001).

In the early '90s, Sega stood for gameplay at the cutting edge of technology and the Mega Drive represented a trendy alternative to Nintendo's toys. However, on its way from 16-Bit hardware to the CD generation, Sega stumbled, then fell. Expensive Mega Drive updates and add-ons confused fans and many had lost their faith by the time Sega launched the Saturn. The technically similar PlayStation became gamers' first choice and Sega was bumped from second to third place in the console race.

At the end of 1998, the introduction of the super console Dreamcast was Sega's last all-or-nothing attempt to catch up with the market's leaders. Optimally scheduled (18 and 36 months prior to the launch of the PlayStation 2 and Nintendo's Gamecube respectively) and retailing for under £200, it was a very promising and powerful console – technically on a par with a 3D-accelerated PC and despite WinCE, trimmed for fast on-screen action. Like the PlayStation 2 and the PC, the Dreamcast used a duo of chips, splitting tasks between the two: The CPU was the new SH-4 chip by long-term partner Hitachi, the graphics processor with PowerVR technology was supplied by NEC

Chips by NEC, Hitachi and Yamaha, operating system by Microsoft: Under the red logo of the Japanese Dreamcast lay state of the art technology.

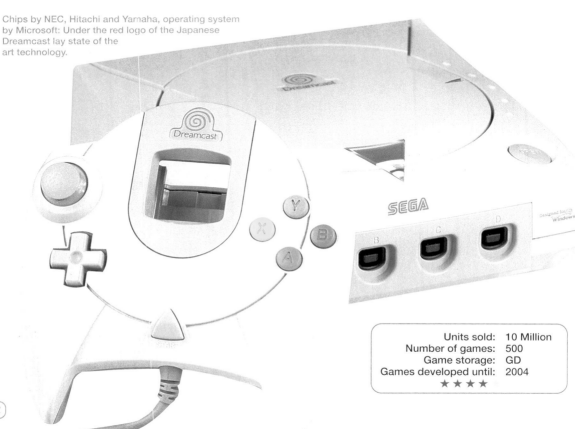

Units sold:	10 Million
Number of games:	500
Game storage:	GD
Games developed until:	2004

★ ★ ★ ★

The Dreamcast was the first console boasting hardware power on a par with current coin-ops. Following Virtua Fighter 3tb,...

...Capcom and Namco also converted their 3D beat 'em up: Soul Calibur from 1998 was released a year later on the Dreamcast.

and Videologic. This graphics chip, originally devised as a 3D accelerator for PCs, but later forced out of the market by 3Dfx and nVidia, was enhanced for Sega to PowerVR 2. Instead of a CD-ROM, the console used so-called GD-ROMs with 1 Gig capacity, another technological novelty.

Sega updated Sony's established Memory Card to come up with the 'Virtual Memory Unit' (VMU), boasting a 48x32 pixel LCD, a miniature direction pad, sleep mode and two fire buttons. The interface was designed so that the VMU could be slotted into the joypad (a window in the centre of the pad made the LCD visible) but could also connect with a second VMU for data exchange. Even before the Dreamcast launch, a green VMU with **Godzilla** games was released. A memory card as mini-handheld – Sony later borrowed the idea for its Pocket Station.

The Dreamcast was the first console to be shipped with a modem, used by Japanese, American and European gamers to enter Sega's online playground Dreamarena. First came the simple, fun multiplayer puzzle game **Chu Chu Rocket**; in 2000 Sega launched the premier console online RPG **Phantasy Star Online**. While Sony and Nintendo's internet ambitions were still nothing but empty promises, Sega had made it reality.

Offline, the Dreamcast was supported with excellent software too. The arcade conversions **Soul Calibur** and **Crazy Taxi** were of a similar

Sega's coin-op Crazy Taxi steered across from the arcades to the Dreamcast in 2000.

standard to the PlayStation 2 games that flooded the world in 2000. Until 2002, the Dreamcast games library grew to accommodate more than 300 titles, half of which were by Sega and its sister company CRI.

Sega's original games won a wealth of accolades: **Jet Set Radio** with its stylistically coloured ('cel shaded') roller-blade heroes and Neo Tokyo turf wars, the retro-chic dance game **Space Channel 5,** and **Virtua Tennis** for up to four players. Many well-known Sony and Nintendo titles were converted: **Rayman 2** (Ubisoft), **V-Rally 2** (Infogrames), **Tomb Raider** and **Soul Reaver** (Eidos) as well as **Tony Hawk's** by Activision. The advantage of strong brands and online connectivity made little difference to the crisis-ridden Sega group, however. In anticipation of new hardware by Sony, Microsoft and Nintendo, third-party publishers dropped

A Pong update for the 21st century: Virtua Tennis (2000)

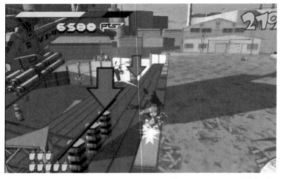

Gollum riding jet powered blades met Tony Hawks on LSD: Cel shading is the name for Jet Set Radio's new look that spawned many PlayStation 2 imitators.

their support for the Dreamcast, particularly in Japan. The 10 million units sold across the globe seemed too insignificant to warrant any R&D. The development scene shrunk in size with only small partners supporting the platform, some of which stood by the Dreamcast even after Sega's hardware division called it a day, early 2001.

The Dreamcast's decline began as early as 1999, when Sega couldn't keep its hardware promises over features such as a DVD player and Zip storage. Sega eventually turned from hardware producer to pure software developer, converting established brands to the platforms of former competitors. And so, since 2001, PlayStation 2, Gamecube and Xbox games carry the blue Sega logo – representing the end of an era. From now on, all console gamers can break the sound barrier with Sonic and collect artefacts in **Phantasy Star Online**.

After the Dreamcast's production ceased, Sega published a new adventure game each month and the occasional 2D shoot 'em up like Treasure's vertical **Ikaruga** in 2002 and **Chaos Field** by Milestone in December 2004.

The white VMU memory card appeared as a green Godzilla variant – in Japan only.

Sporty Dreamcast: The black model with blue and white logo was produced for the US market. Two sports games were included.

The Dreamcast was blessed with a ton of original peripherals, including the only fishing rod controllers marketed and sold outside Japan by a first-party.

Inspired by early iMac and the design of Sonic and Space Channel 5, Sega threw the Dreamcast into a rounded monitor case with blinking sides and Sonic head/antennae-look.

The CX-1 was packaged with software, keyboard, webcam and browser for a massive 88,888 yen – the most expensive Sega console.

Dreamcast variants and successors

Sega Partners Special Model	1998	The first limited edition debuted along with the original on 27 November exclusively for Sega's business partners. With colour and technology identical to the original, a signed metal plate on the lid proudly showed its limited status.
Mazyora Dreamcast	1999	This case variant was painted in a special glowing purple (provided by Nippon Paint) and was apparently limited to 500 units.
Model Seaman	1999	Console variant bundled with the unusual artificial life sim Seaman, joypad, VMU and microphone. The translucent lid of the machine displays a small Seaman silhouette as a logo. Five months later, the package appeared as a Christmas bundle featuring a seasonally red console.
Hello Kitty DC Set	1999	Bundled with the licensed game of the same name, the console came in translucent case (similar to the Seaman variant), with pad, VMU and mini keyboard in the same pastel tone. Both versions, Skeleton Pink and Skeleton Blue, retailed for 34,800 yen.
Sakura Taisen Set	1999	25,800 yen bundle with a slightly pink shaded console and fitting extras included: Pad, VMU, game and Sakura Taisen mail program.
DC Code: Veronica	2000	The translucent Dreamcast with S.T.A.R.S. logo was available in two versions. Limited Box S.T.A.R.S. (blue) and Limited Box: Claire (in a dark, bloody red) both retailed for 34,800 yen.
Colour versions	2000	Price reduction to 21,000 yen: Super Black Model (July 2000), Metallic Silver, Bubble Pink and Bubble Blue (all three shipped in March 2001)
Sega Sports Model	2000	The black Dreamcast with blue and white Sega Sports logo is the only case variant shipped in the US, where it retailed for $170 including the sports games NBA 2K and NFL 2K.
CX-1	2000	The all-in-one desktop was clearly inspired by Apple's iMac computers and a combination of console and TV tube in a rounded, blue case, separate keyboard, digital camera and joypad – a collector's dream for a hefty 88,888 yen.
DC R7	2001	Retailing for 9,900 yen, this was the cheapest Dreamcast console – and the final one. Shipped in September 2001 in a black case with yellow R7 logo.

With its final hardware invention, arcade specialist
SNK took a bit(e) out of the Game Boy market: At first with a
monochrome handheld, then with a screen update to 146 colours.

Neo Geo Pocket

Japan, 1999

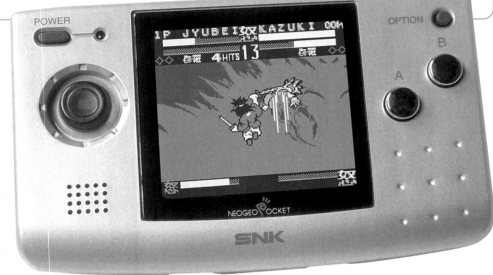

This arcade-for-your-pocket is smaller and simpler than other handhelds. The action is controlled via a digital thumbstick.

It wasn't a technical milestone like SNK's arcade power-house of 1989, but a quite conventional game handheld in 122x74x24 mm size, with a black/white screen, 16-Bit CPU and Z80 co-processor. Apart from sharing a name and several franchises and heroes, there was no similarity or even compatibility between Neo Geo Pocket and the big Neo Geo console. Instead of linking the new device to its older hardware, SNK created a port to the Sega Dreamcast. Thus, in the **King of Fighters** and **Capcom vs SNK** conversions, character features and codes could be swapped.

By chance, just a few months after the Neo Geo Pocket's launch, the WonderSwan was released, a technically similar handheld by Bandai. It was a little smarter and sold – thanks to Bandai's marketing and software – twice as many consoles and games as SNK's baby.

Half a year into its lifespan, SNK replaced the handheld with the backward compatible Neo Geo Pocket Color. But in spite of the new screen, third-party interest remained low, and only minor companies like Yumekobo, Sacnoth, Asmik,

Cute heroes: After a black and white start, SNK published colour software only. Dark Arms (left) and Baseball Stars right.

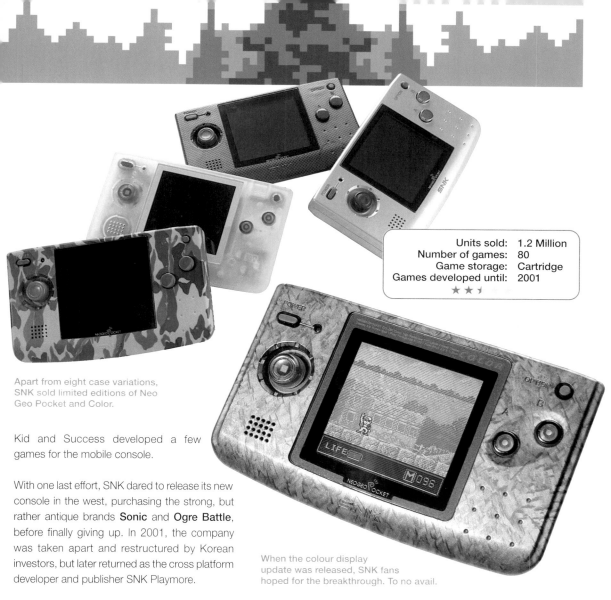

Units sold:	1.2 Million
Number of games:	80
Game storage:	Cartridge
Games developed until:	2001

★ ★ ⯪

Apart from eight case variations, SNK sold limited editions of Neo Geo Pocket and Color.

Kid and Success developed a few games for the mobile console.

With one last effort, SNK dared to release its new console in the west, purchasing the strong, but rather antique brands **Sonic** and **Ogre Battle**, before finally giving up. In 2001, the company was taken apart and restructured by Korean investors, but later returned as the cross platform developer and publisher SNK Playmore.

When the colour display update was released, SNK fans hoped for the breakthrough. To no avail.

Variants and successors

Neo Geo Pocket	1998	The first model came in eight case variations (including Crystal White, metallic and camouflage design), as well as a limited, half-transparent Samurai Spirits version. The machine ran nine black and white games and 40 colour cartridges (displaying colours as shades of grey). Released for 7,800 yen, the last units sold for under 1,000 yen in 2003.
Neo Geo Pocket Color	1999	The second hardware model displayed 146 colours (out of a 12-Bit palette) and retailed for 8,900 yen in six different cases, which were partially taken from the predecessor. The most unusual model is Hanshin Tigers, carrying the famous Baseball team's black and yellow stripes. The Pocket Color shipped the same year in the States and UK and was fully compatible with the monochrome predecessor.

Bandai WonderSwan

Japan, 1999

Units sold:	3.5 Million
Number of games:	200
Game storage:	Cartridge
Games developed until:	2003

★ ★ ★

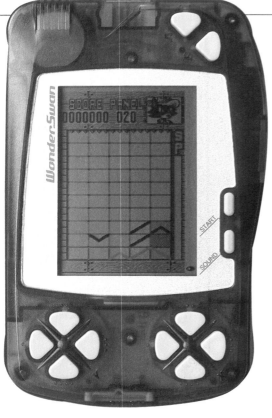

For brain teasers like the highly addictive launch-title Gunpey, the WonderSwan is held vertically.

Instead of a direction pad, it had two sets of four buttons each to the left of the display. Depending on the game, it could be held vertically or horizontally like the Neo Geo Pocket released in the same year.

The smart design and 16-Bit CPU did not stem from an internal Bandai team, but from a small company called Koto, founded by Gunpei Yokoi in 1994. In previous years, Yokoi had been chief developer at Nintendo and bestowed his company with a row of successes: Mechanical toys in the '70s, the Rubik's Cube clone `Billion Barrel´, the Donkey Kong arcade machine, Game & Watch handhelds and ultimately the Game Boy. The 30-year long partnership came to a sudden end with the Virtual Boy – Yokoi's overambitious flop had cost him the grace of company boss Hiroshi Yamauchi. Yokoi died at the age of 56 in a traffic accident, just a year after his restart with Koto and 18 months before the WonderSwan debut.

The addictive launch title **Gunpey** was homage to the man and Bandai's answer to Tetris. The puzzle game was the best game of the WonderSwan's initial years, and played vertically like the famous Game Boy title. Most other cartridges were conversions of well-known series such as **Densha De Go**, **Puyo Puyo**, and **Nobunaga's Ambition**, as well as Bandai's own brands **Gundam**, **Robo Wars** and **Digimon**. Square became a specialist partner for RPGs, licensing **Chocobo No Dungeon** to Bandai and supporting the start of the WonderSwan Color with **Final Fantasy**. As the most important title from a commercial point of view, the RPG remake was bundled with the colour handheld in a stylish box. Later, Square released further episodes and programmed new strategy and RPG games for the WonderSwan. Namco and Sony followed suit.

Neither Atari's Lynx nor Sega's Game Gear were a match for the Game Boy and for a number of years, no one challenged Nintendo's dominance of the handheld market. It wasn't until 1996 that rumours of imminent competition reached industry insiders: The toy manufacturer Bandai, known for Gundam, Power Rangers and Tamagotchi, planned a handheld which would utilize a power saving monochrome LCD just like the Game Boy, which was linkable, but which was – thanks to its 16-Bit CPU – more powerful than Nintendo's. In March 1999, the device with the strange name hit Japan.

The WonderSwan was slimmer and smaller and with its seven colour variants, prettier than the old Game Boy.

Thanks to this backing, the Wonderswan sold twice the amount of its contemporary rival Neo Geo Pocket. Whilst SNK targeted its console at die-hard action fanatics, Bandai

used sympathetic marketing to appeal to young trendsetters and school girls. The add-ons were both modern and original: The fishing add-on 'Wonder Sonar' was followed by the 'Wonderborg' robot kit in 2000. The crawling and rolling toy received its orders via infrared signal, monitoring its surroundings with optical sensors and mechanical feelers.

A link cable was used to connect two WonderSwans; further connectivity was made available via optional peripherals:

The 'Wondergate' adapter, a 9600 Baud modem for the mobile net, shipped with browser and mail functionality for downloading game characters and scenarios. A 'Wonderwave' infrared adapter interfaced to Sony's Pocket Station, the 'WonderWitch' to the PC. Close to 400 hobbyist programmers participated in the WonderWitch competitions in 2001, 2002 and 2003. One of the winning entries (**Judgement Silverfish**) was released in 2004 as the final WonderSwan cartridge.

The Wonderborg DIY robot got his master's commands via infrared download.

Variants and successors

WonderSwan	1999	The first generation was available for 4,800 yen in three colours (Metallic Blue, Metallic Silver and Pearl White) and as the translucent 'Skeleton' variants (pastel colours and black). Later, 'summer' models followed (blue, green and yellow), six case variants in the style of Digimon and Gundam: MSVS, and pretty bundles with Chocobo or Tare Panda Gunpey. WonderSwans in gold and military camouflage look were available at some events, but not sold in shops.
WonderSwan Color	2000	Technically improved, backward compatible hardware successor with an enlarged colour display. At launch (6,800 yen), five case variants were available: Pearl Blue, Pearl Pink, the half transparent Crystal Black, Blue and Orange. At a later stage, six variants were released in new colour and bundle versions, for example the RX-78-2 Gundam in white, blue and yellow case.
Swan Crystal	2001	Originally somewhat more expensive (but soon sold dirt-cheap) successor with larger, modified case and improved 2.8" TFT screen. Initially available in a blue-violet and wine red case, then in 'crystal' black and blue.

Sony succeeded where Atari, Sega and Nintendo failed.
The market's leading player seamlessly superceded the first PlayStation
with DVD drive, fast 3D chips and backward compatibility.

Sony PlayStation 2

Japan, 2000

Units sold:	80 Million
Number of games:	2,000
Game storage:	CD, DVD
Games developed until:	Still on
★ ★ ★ ★ ★	

Survival horror during feudal times:
Onimusha by Capcom.

Lean, mean, black and pretty expensive for a console: At the end of the millennium, the successor to the biggest selling game console was ready to go. In Sony's long history, this was to become the company's biggest feat, releasing the machine across the world within nine months, in March in Japan, in October in the US and on 24 November in Europe. Compared with the first shipment of original PlayStations, Sony Computer Entertainment (SCE) poured three times as many machines into shops and sold 20 million units in the first year. The plan worked out: The hardware successor defended Sony's market leadership. There was no single system to receive more support from developers, retail and consumers.

According to Sony, the massive launch price of around €450 was due to the integrated DVD functionality of the console: The PlayStation 2 is not just a toy for games, but doubled as a DVD movie player. Although it lacks RGB output for movies (Sony chose to leave it out for copy protection reasons) and suffers somewhat due to clumsy DVD controls, older gamers soon consented and purchased the console. After a price reduction, the mass-market followed. Video gamers got their RGB signal via the Multi-AV port, but there's also a Firewire (iLink) and two USB ports. This way, it was possible to connect Microsoft's Intellimouse to the Sony console but not to the Xbox – a crazy situation.

As nobody doubted that the PlayStation 2 would be a success, all big-name publishers delivered games just as they did in the predecessor's days: Activision, EA and THQ, Infogrames, Take 2, Interplay and Ubi Soft, Sega, Capcom and Konami. Even those who notoriously shunned consoles, like Sierra's heirs Vivendi Universal, released DVDs. The speed at which the software library expanded was great for gamers. Microsoft and Nintendo, who came later with their next gen hardware, never caught up.

The system stayed competitive for years. The `High Bandwith Superscalar Multimedia Processor´, known by the more catchy moniker Emotion Engine was developed in cooperation with Toshiba. Next to its 128-Bit RISC core, this CPU contains two Vector Units (floating point accumulator, FMACS), 10 DMA channels and MPEG2 decoder. An additional Graphics Synthesizer turns the rendering power around into 3D graphics and has access to the embedded video RAM at 48 Gigabytes per second. But the VRAM is somewhat sparse with just a measly 4 MB, making western programmers wonder.

An exotic train station for travellers in Final Fantasy X. The lavish adventure by Square blurred the border between computer animated film and real-time interaction.

Despite a delayed release, the balanced car physics, the intimidating automobile pool and RPG mechanics made Gran Turismo 3 A-Spec the best racing title for years to come.

But the bottom line is that the architecture is powerful enough to display particle effects and transparency at 600 frames per second, at the same time rendering cinematics and physics in real-time. A novelty is the technically harmless I/O chip: The MIPS3000-related unit is basically the first PlayStation in miniature, making the new hardware instantly compatible with several thousand game CDs for the old console. The double-feature – controlling the pad/memory card, USB and iLink ports on the one hand, and the PlayStation emulation on the other, was SCE's best design idea of the lot.

Other than data ports, the PlayStation 2 features a digital audio output (optical fibre), which gives surround sound to external receivers and amps. The biggest port is the Expansion Bay on the back, a replacement for the PCMCIA port found in the first series. It's only used for net access and connects with hard-drive and modem for this purpose (2002). The foremost PlayStation 2 online games were **Final Fantasy XI**, and in the west **Tony Hawk's 3**, **Twisted Metal: Black** and the first person shooter **Socom**.

Unimpressed by Nintendo and Microsoft, the PlayStation 2 took over market leadership from its 32-Bit predecessor and made Sony

The set-top box PSX comprises games technology, TV and music recording plus storage features in a bulky case. A remote is included, a Dualshock2 pad available separately.

Computer Entertainment the corporation's spearhead division on the way into the digital age. With Ken Kutaragi's technology, Sony devised the set-top box PSX, a 6 kg home server with hard-drive, DVD burner and broadband connection. But because of various compatibility issues, the launch in Japan was followed up with several software updates: Released in February, version 1.1 accelerated DVD recording to 24-speed and added MP3, TIFF and keyboard support. The 1.2 update provided further picture formats, playback of CD-R movies, DVD+RW recording and the ability to record both audio channels of two-channel TV.

The PSX retailed for a considerably higher price and is mildly more flexible than an Xbox. It is widely regarded as the technical link and field test for the next PlayStation generation. Whilst the parent company experimented with it, SCE launched a mini version of the PlayStation 2 at the end of 2004. The hardware for the masses was reduced to 25% of its original size, and is as light and slim as a DVD case.

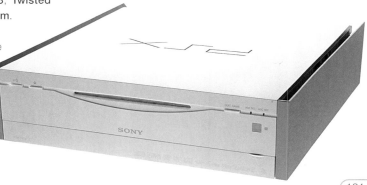

Sometimes, crime pays off in the neon and asphalt jungle of GTA by Rockstar UK.

While the compact, final model is generating more revenue, SCE is tweaking the PlayStation 3 concept, fully devised for broadband access.

The `Cell' technology by Sony, IBM and Toshiba, and its `16 Terraflops' and `trillions of floating point calculations', is unlikely to become part of a conventional console for private homes. It's more probable that the Cell processors shall power the at home on-screen action over the net. Graphics will be handled by a new GPU by nVidia (based on the next GeForce generation developed for SCE). Soon it'll be PS3 versus NeXt Box. Watch this space.

As Sony reduced manufacturing costs and size, the console was transformed from front-loading to top-loading device.

PlayStation 2 variants

SCPH-10000	**2000**	The first series was shipped with a PCMCIA port, memory card and a region free DVD Player 1.0. The second version, SCPH-15000 was internally redesigned, the DVD player improved a little; the third variant (-18000) had the movie player in ROM and came with a remote control but without a memory card. All units are black and can stand vertically – a widespread method even used back in PlayStation days (to ensure stable CD-ROM operation).
SCPH-30000	**2001**	From this model on, all variants (ie. all US and European machines) sported an Expansion Port instead of PCMCIA and a stronger (and louder) cooling fan. The SCPH-30000 hardware is the basis for the PlayStation2 bundled with Gran Turismo 3 in red packaging (-35000), as well as the ...
European Automobile Color Collection	**2001**	... which was limited to 2,000 units and released to celebrate the sale of 20 million consoles. It was available in white (RSW), red (RSR), yellow (RLY), blue (RAB) and silver (RMS) and distributed only through the Sony Style stores: 666 Units each for Japan, USA and Europe. Launch price: 50,000 yen.
Ocean Blue, Zen Black	**2002**	Console, base, controller and DVD remote retailed for 30,000 yen and were limited to 350,000 units each: The SCPH-37000L appeared in July in a translucent Ocean Blue, the –37000B was released on 1st August in a matt Zen Black. Later, Japan saw the colour variants Toy's Blue (Ratchet & Clank bundle) – and to celebrate 50 million units sold: Silver, Sakura and Aqua.
SCPH-50000	**2003**	This major hardware revision replaced the Firewire port on the front with an infrared receiver for the DVD remote control, which was redesigned and now featured an on/off button. The 50000 series runs DVD-R and DVD+R discs, outputs a progressive signal and is quieter than the previous models. Colour variants were ...
Midnight Black, and Satin Silver	**2003**	... the latter was also available in Europe as the Silver Prestige Line. In Japan, there was the golden SCPH-55000GU, bundled with Mobile Suit Z Gundam, Sakura (-50000SA) and Ceramic White (-50000CW). The latter was also sold as part of the Racing Pack bundle with GT3 Prologue (-55000GT). And, retailing for 20,000, came the Pale White PS2 in July 2004.
PSX	**2003**	The home server based on PlayStation 2 contains a hard-drive, DVD burner, TV tuner and net connection, plays and stores music, photos and movies. Retailing for 105,000 and 83,800 yen respectively, the PSX contains either 250 GB hard-drive (DESR-7000) or 160 GB (DESR-5000). The DESR-5100 and –7100 appeared in 2004 with updated and enhanced firmware in a limited, silver case. In September, the cheaper models were equipped with new players: -5500 (160 GB hard-drive, 70,000 yen) and –7500 (250 GB, 90,000 yen). Other than memory cards, the PSX is also compatible with Memory Stick, has two USB ports and digital video (D1/D2) and audio outputs (SPDIF).
Aqua Blue	**2004**	This limited PS2 variant for Europe retailed for €200, bundled with a PS2 stand and memory card. Available since March, shown right.
SCPH-70000	**2004**	While keeping its black look, this radically scaled-down PS2, is about as slim as a DVD case – and that alone makes it irresistible. At the back, the port for the hard-drive (which was only shipped in Japan) has been removed, and instead the Ethernet port has been made standard. American models are equipped with an analogue modem, too.

Nuon

GB, 2001

Units sold:	Unknown
Number of games:	8
Game storage:	DVD
Games developed until:	2001

★☆☆☆☆

Little interactivity despite 128-Bit: The Nuon machines are great DVD movie players but poor games machines.

The Nuon chipset represented a strange hardware evolution. John Mathieson's vision for the Konix in the '80s indirectly resulted in Atari's last console. When the Jaguar flopped, the development team continued enhancing the technology on their own: Under the name VM Labs, Richard Miller, Jeff Minter and other Atari veterans invented `Project X´. In 1999, its name was changed to Nuon.

Instead of building their own console, VM Labs showcased the Nuon technology to electronics manufacturers: The 128-Bit processor took over DVD movie MPEG2 decoding and had enough power for an improved user interface and digital effects. In 1997, prototypes were built, but it took until 2001 for Samsung to ship the first Nuon 'Enhanced' DVD player.

The home-cinema fraternity took interested note of the Nuon. The attention was aimed at the 15-fold zoom, digital fast-forward and frame scaling – features that other DVD players lacked. But the promise of specially enhanced DVD movies was never kept. After the Liz Hurley comedy `Bedazzled´, only half a dozen Nuon-improved movies appeared.

The games on offer were just as sparse. As with the Jaguar years before, international games were announced by Acclaim, Capcom, Hasbro and THQ, but when the Nuon players were delayed (Samsung quickly removed them from their product catalogue), Hasbro and others stopped development. In the end, only eight titles (and a Logitech gamepad) made it to the shops. At least they were unusual: Tony Takoushi, a well-known '80s video game journalist, produced **Freefall 3050 A.D.**; in Indonesia conversions of **Space Invaders DX** and the unreleased Bust-A-Move 4 were coded; Belgian developers provided the Mario Kart clone **Miracle Racing**. The two best games were improved Jaguar conversions **Tempest 3000** and the German-developed mech simulation **Iron Soldier 3**.

In 2001, the Nuon story ended with VM Labs going bust. Prior to that, Motorola had licensed the technology for its StreamMaster set-top boxes, and Summer 2002 saw two Nuon-driven DVD players by US manufacturer RCA (DRC 300N, 480N) appear, which weren't compatible with games and game peripherals anymore – it was Game Over.

Variants and successors

Samsung Extiva N2000	2000	The first Nuon enhanced DVD player was launched in the US including a joypad and a demo disc, and retailed for $350. When playing music, the built-in `Virtual Light Machine´ (VLM) threw some 100 effects onto the screen.
Toshiba SD2300	2000	The only Nuon player to be manufactured by Toshiba came in a dark case and was sold in the US only. Instead of a game controller, the unit was shipped with a remote control holding a mini-joystick as well as Hasbro's conversion of The Next Tetris. In comparison with the Samsung machines, the VLM was stripped down considerably to eight effects.
Samsung N501	2001	The third Nuon player came in a slimline, silver case and retailed for only $230 in the US. Unlike its predecessors, it runs self-burned MP3 CDs. Jeff Minter's VLM was enhanced to 152 effects. The test market Switzerland was treated to the N504 variant, at home in Korea came the N591 with an awkward digipad; due to region-protection, the included game CD Crayon Shin-Chan ran on this Korean hardware only.

Game Boy Advance

Japan, 2001

Units sold:	70 Million
Number of games:	800
Game storage:	Cartridge
Games developed until:	Still on

★ ★ ★ ★ ⫟

The Game Boy, launched in 1989, was a bold and ingenious move. Its successor, the Advance wasn't. Externally, the appearance of Nintendo's handheld for the 21st century was reminiscent of the Game Gear and Neo Geo Pocket, sporting the tried and tested D-pad seen in all previous Nintendo hardware, shoulder buttons and two fire buttons to the right of the display. It was not the smallest but the largest and heaviest handheld on the market. Nonetheless, no one seriously thought that it would fail.

The Game Boy Advance was released in six case variants: Black, White, Violet, Orange, Milky Pink and Milky Blue, and at the end of 2002, two metallic versions, Silver and Gold.

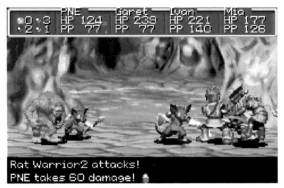

Golden Sun is an epic role-playing game developed by the Shining Force team Camelot for Nintendo.

Polygonal beat 'em ups like Tekken have been ported to 2D; the gameplay was left intact.

Instead of reinventing the wheel, Nintendo upgraded the specs: A 32-Bit RISC CPU, colour graphics in 244 x 160 pixel resolution (the Game Boy had 144 x 160) and simple 3D effects (thanks to bitmap zooming and rotation) elevated the handheld to Super Nintendo level, which made game development considerably easier. Nintendo itself revitalised its '90s classics **F-Zero**, **Mario-Kart** and **Super Mario** on the Advance and third-parties began porting their back catalogues of 16-Bit titles: **Rayman**, **Earthworm Jim** and **Sonic**, **Street Fighter**, **Mega Man** and the RPG troops of **Breath of Fire**. Attempts at converting 32-Bit polygon figures and concepts to the mini-display were pretty feeble: Japan provided 2D adaptations of **Tekken Advance** and **Klonoa**. But the European **V-Rally 3** was proof that the Advance is capable of fast 3D.

Nintendo's 'Multi Boot' is sadly a rarely used feature – networking up to four players at the same time to the same cartridge. **Bomberman** from 2000 supports it very well, as do **Mario Kart Advance**, **Colin McRae Rally 2.0** and the **Advance Wars** strategy field-campaigns. But although most games are link compatible, they're not Multi Boot capable: For instance, **Ecks vs. Sever** death-matches require a separate cart for each player.

A special cable connects the Advance with the Gamecube, turning the handheld into an intelligent controller and personal status screen. The first game to make use of this was **Sonic** – for raising and breeding the cute Chao creatures. In 2002, **Zelda** sailors on Gamecube were using the Game Boy Advance as the 'Tingle Tuner'; half a year later,

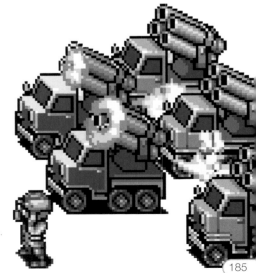

Up to four handheld generals network for Advance Wars. The high-tech turn-based battles are great even in solo mode.

Classic mechanics met new ideas on the Game Boy: After three Castlevania episodes, Konami created a vampire adventure that reacted to sunlight.

the multiplayer Final Fantasy Chronicles allowed every player to have his own menu screen. Nintendo bundled a radio transmission adapter with **Mario Golf Tour** (and also with Pokémon) to enable wireless data exchange between handhelds. The adapter was available separately later.

Sustained by its success and the worldwide support from developers, Nintendo was confident and valiant enough to bestow the handheld with an all-round update. The Advance SP reduces the boring design to a flip-down square that's reminiscent of a cigarette case. The SP is sturdy, practical and much more stylish than its chubby predecessor, with a backlit LCD as well as rechargeable battery unit as standard – finally, the smart architecture

The SP has an improved case and technology and prolonges the battery time to 10 hours, or with disabled LCD backlight up to 18 hours. In standby, the handheld can be collapsed to a sleek box.

There are several case variants, like the Rockstar edition shown above.

Where hardware generations merge: After the Famicom Mini success, Nintendo sold a grey NES edition in the US and Europe.

arrived at a perfect, matching chassis. Unfortunately, the small size meant that the headphone jack had to disappear, necessitating the use of a special adapter.

The 20-year anniversary of the Famicom brought forth the prettiest model, as new technology was coupled with '80s colour design. In addition to the SP Famicom version of the hardware, Nintendo started the Famicom Mini series: The 8-Bit classics by Nintendo, Namco, Konami and Hudson were shipped in packaging and cases in the style of the originals and retailed for – Japan is seemingly experiencing deflation – 2,000 yen, just a third of the original Famicom

cart price. The first series (20 games) sold 1.5 million units in Japan (a third of that accounted for by **Mini 01: Super Mario Bros**), before Nintendo released a second series of ten titles in May 2004 and shipped the oldies over to Europe, introducing the NES Classics brand.

The Game Boy's evolution proves Nintendo's respect for the past and its courage for the future: The stationary console market may be lost, but the Game Boy remains number one in the mobile sector. The SP combines and plays 15 years of game history – across generations and compatible all over the globe.

GBA variants and successors

GBA (AGB-)	2001	The first case variant was conservative and reminiscent of the Game Gear and Neo Geo Pocket: To the left, the control pad; to the right, the buttons; in between, a colour display. In Japan, variants in white (AGB-s-WA), violet (VTA) and a translucent Milky Blue (MBA) were released on 21 March. On 27 April, came Milky Pink (MPA), in December orange (OA) and black (KA). The 2002 models Gold (DA) and Silver (PLA) were the last. Of the eight Japanese versions, six were sold in Europe: Clear Blue, Clear Red, Purple, White, Black and finally Platinum. After Nintendo had shipped the unit in China, production ceased in favour of the SP. Worldwide, 34 million units of the old version were sold before March 2004.
GBA SP (AGS-)	2003	The flip-down GBA is the most practical and best handheld – but its outside is not as invulnerable or metallic as it looks. In the hands of children, the case's die-cast surface will be scratched, but the display is protected. Silver (ZVA), `Earthlight´ Blue (ZBA) and 'Onyx' Black variants were shipped in October in Japan, and four weeks later in the west. In Europe, from October on, the `Flame Red´ and `Arctic Blue´ versions were released, and at the end of 2004, a pink variant as well as a golden SP with Triforce logo on top. In Japan, September 2003 saw the pastel variants Pale Blue (-PBA) and Pale Pink, before the …
SP Famicom	2004	… retro model came along – the coolest Game Boy available. Following the Japanese hardware released on 14 February, the grey Classic NES Edition was launched in July in both Europe and USA.

Four kilograms of high tech: Microsoft's first games console trumped Sony and Nintendo with LAN connectivity, a case of huge proportions and sheer technical power.

Microsoft Xbox

USA, 2001

Units sold:	20 Million
Number of games:	700
Game storage:	DVD
Games developed until:	Still on

★ ★ ★ ★

In the '80s, Microsoft took over the office market and put other operating systems out of business or forced them into niches. In 1995, the Gates empire began its entertainment offensive with DirectX.

Before that, Windows PCs were unconvincing games machines, cursed by driver and compatibility problems. DirectX, originally presented as `Game SDK´ and introduced as part of Win95, unified and simplified game development. Its most important element was the Direct3D component.

Microsoft established DirectX as a games platform, began involving itself in the peripheral and controller market (IntelliMouse, Sidewinder) and invested in well-known games studios: Access, Digital Anvil, Ensemble (Age of Empires), FASA (Mechwarrior) and Bungie – prior to that the most successful Mac developer. Five years after DirectX had debuted at the American Game Developers Conference (GDC), Bill Gates revealed the first Microsoft console at the same event: The Xbox was based on PC components and DirectX 8, but unlike PCs, was optimised for games only.

The Xbox is well equipped with hard-drive, ethernet port and four joypad ports. To unlock the DVD movie player, you have to buy the remote control.

An explosive start: Marines comb the ringworld Halo either solo or as a team.

Sega developed its House of the Dead 3 simultaneously for Xbox and arcades.

The PC-relation is a guarantee for strong US ports: Morrowind.

To lift the hardware above the PlayStation 2 and the announced Nintendo console, hard-drive and network connectivity was incorporated from the outset. The unit shipped in the States at the end of 2001, early 2002 in Japan and Europe.

Technically, the Xbox is slightly more powerful than both the PlayStation 2 that arrived in 2000, and the contemporary Nintendo Gamecube. Microsoft opted for a 733 MHz Pentium III chip as main processor, while graphics acceleration was handled by the latest GeForce generation. With 64 MB RAM and a 10 GB hard-drive, the Xbox had more memory than its competition. And, at cost, Xbox owners can activate the DVD functionality and transform their games machine into a movie player.

The size of the machine is off-putting – reminiscent of Atari's giant 5200 console, but much heavier. Whilst Japanese manufacturers manically miniaturise technology, Microsoft rampaged about like Godzilla in the video game scene. The

case is sturdy yet rounded and not very good as a base for other electronics components. The original joypad was huge. Later, Microsoft shipped a smaller one.

With its launch titles, the Xbox flexed its muscles. Tecmo's beat 'em up **Dead or Alive 3** was an audiovisual treat, and the first person shooter **Halo** featured excellent playability. As an alternative to net matches, a cooperative mode was added – two marines blazed their way through the ringworld. Next to Microsoft, Sega became the biggest games supplier, shifting its Dreamcast projects like **Jet Set Radio Future** and **Gun Valkyrie** to the Xbox.

The European hardware launch was a disaster. At €480, the PAL machine was 70% more expensive than the US variant and all other game machines (excluding a PC with GeForce card, of course). Microsoft reacted to the disappointing sales with several price reductions. In autumn 2002, the price came down to €250 and to €150 in mid 2004.

Pretty faces and bodies, fast moves: Dead or Alive (far above) and Soul Calibur (right).

Sam Fisher leads the squad of military shooters and stealth adventures on the Xbox: Splinter Cell (Ubisoft, 2002).

The first special edition was a green translucent Xbox, shipped with high-end AV cables and a Bill Gates key tag.

As Japanese gamers ignored the Xbox, development of the RPG True Fantasy Online was cancelled.

In Japan, despite aggressive marketing and games by Sega, Konami and Capcom, the Xbox never got on its feet, struggling with sales of a few thousand units per month compared to Gamecube sales that were four times larger, and PlayStation 2 that were tenfold. After selling 330,000 consoles in 2002, sales in Japan crashed to a meagre 100,000 units the next year. By early 2004, half a million consoles were in use, and not a single game made it to the weekly Famicom Tsushin cross-platform charts.

In the high-end market however, the Xbox is the works. A year after launch, games with 5.1 Dolby Digital soundtracks and HDTV graphics appeared: The additional Component AV Pack delivers double the scan lines (Progressive Scan) and hence a maximised resolution to digital TVs, plasma monitors and projectors (only for games, not for DVD movies however). Games that are released for multiple platforms look and sound better on the Xbox – if you have the right home cinema equipment that is.

Microsoft might fail in some areas or territories, but easily leads the race in the area of networking, making the 10/100 LAN connectivity a standard right from the beginning. The console took off fullscale into the internet on November 15 2002, launching Xbox Live worldwide. The starting package for the online service contained the Communicator – a set of headphones and microphone for communicating with other gamers, and since 2003, for chatting with the Japanese cyber beauty **N.U.D.E.**

By autumn 2004, more than a million users had registered for Xbox Live worldwide, most of them in the US, where EA Sports, Ubisoft and other major publishers support the network with multiplayer games and downloads.

Xbox variants and successors

Special Edition	**2002**	Following the black original, Microsoft released 50,000 units of a limited green, translucent Xbox in Japan. The machine was shipped with a smaller joypad as well as HDTV and Dolby Digital cable and a numbered key tag with Bill Gate's signature. After that, small became the standard size for all joypads.
Pure White	**2003**	An Xbox version limited to 100,000 units, with DVD player and online kit as standard, retailed for 20,000 yen and was available via the Japanese Xbox Live site.
Crystal Edition	**2004**	The European variant in a colourless, translucent case was criticised for its noise level. After release at the beginning of the year, came a second series in October – available in some regions, but not in Germany for instance.

It's no multimedia all-rounder – instead Nintendo did what it does best:
To face off its rivals Sony and Microsoft, the console pioneer
sent in a small cube which packed a powerhouse punch.

Nintendo Gamecube

Japan, 2001

Sega provided online-compatible and launch games for Gamecube, but ...

... most games came from Nintendo. Eternal Darkness scared grown-ups ...

... the Smash Brothers entertained a four headed family (both in 2002).

After five years of Sony's dominance, the console market began to get interesting again. The two most successful software manufacturers tried to tempt gamers with new consoles: Microsoft, as a newcomer on the scene, Nintendo as the veteran. After NES, SNES and the N64, the pioneer turned away from the tried, yet expensive ROM cartridges and finally decided to ship its games on an optical medium. Just behind the Xbox, the Gamecube rolled out onto the shelves – a cute and compact console with a handle.

To undermine the other consoles, Nintendo saved money wherever possible: A top instead of front loader, no Ethernet or Firewire ports, no modem, no Dolby Digital sound. According to Nintendo's software genius Shigeru Miyamoto, the manufacturer wanted to create the `image of an easy to use and portable games machine´. Unlike PlayStation 2 and Xbox, the Gamecube can't run DVD movies or music CDs – it wasn't meant to be a multimedia player. Four controller ports allowed for multiplayer sessions, and there was a second AV port on the back: The digital output connected the cube to

Black or purple were the first case colours in the west; later a platinum look version appeared.

Units sold:	20 Million
Number of games:	600
Game storage:	Mini-DVD
Games developed until:	Still on

★ ★ ★ ★

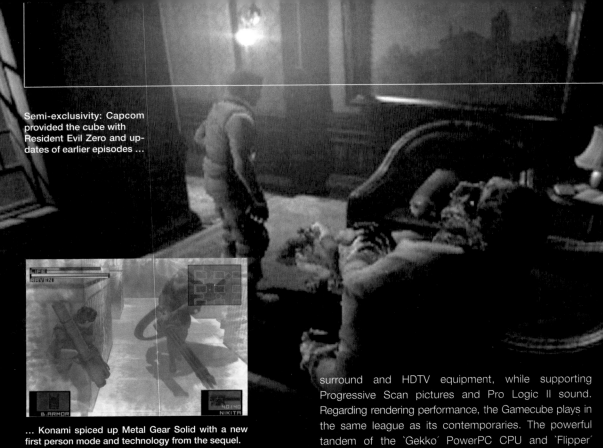

Semi-exclusivity: Capcom provided the cube with Resident Evil Zero and updates of earlier episodes ...

... Konami spiced up Metal Gear Solid with a new first person mode and technology from the sequel.

At the end of 2002, the Game Boy Player made the cube compatible with handheld software. The base connected to the High-speed port and was available either separately or bundled with special edition hardware like this pretty Tales of Symphonia unit.

surround and HDTV equipment, while supporting Progressive Scan pictures and Pro Logic II sound. Regarding rendering performance, the Gamecube plays in the same league as its contemporaries. The powerful tandem of the `Gekko´ PowerPC CPU and `Flipper´ multimedia processor was given access to 40 MB RAM, while buffer and fast bus provided for smooth and speedy data transfer. Depending on the component, the internal bandwidth can reach up to 12.8 GB per second – faster than a fully upgraded PC. One of the Gamecube's specialities is texture compression: The Flipper packs graphics data in real-time – the PlayStation 2 is short of such video RAM optimisation. The powerful hardware was conceived with know-how from the PC world: IBM helped with the development of the CPU, 3D specialist ATI, known for its Rage accelerators, came up with the graphics and sound chip Flipper.

Matsushita invented the exclusive storage medium: The 8 cm small 1.5 GB disc is a physical copy protection and loads data faster than a normal DVD. For Nintendo's western marketing the disc looked too insignificant: Whilst Japanese games were released in a cute miniature box, PAL discs are packed into ordinary DVD cases.

Game manufacturers welcomed Nintendo's break with the cartridge and the ease of programmability of the console. As US and European companies started work on new games in advance, most major PlayStation characters and

Nintendo left the DVD movie market to its partner Panasonic: The Q runs audio and video discs and offers more functionality and ports than a standard Gamecube.

brands (**Rayman**, **Tony Hawk's**, **XtremeG**) made their appearances on the Gamecube. Back home in Japan, where PlayStation sales exceed Nintendo on a 3:1 basis, companies are more reserved. Konami, a partner since the '80s, delivered no original game in the first twelve months, and Namco was just as careful. On the other hand, one of the launch titles was by Sega, **Super Monkey Ball**. After retreating from the hardware business, the old arch enemy now programs for Nintendo hardware.

Capcom supported Nintendo with a conversion of its horror series and even brought a Nintendo-exclusive prologue to the Gamecube with **Resident Evil Zero**. Seen by many as a sensational return, was the reappearance of Square games to the Big N. After eight years of absence and PlayStation exclusivity, the Gamecube finally witnessed a new **Final Fantasy** episode in 2003.

Sailing on, backed by strong technology and Shigeru Miyamoto's enchanting game design: The Wind Waker, 2002.

Gamecube variants and successors

Gamecube	2001	The originally announced five colours turned out to be four at release: Purple, black and – in Japan – orange and metallic cubes were shipped. The Gamecube has four joypad ports and three expansion slots, plus there's an analogue and (for the first time) digital AV connection for projectors, Plasma-screens or HDTV. A modem for playing Phantasy Star Online was shipped as an add-on from the start.
Panasonic Q	2001	The combo of games console and DVD movie video player was sold only in Japan and was nearly twice as expensive as the Gamecube, at 35,000 yen. The case is larger, features an LCD, new controls and enhanced connectivity. The metallic machine was shipped with a grey Panasonic joypad and a remote control. Matsushita stopped the Q production in 2003.
GB-Player-Bundles	from 2003	In Japan, Nintendo sold limited Gamecube/GB Player bundles. In September 2003, it was a black/white striped Hanshin Tigers special model (with the Baseball team's shirt), a little later the Emerald variant with a Tales of Symphonia plate in the lid.

Gamepark GP32

Korea, 2002

Units sold:	Unknown
Number of games:	25
Game storage:	Card
Games developed until:	2004

★ ⌐

Prior to the backlit unit, white and dark case variants were sold in Korea. With two AA batteries, you can use the multimedia handheld for 12 hours.

Before 2002, to play games, watch movies and listen to MP3s whilst on the move, you'd need either several single gadgets or an expensive PDA. Although Sony eventually became busy with development of the multimedia handheld PSP, the Korean company Gamepark had long finished the technology to do just that. The GP32 is a handheld with built-in music and movie player, is somewhat larger and heavier than a Game Boy but has a similar design: The direction pad is to the left of the display, to its right are two

An ARM CPU, USB and SmartMedia slot – the GP32 is well specced. The multiplayer RF connection costs extra.

fire buttons. Shoulder buttons, Start, Select, headphone jack and volume control – as shown by Nintendo.

To exchange data with a PC and other digital gadgets, the GP32 uses its USB port. The storage medium also follows an established standard: The Korean handheld stores and swaps applications and emulators, pictures, music and movies via SmartMedia Cards (SMC).

Technically, the GP32 is ahead of both GBA and the N-Gage; it has a faster processor, more memory, more colours and a higher resolution. Apart from the power and headphone jack, it sports stereo speakers and a 7.2 x 5.3 cm display. But the notorious display light problem haunted the first generation of the GP32 too. To recognize every pixel, you needed a good light source. A GP32 version with backlight was shipped later.

Despite its power, major publishers didn't support the handheld and the games on offer were few and far between. Fans of funky anime action grabbed a copy of the fantasy beat 'em ups **Her Knights** and **Dungeon & Guarder** or the 2D shoot 'em up **Tomak**, but sports, strategy or 3D games are missing. As it is possible to program the GP32 via USB and PC, there's more of a hobby developer than game user scene. The launch in the west was put off entirely.

Nokia N-Gage

Finland, 2003

Units sold:	1.3 Million
Number of games:	40
Game storage:	Card
Games developed until:	Still on

★ ★ ✦ ☆ ☆

By the end of the '90s, Nokia had developed into a bold and successful mobile phone manufacturer and amazed with handsets that were capable of more than just, well, phone calls. In 1997, the world was astounded by the launch of the clamshell Communicator 9000, the first mobile phone/computer hybrid. From 2001 on, the Finnish company began using the open source operating system Symbian for its Smartphones, researched in the UK by Psion (see page 59). With a CPU and RAM, Java and Symbian, the Series 60 mobile phones attracted the interest of both gamers and game developers.

In 2000, Nokia started an aggressive campaign, focusing on games for its mobile phones. Then, the company presented a consequent combo of phone and handheld: The N-Gage has an ARM CPU, and with it, it's fast enough for real-time 2D and 3D animation. One of the first titles to prove it was **Tony Hawk's Pro Skater**.

Aiming at grabbing market share from the Game Boy, Nokia engaged big names. Most games were conversions of successful PlayStation or Sega brands; however, the 3D architecture of **Pandemonium** and **Super Monkey Ball** lost some of its original thrills due to the small vertical screen format and 12-Bit colour depth, while in **Tomb Raider**, it's hard to spot wolves against the grey stone walls. Scrolling

No fun without a mobile contract: The N-Gage runs games only with a SIM card inserted.

2D games like **Rayman 3** and **Sonic N** also suffer from the unusual screen format. Nonetheless, it is well suited for classics like **Puzzle Bobble VS** and **Puyu Pop**.

With radio and media players, N-Gage is multitalented but feels somewhat overburdened and clumsy. Pressing the handheld to your ear looks silly – Nokia had to pay the price with worldwide ridicule. One major fault was the card slot: To exchange games, the battery had to be removed. Reacting to the critics, Nokia shipped the smaller QD, which is easier to hold and consumes less battery power.

While the USB port is used to synchronize with the PC, handhelds connect wirelessly – apart from three, all games offer local Bluetooth matches. The phone's networking potential remains untapped; due to GPRS costs, **PGA 2004**, the first online game, ended up as an expensive leisure activity. N-Gage Arena started as a forum for downloads and hi-scores, but is now visited by people from **Pocket Kingdoms,** the first MORPG for N-Gage. Military sims also made their much-awaited appearances at the end of 2004.

The successor

N-Gage QD	2004	Nokia doubled the battery life and threw most bells and whistles overboard. Without MP3, triband and shortwave radio, the N-Gage QD is more handy than its predecessor. Games can be swapped without dismantling the battery and making calls is more comfy, as the QD can be held to the ear just like a normal mobile phone.

Nintendo DS

Japan, 2004

Units sold:	3 Million
Number of games:	20
Game storage:	Card, Cartridge
Games developed until:	Still on

★ ★ ﹜

The introduction of the Advance SP surprisingly prolonged the Game Boy's longevity and suddenly, Nintendo holds two mobile platforms in its hands: The Game Boy Advance format has been joined by the futuristic DS; the abbreviation doesn't denote a simple update of the Game Boy, but stands for a technical revolution.

This book is full of pioneering efforts and inventions, and Nintendo's DS manages to score in many categories: It's the first portable console with two displays and it sports touch-screen control. The DS sets up Wireless LAN as soon as another handheld is in vicinity and features user-friendly software (**PictoChat**) for connecting and exchanging data, plus a plastic stylus for scribbling on screen and a microphone to allow speech input.

Prior to the hardware launch (in December in the US and Japan, 2005 in Europe), confusion reigned: Isn't that too much innovation? How can the double screen be used for new gameplay? The launch title **Super Mario 64 DS**, a graphically polished remake of the N64 bestseller, proved the sense and functionality of touch-screen control within a third-person environment: Instead of pressing the pad with your thumb, Mario is controlled by gently touching the lower display. Point your finger and Mario sprints; do it again and he'll swerve around, glowing heels and all. When Mario runs, your finger rests.

Metroid Prime Hunter, which was included with the US DS as a multiplayer demo, also works very well. To aim your weapon in this first person shooter, your thumb slides over the touch screen. This gives the precision of an optical mouse. Tapping the display twice makes the heroine jump. In order to avoid smudging the screen with greasy fingers and to maintain a point of precise control, a little piece of rounded plastic rests on the tip of your finger – attached to the device's wrist strap.

At the time of Gameplan's editorial deadline, it is hard to tell how the market will react and how developers will come up with new game mechanics for the unusual technology. The worldwide race between Sony's PSP and Nintendo's DS starts in 2005. Launch titles by Electronic Arts, Sega and Namco and fresh concepts by renowned Japanese designers like Tetsuya Mizuguchi (after Rez and Space Channel 5, the enfant terrible has founded a handheld label for Bandai) and Sonic inventor Yuji Naka have proven that the DS has passed its initiation test.

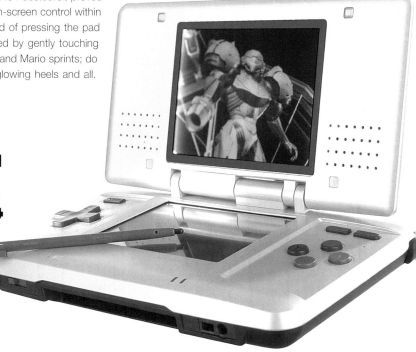

It's like seeing double: The DS has two ARM processors, two displays and two cartridge slots – one for Advance carts and the other for Nintendo's new Flash Cards.

Now that the PlayStation's dominance has been consolidated across the world, Sony intends to conquer the handheld sector: The PlayStation Portable is a pocket computer for anyone looking for consistent, mobile entertainment.

Sony PSP

Japan, 2004

Units sold:	1 Million
Number of games:	20
Game storage:	Mini-DVD (UMD)
Games developed until:	Still on

★ ★ ⸜

The PSP plays all sorts of media and is compatible with Sony's UMD and Memory Stick Duo formats. It is a hip, high-tech accessory for trendy gamers, not for nerds.

SCE's step into the handheld business has taken time, allowing other Sony divisions to have a go at the mobile market. After the failure of pocket computer Clié, the group launched another attempt with the PlayStation Portable (PSP), the latest of Ken Kutaragi's inventions. With this sleek gadget, Sony breaks into the market of mobile, all-round game and media players.

The PSP turns the PocketPC trend around: Instead of being a multimedia player capable of the odd game, the PSP is a pure-bred mobile console with film and music as extra features. Normal CDs don't fit into the handheld, which is designed to use Sony's new UMD format, a mini-DVD for games, movies and music. The recordable medium for MP3s and pictures on the PSP is the Memory Stick Duo, Sony's own, not-quite-so-cheap flash card format.

The PSP lacks the ground-breaking new features of the DS, but it has more power under its hood than any other handheld. Whereas Nintendo economised, Sony has been extravagant to the point of wastefulness: A large 16:9 display with 16 million colours, an optical storage medium and PS2-comparable specs deprive the Lithium-Ion batteries of power within five hours. Sony has price-positioned its baby a level higher than Nintendo, but has also managed to keep the launch price down to 20,000 yen (€180), despite all its lavish components. The `Value Pack´, including headphones, Memory Stick and carrying case, retailed for 26,000 yen.

Like the DS, it's too early to write home about the PSP's history. In Japan, it appeared just in time for Christmas, in the west it is released in 2005. Sony has already shipped 300,000 PSP units in Japan, but as Gameplan goes to press, nothing can be said about European pricing, internet strategy or launch line-up. One thing is certain though: Major publishers in Japan, USA and Europe (and even a handful of Korean studios) are working on and releasing a lot of PSP games in 2005. Nobody wants to miss the next step in the PlayStation evolution.

Comeback for an entire decade of PlayStation thrills and action: Ridge Racer, Need for Speed and Gran Turismo start their engines with polished graphics and over wireless LAN. In the UK, updates of MediEvil and wipEout are coded, and RPGs in Japan.

Dragon 32

GB, 1982 | Games: 140 | Games on: Cartridge, Tape | Development until: 1986 | ★ ⌁

This early Spectrum and BBC B competitor hid TRS-80 architecture (featuring the same Motorola CPU and video chips) under a rather dull typewriter case, yet it did have improved BASIC and small modifications. Initially, the Dragon micro was produced in Wales. It's not compatible with the American CoCo, but it's technically so similar that, US software was converted for the UK market very quickly.

Dragon Data published a dozen cart games at launch, but then slacked off. Microdeal stepped in, producing and marketing nearly 100 tape games and inventing the Cuthbert mascot. With **Cuthbert in the Jungle**, a straight clone of Pitfall, imported from the States and renamed, Microdeal faced a law suit. Further adventures of the glasses-wearing hero included ...**goes Walkabout** (Amidar), ...**goes Digging** (Space Panic) and ...**in the Mines**. Nearly all contemporary arcade hits had a Dragon counterpart: Galaga (**Galagon**), Time Pilot (**Fury**), Joust (**Buzzard Bait**) or Bosconian (**Draconian**), but there were also text adventures and the ingenious original RPG **Ring of Darkness** by tiny software house Wintersoft. In 1983, the eventual C64 wizard Andrew Braybrook sat behind a Dragon: His conversion of the **Seiddab** shoot 'em up trilogy by mentor Steve Turner was evidence of his talent and shape of things to come.

At the end of the year, the externally unchanged Dragon 64 with 64 K (ie. double) memory appeared, but interest by dealers, press and users had waned. Attempts to gain ground in the US failed, the company went bankrupt and was handled by investor General Electric. At the last minute, the Spanish company Eurohard took over the technology and continued production and marketing on mainland Europe. In 1986, the last Dragon rolled off Spanish production belts.

Fujitsu FM-7, FM-77

Japan, 1982, 1984 | Games: 700 | Games on: Tape, Disk
Development until: 1989 | ★ ★ ★ ⌁

In Japan, Fujitsu shipped the FM-7 micro as compatible hobby successor to the office machine FM-8, released in May 1981. All its variants contained two CPUs, hi-res graphics (640x200 in eight colours) and a programmable sound generator (PSG). With this specification, the FM-7 became the most successful platform after the PC-88 range. Tape and disk software was supplied by Technosoft, Koei and Hudson, Enix, Falcom and Square. One well-known original game on the FM-7 was the economics simulation **A-Train** (1985) by Artdink.

The backward compatible successor FM-77 had 64 K RAM, 48 K video RAM and was shipped with two drives for Sony's new 3.5" disks. At first it retailed for 228,000 yen, while its successor FM-77AV (October 1985) sold for 170,000 yen. AV stands for improved graphics (4,096 colours, at least 96 K video RAM) and FM sound. The last model was the 40SX from 1988 with two times 192 K RAM as standard, four graphics modes and a maximum of 262,144 colours.

Mattel Aquarius

Hong Kong/USA, 1983 | Games: 10 | Games on: Cartridge | Development until: 1984 | ⌐

Parallel to the Intellivision II development, came a cheap computer designed and manufactured in Hong Kong, with 4 K RAM, rubber keys and BASIC. The Mini Expander released simultaneously, was the most important expansion for gamers; it added two joypads (disc, six buttons), two cartridge ports and the sound chip from the Intellivision console. Other add-ons for Mattel's weakly marketed computer slip-up were Datasette, memory expansion and a 300-Baud modem for the cartridge port. In Europe and Asia, the machine was marketed by the manufacturer Radofin itself (Radofin Aquarius).

NEC PC-98

Japan, 1982 | Games: 2,000 | Games on: Disk | Development until: 1997 | ★ ★ ★ ★ ⌐

The first Japanese 16-Bit PC and most successful games machine was the counterpart to western DOS computers. The 98 range took over from NEC's 8801 PCs and like its predecessor, it was continuously enhanced, resulting in unaccounted numbers of variants much like the western IBM-compatible. Since the PC-9801VM, NEC replaced the Intel CPU (8086 at 5 MHz) with their own 8 MHz V30 processor. From early 1990, the PC-98 micros returned to Intel processors and used 386, 486, Pentium and variants (eg. 386SX in the PC-9801DS from 1991).

Unknown in the west, the PC family of computers provided breeding ground for many franchises popular today: In 1983, Technosoft published its first **Thunderforce** shoot 'em up on the PC-98, two years later came the debut of Systemsoft's WWII strategy epic **Daisenryaku** (aka Military Commander) and various historical simulations by Koei. Prominent RPGs like **Ys 2** in 1988, **Dragonknight** in 1989, and **Princess Maker** in 1991 tagged along. Simulations like **Derby Stallion**, **Winning Post** were followed up on games consoles. In the mid-'90s, NEC replaced its PC-98 range with MS Windows computers.

Sinclair QL

GB, 1984 | Games: 30 | Games on: Microdrive | Development until: 1986 | ★ ⌐

The professional successor to the Sinclair Spectrum is based on an 8-Bit variant of Motorola's 68000 CPU. Unlike the chips used in Atari ST and Amiga, the 68008 has an 8-Bit wide data-bus and is clocked at 8 MHz. The QL had 128 K RAM as standard, graphics resolutions of 256x256 pixels with eight and 512x256 in four colours, two RS232 as well as RGB, joystick and power connections but no specialised sound chip.

The externally elegant QL fell prey to delays, technical problems and its storage medium. The 100 K 'Microdrive' couldn't even hold its ground against the disk in its homeland. In Japan and the US, the QL wasn't available at all. The only games worthy of note are the Games Workshop strategy **D-Day** and adventure **The Pawn**, originally developed for QL, and later famous on the Atari ST and Amiga. The new software house Psygnosis intended to support the ill-fated 68000 pioneer too, but quickly switched over to Amiga and Atari ST development. After 60,000 units sold, the QL was reduced to half price (£200) in autumn. A little later, it was cancelled altogether.

Sord, Takara M5

Japan, 1982 | Games: 50 | Games on: Tape, Cartridge
Development until: 1983 | ★ ★

This Japanese games computer with rubber keys and a Z-80A CPU (3.58 MHz) was launched at the end of 1982. Despite a puny 3 K of RAM, both variants, the Sord M5 (49,800 yen) and the Takara Game PC (59,800 yen) were short-lived but quite successful games machines with cartridge port, good graphics (16 colours, 32 sprites) and 3-channel sound. Two joypads with direction disc were included. About 25 games

were released on cartridge – including arcade conversions **Dig Dug**, **Pac-Man**, **Moon Patrol**, **Pooyan** and **Super Cobra**. Peripherals included: Printer, data recorder, joysticks and a disk drive. The M5 was replaced by the cheaper M5 Junior early in 1984 (29,800 yen including joystick) and its big brother M5 Pro (39,800 yen). In Europe, it was available from 1983 on, but it was more expensive than Commodore, Sinclair and Atari computers. With only 3 or 16 K RAM, it was hopelessly underpowered and unsuccessful.

Spectravideo SVI-318, SVI-328

USA, 1982 I Games: 50 I Games on: Tape, Cartridge I Development until: Unknown I ★ ★

The games and home computer with calculator style keys was technically related and a predecessor to the MSX machines by Spectravideo. The hardware is nearly identical but not compatible. One distinctive feature was the embedded red joystick. The successor SVI-328 (64 K RAM, 16 K VRAM, two controller ports) lacked the mini joystick, but did have a proper typewriter keyboard.

Thomson TO7

France, 1983 I Games: 100 I Games on: Cartridge, Tape, Disk I Development until: 1988 I ★ ★

Based on the 6809 CPU by Motorola, the government-supported company Thomson built this home computer for France only. Internally, the TO7 and its compact successor MO5 were similar to British micros: Up to 32 K RAM, graphics resolutions of 320 x 300 pixels in eight colours. Additionally, the `Tele Ordinateur´ offered RGB output and a light pen concealed beneath a case flap. The light pen test was the only program inside the ROM, but BASIC was available on cartridge. The Datasette was incorporated in the wedge-shaped case.

Thomson saved bucks on the keyboard, shipping the first model with useless membrane keys and the MO5 with a rubber keyboard. The improved micros MO6 (1986), TO8 (256 K, 1985) and TO9 (128 or 512 K, 1985) came with a full-blown keyboard. Light pen, Datasette and floppy drive were optional.

At first, Thomson competed with the Oric Atmos, then with the Amstrad CPC, and just like the competition, it earned tape and disk support from French software houses Infogrames, Titus, Loriciels, Cobra and Ubisoft. Country wide, the computers were used by schools, where the light pen ended as a weapon rather than an input tool. In Italy, Olivetti manufactured and marketed Thomson's micros.

The limited model with football star Michael Platini's signature is a funny version of the MO5 built in 1984.

Tomy Pyu-Ta

Japan, 1982 I Games: 28 I Games on: Cartridge I Development until: 1984 I ★ ★

A games micro introduced in 1982, with a TI 9995 16-Bit CPU, RGB output and BASIC operating system, retailed for 59,800 yen – one of the most expensive game machines. The 30 odd cartridges published included officially licensed Konami arcade conversions (**Scramble**, **Frogger** and **Gattan Cotton**) and Universal titles (**Mr.Do!**). **Rescue Copter**, a vector graphics game, and the scrolling Disney jump 'n run **Mickey Athletic Land** were the two most interesting titles. Retailed for a mass-market compatible 19,800 yen, came the Pyu-Ta Jr. variant (stripped of the keyboard), which was released in the west as the Tomy Tutor. A professional version with a proper mechanical keyboard, called Mk. II, was also available. The Tomy-Pa controllers were pads with a control disc and two buttons kept in the same colours as the computer, namely blue and white.

APF M1000

USA, 1978 | Games: 12 | Games on: Cartridge | Games developed until: 1978 | ★

This was an obscure TI99/4a relative that never made it to Europe and also, without ado, bit the dust in its homeland. The **Rocket Patrol** game was built-in, the controllers were similar to the later Coleco pads (control stick and numerical buttons). The dark console became the heart of the Imagination Machine in 1979, a computer system with keyboard, Datasette, music chip, 9 K RAM and 14 K ROM including BASIC. Without the $600 computer set, the console had a mere 1 K RAM. The Motorola 6800 (8-Bit, 3.58 MHz) is used as CPU.

Bally Astrocade

USA, 1976 | Games: 50 | Games on: Tape, Cartridge | Games developed until: 1983 | ★ ⊁

The Astrocade was an early programmable console by American arcade manufacturer Bally. It had three built-in games, calculator and a mini keyboard. In 1978, Bally shipped its BASIC cart that upgraded it to a home-micro. The technically superior system, based on a Z-80 CPU, remained an outsider due to its high (in comparison to the Atari VCS) street price of $299 and weak marketing. Following some Bally cartridges like **Wizard of Wor**, only a few tape games made it to the shops from 1980 on, programmed by semi-pros, for whom an improved BASIC cart was included in 1982. The edgy, two-level console appeared in two versions: A limited one in a white case as well as the standard system in a wood-look. The controllers were an unusual combination of stick, paddle and triggers in one unit. The console was upgradeable with four to 32 K. Jay Fenton, who wrote the BallyBASIC, later became famous for the shoot 'em up Gorf and as founder of Macromind.

Bandai Playdia

Japan, 1994 | Games: Unknown | Games on: CD | Games developed until: 1995 | ⊁

This was a CD-ROM console for kids, launched only on the home market by the Japanese toy and anime conglomerate Bandai. When not used, the infrared remote controller is firmly embedded in the colourful case of the ill-fated machine. Bandai was the only publisher to support this exotic hardware with CD-ROM titles, based on well-known manga and anime brands, prior to production stop. Original price: 24,800 yen.

Casio PV-1000

Japan, 1983 | Games: 15 | Games on: Cartridge | Games developed until: 1984 | ★ ⊁

A Japanese video game console that was released simultaneously with the home computer version PV-2000 in October 1983, The PV-1000 retailed for an initial 14,800 yen; the keyboard and BASIC variant sold for double that. In 1984, the Nintendo Famicom blew this Casio system out of the market, along with the Super Cassettevision by Epoch and other rival formats.

Nintendo Pokémon Mini

Japan, 2001 | Games: 10 | Games on: Cartridge | Games developed until: 2002 | ★

A tiny handheld with a 48x31 pixel resolution, Nintendo's typical direction pad, two fire and one shoulder button, built-in shock-sensor and rumble feature, clock, infrared connection and battery buffered memory. With its 74x58x32mm dimensions and 70g weight, it was the smallest and lightest games console yet. It was devised specifically for puzzle and reaction games set in the Pokémon world: By 2002, the mini's games selection consisted of **Pokémon Puzzle Collection**, **Pokémon Pinball Mini**, **Pokémon Party Mini** and six more carts. Three case variants were available: Purple, blue and green.

8-Bit and BASIC home computers

Manufacturer Type	Apple Apple II/+	Commodore Pet	Atari 800	Tandy TRS-80 Color Computer	Texas Instruments TI99/4a	Sinclair ZX 81	Sharp MZ-80B, -700
Year	1977, 1979	1977	1979	1980	1981	1981	1981, 1982
CPU							
Type	6502	6502	6502A	MC 6809E	TMS9900	Z80A	Z80A
Clock speed	1 MHz	1 MHz	1.79 MHz	0.9 MHz	3 MHz	3.5 MHz	4 MHz
Memory (in Byte)							
RAM	4 K to 48 K	4 to 32 K	16 to 48 K	4 K	16 K	1 K	to 64 K [1]
expandable to	64 K	32 K	48 K [24]	64 K	to 48 K	16 K	to 64 K
ROM	12 K	14 K	10 K	8 K	26 K	16 K	4 K
Graphics							
Coprozessor	–	MOS6545 CRTC	GTIA/Antic	–	TMS9918A	–	–
minimum resolution/colours	280x192/6	40x25(x8x8)	80x192/16	128x128/4	40x24	24x32(x8x8)	40, 80x25(x8x8)
medium resolution/colours	–	–	160x192/4	–	240x192/2	–	320x200 [21]
maximum resolution	560x192	–	320x192	256x192	256x192/16	–	640x200 [22]
Colour palette	8	0	128, 256	9	15+1	0	0 [21]
Sprites	no	no	8 [3]	no	32	no	no
Sound							
PSG chip	no	no	Pokey	no	TMS9919	no	no
Channels [18]	1 Beeper	–	4 PSG	1 Beeper	3 PSG	–	1 Beeper
Sound wave type(s)	–	–	square	–	square	–	–
as well as	–	–	Beeper	–	noise	–	–
Channel modulation							
Frequency (pitch)	–	–	8 bit	–	6 bit	–	–
Volume	–	–	4 bit	–	4 bit	–	–
Envelope	no	no	yes	no	no	no	no
app. voice range	unknown	–	3 octaves	unknown	5 1/2 octaves	–	unknown
Features							
Joystick ports	internal	no	4	2	1	no	no, 2
Built-in drive	no	Datasette [6]	no	no	no	no	Datasette
Built-in monitor	no	10", 12"	no	no	no	no	9" [23]
Cartridge port	no	no	2	no	yes	no	no
Keyboard							
Keys	solid, 62	mini, 73 solid, 76 [9]	solid, 61	solid, 53	solid, 48	membrane, 40	mini, 78, solid, 92
Large SPACE	yes	yes [11]	yes	yes	yes	no	yes
Numerical keypad	no	yes	no [26]	no	no	no	yes
Separate Cursor keys	no	no	no	no	no	no	yes
Separate Function keys	no	no	no	no	no	no	10

Without built-in
monitor, but with integrated
Datasette: Sharp MZ800

[1] as well as 16 K VRAM
[2] VIC-2 is either a MOS 6567 (NTSC models)
or a MOS 6569 (PAL)
[3] `players & missiles´
[4] Texas Instruments SN76496N inside PC Jr.
[5] two joystick ports and cartridge port via add-on Interface II
[6] only the first model (Pet 2001) had the tape drive
integrated in case
[7] depending on series, differing configuration, partially with
Datasette
[8] disk drive integrated in CPC 664 et.al.
[9] 76+ solid keys with all variants starting with 3001
[10] small `Mickey Mouse´ keyboard with the PC Jr.

Commodore VC20	IBM PC, PC jr.	Sinclair ZX Spectrum	Commodore C 64	Acorn BBC B	various MSX,[7] Spectravideo SVI	Coleco Adam	Amstrad CPC 464
1981	1981, 1983	1982	1982	1982	1982, 1983	1983	1984
6502	8088	Z80A	6510	6502A	Z80A	Z80A	Z80A
1 MHz	4.77 MHz	3.58 MHz	1 MHz	2 MHz	3.58 MHz	3.58 MHz	4 MHz
3.5 K	64 K	16 K or 48 K	64 K	32 K	8 to 64 K [1]	64 K [1]	64 K
16 K	128 K	128 K	128 K	64 K	64 K	144 K	80 K
20 K	64 K	8 K,16 K	20 K	32 K	32 K	32 K	32 K
MOS 656x (VIC)	(CGA)	–	MOS 656x [2]	6845 CRTC	TMS-9918	TMS-9918A	6845 CRTC
88x184/4	320x200/4	256x192/8	160x200/16	160x256/16	256x192/16	256x192/16	200x160/16
–	–	–	–	320x256/4	–	–	320x200/4 [15]
176x184/2	640x200/2	–	320x200/16	640x256/2	255x211/256	320x200/4	640x200/2
16	16	8	16	8 + 8	16	16	27
no	no	no	8	no	32	32	no [17]
MOS 656x (VIC)	no [4]	no [25]	MOS 6581SID	TI SN76489	AY-3-8910	TI SN76489	AY-3-8910
3 PSG	1 Beeper	1 Beeper	3 PSG [19]	3 PSG	3 PSG	3 PSG	3 PSG
square	square	–	flexible	square	square	square	square
noise	–	–	–	noise	noise	noise	noise
8 bit	yes	yes	16 bit	10 bit	12 bit	10 bit	12 bit
4 bit (global)	no	no	8 bit	4 bit	4 bit	4 bit	4 bit
no	no	no	flexible	yes	yes	yes	yes
unknown	unknown	5 octaves	8 octaves	8 octaves	8 octaves	8 octaves	8 octaves
2	1	no [5]	2	1	1 or 2	2	2
no	Disk	no	no	no	no [7]	Tape	Datasette [8]
no	optional	no	SX64 only	no	no	no	no [20]
yes	no	no [5]	yes	no	1 or 2	no	no
solid, 66	solid, 82 [10]	rubber, 40 [16]	solid, 66	solid, 74	solid or rubber, 60+	solid, 76	solid, 74
yes	yes	no	yes	yes	yes	yes	yes
no	yes	no [12]	no	no	no	yes [14]	yes
no	yes	no	no	no	yes	yes	yes
4	10	no	4	10	yes	6	no

[11] from the 3001 series on

[12] only Spectrum 128 had a seperate keypad

[13] SVI-318 had a mini-joystick built in

[14] numerical keypad on each joypad

[15] four colours in three levels of brightness (12 tones plus black and white)

[16] Spectrum+, +2, +3 had solid keyboards

[17] CPC+ and GX had 16 sprites

[18] primitive 1 channel sampling possible, for example via the noise generator

[19] thanks to flexible waveforms, filters and ADSR envelope for each channel, as well as ring modulation, the SID was far ahead of other sound chips

[20] monitor was not integrated but included, and was the power source for the whole system.

[21] while the 80B basic configuration had no colours, the 700 displayed four (out of 16).

[22] with special chip only (but standard on MZ800)

[23] only MZ80B. 10" in earlier models, no screen integrated in later model.

[24] Atari 800XL had 64 K

[25] Spectrum+ and later had the common sound chip AY-3-8912A

[26] official add-on for the controller port (CX-85)

Manufacturer Type	Fairchild Channel F	Atari VCS 2600	Interton VC 4000	Philips G7000	Mattel Intellivision	GCE Vectrex	CBS Colecovision	Entex Adventurevisic
Year	1976	1977	1978	1978	1979	1982	1982	1982
CPU								
Type	F 3850	6507	Signetics2650	8048H	GI CP 1610 [1]	MC 68A09	Z80A	Intel 8048
Clock speed	1.78 MHz	1.2 MHz	0.9 MHz	1.79 MHz	0.9 MHz	1.6 MHz	3.58 MHz	0.93 MHz
Memory (in Byte)								
RAM	64 [22]	128	43	64	2 K [3]	512	1 K	64
Video RAM	–	–	–	256	512, 256	–	16 K	–
expandable	no	yes [4]	no	no	yes [5]	no	no	–
max. Cartridge size	2 K	32 K	8 K	8 K	16 K	8 K	8 K	4 K
Other media	no	Tape [4]	no	no	no	no	no	no
Graphics								
Chip	–	TIA	Signetics2636	Intel P8245	GI AY-3-8915	–	TI TMS9928A	–
Resolution	75x55	160x200	208x128	144x96	160x96	–	256x192	150x40
Colours	4	16	8	8	16	–	16	–
Palette	16	128	8	12	16	–	16	–
Sprites	5	5	4	4	8	–	32	–
Resolution	unkown	8xX	8x10	8x8	8x8, 8x16	–	8x8, 16x16	–
Sound								
Chip	–	Atari TIA	Signetics	Intel P8245	GI AY-3-8914	GI AY-3-8912	TI SN76489AN	–
Channels								
PSG	2	2	1	1	3	1	3	
Noise	–	–	–	–	1	1	1	1
FM	–	–	–	–	1	1	1	
Digital/PCM [27]	–	–	–	–	–	–	–	
Channel modulation								
Frequency	unknown	5-Bit	unknown	1-Bit	12-Bit	12-Bit	10-Bit	
Volume	unknown	4-Bit	unknown	2-Bit	4-Bit	4-Bit	4-Bit	
Others	–	4-Bit wave-form selector	–	–	envelope	envelope	–	
Expandable	no	no	no	yes [17]	yes [17]	no	no	no
Official add-ons								
Modem	no	yes [12]	no	no	no	no	no	no
Keyboard	no	yes	no	no	no	no	no	no
Trackball	no	yes	no	integrated	yes	no	yes	no
Light Gun	no	no [23]	no	no	no	no	yes	no
Music keyboard	no	no	no	no	no	no	no	no
Graphical input	no	no	no	no	yes	no	no	no
Removable storage	no	no	no	no	no	Light Pen	no	no
3D glasses	no	no	no	no	no	no	no	no
Joypad ports	– [20]	2	2	– [20]	– [20]	yes	no	no
						2	2	–

16-Bit
as well as 8-Bit coprocessor
Z80A clocked at 4 MHz
even first class sources
(such as IEEE, Blue Sky Rangers) can't
define the Intellivision RAM precisely
via Supercharger
with ECS or Keyboard Component
up to 2 MBit via Arcade Card
with 32X and Mega CD
for Japanese consoles only
special variants only or via external drive

10) variants Neo Geo CD and Neo Geo CD-Z
11) with add-on Satellaview and BS-X adapter,
containing 64 K RAM and 32 K flash RAM.
External flash cards (BM Memory Packs)
hold 128 K each.
12) for GameLine download service (USA only)
13) vertical size 128 or 256 pixel
14) CPU is a 6502 variant enhanced
with a sound generator
15) (in Japan, with additional FM chip YM2413
(9 channel, ADSR envelope); for Mark III in 1987
shipped as add-on FM Sound Unit)
16) CPU contained a programmable sound generator (PSG)
17) with add-on voice cartridge
18) ... but custom chips inside cartridges

19) with Mega CD
20) two controllers hardwired to the console
21) X-Band add-on and matching
service in USA and Japan
22) scratchpad in CPU
23) ... but compatible to later
XE GS light gun

AV jacks		
RF tuner and cable		
special AV out		
separate audio out		
Video out		
Component (RGB)		
SVideo (Y/C)		
Video (CVBAS)		

Hanimex HMG 2650	Atari 5200	Nintendo Famicom, NES	Atari 7800	Sega Master System	NEC PC-Engine	Sega Mega Drive	Nintendo Super NES	SNK Neo Geo
1982	1982	1983, 1985	1984	1987	1987	1988	1989	1990
Signetics2650	6502	Ricoh (6502)[14]	6502	Z80A	HuC6280	MC 68000[2]	65C816	MC 68000[2]
3.58 MHz	1.79 MHz	1.79 MHz	1.79 MHz	3.58 MHz	7.16 Mhz	7.6 MHz	3.58 MHz	12 MHz
1 K	2 K	2 K	4 K	8 K	8 K	64 K	128 K	8 K
–	unknown	2.25 K	unknown	16 K	64 K	64 K	64 K	8 K
no	no	no	no	no	yes[6]	yes[7]	yes[11]	no
8 K	32 K	512 K	128 K	512 K	2.5 M	4 M	6 M	100 M
no	no	Diskette[11]	no	MyCard	CD-ROM[9]	CD-ROM[9]	Flash[11]	CD-ROM[10]
Signetics2637N	Antic, GTIA	PPU	Maria	–	HuC6270	–	PPU2 (16-Bit)	–
262x192	320x200	256x240	160x242, 320x242	256x192	320x224, 512x256	256x244, 320x244	256x224, 512x448	320x224
9	8, 16	16	16	16	32	64	256	4.096
9	256	52	256	64	512	512	32.786	65.536
4	8	64	unknown	64	64	80	128	380
8x8	8xX + 2xX[13]	8x8, 8x16	unknown	8x8	16x16~32x64	32x32	8x8~64x64	16x512~1x16
Signetics 2637N	Atari Pokey	Nintendo PPU[14]	Atari TIA	TI SN76489 AN[24]	NEC PSG[16]	TI SN76489, YM2612	Sony SPC700[28]	Yamaha YM2610
1	4	3	2	3	–	3	–	3
–	–	1	–	1	–	1	–	1
–	–	–	–	–[24]	–	6[26]	–	4
–	–	1[25]	–	–	6	1[26]	8 ADPCM	6+1 ADPCM
unknown	8-Bit	11-Bit, 4-Bit	5-Bit	12-Bit	12-Bit	flexible	16-Bit	flexible
unknown	4-Bit	flexible	4-Bit	4-Bit	8-Bit	flexible	16-Bit	flexible
–	envelope	flexible wave-form, envelopes	4-Bit wave-form selector	-	–	Stereo, envelopes	Stereo, ADSR envelopes	Stereo, envelopes
no	no	no[18]	no[18]	no	no	yes[19]	no[18]	no
no	no	yes[8]	no	no	no	yes	yes[21]	no
no	no	yes	no	no	no	no	no	no
no	yes	no	no	no	no	Mouse	Mouse	no
no	no	yes	no[23]	yes	no	no	yes	no
no	no	yes	no	no	no	no	no	no
no	no	no	no	Graphics tablet	Graphics tablet	no	no	no
no	no	yes[8]	no	no	no	no	no[11]	Memory Card
no	no	yes	no	yes	no	no	no	no
–[20]	4 or 2	2	2	2	1	2	2	2
	yes	yes	yes	yes	yes	yes	yes	yes
	no	yes[29]	no	DIN 8pin	no	DIN 8pin[33]	MultiAV 12pin	DIN 8pin
	no	no (Cinch)	no	no	no	Phone jack[32]	no	Phone jack[32]
	no	no	no[30]	yes[30]	no	yes[34]	yes	yes
	no	no	no	no	no	no[35]	yes	yes
	no	yes[29]	no	yes	yes[31]	yes	yes	yes

[24] in Japan, with additional FM chip YM2413 (9 channel, ADSR envelope); for Mark III in 1987 shipped as add-on FM Sound Unit
[25] NES only (not Famicom)
[26] if PCM sound, maximum of 5 FM channels
[27] primitive 1 channel sampling via noise or PSG channel possible
[28] an 8-bit (2 Mhz), 16-Bit DSP, 16-Bit DAC and 64 K RAM
[29] in Japan, on Twin Famicom and Famicom AV only (12-pin MultiAV)
[30] in France, RGB-Scart as standard (peritél)
[31] with add-on AV Booster
[32] Miniature phone jack and volume control
[33] Mega Drive 2, MegaJet, 32X: 9pin MiniDIN
[34] special cable, not a first-party add-on
[35] Wondermega models with SVideo

Manufacturer Type	Apple Mac	Sinclair QL	IBM PC-AT	Atari ST
Year	**1984**	**1984**	**1984**	**1985**
CPU				
Type	MC 68000	MC 68008	Intel 80286	MC 68000 [1]
Clock speed	8 MHz	7.5 MHz	8 bis 12 MHz	7.9 MHz
Operating system	MacOS	QDOS	DOS	TOS
Graphical user interface	yes	no	no [6]	GEM
Memory (in Byte)				
RAM	128 K, 512 K	128 K	640 K	256 K - 1 M [4]
max.	512 K	640 K	16 M	4 M
ROM	64 K	32 K	unknown	192 to 256 K
External storage				
Main media	3.5" disk	2 Microdrives	5.25", 3.5" disk	3.5" disk
Capacity	400 K	100 K each	360 K, 1.2 M	720 K
CD-ROM	after 1990	no	no	no
First internal hard disk	Macintosh SE (1987)	no	1984	MegaST (1989)
Graphics				
Coprozessor	–	–	– [8]	– [9]
minimum resolution/colours	512x342	256x256/8	320x200/16	320x200/16
maximum resolution	–	512x256/4	640x200(350)/16	640x400/2
Colour palette	–	8	64	512
Sprites	no	no	no	no
Sound	–	Intel	Yamaha Adlib [13]	Yamaha
Chip	–	integrated in 8049 [12]	YM3812	YM2149 [14]
DAC	no	no	no	yes
Channels	1 Beeper	1 Beeper	9 FM	3 PSG, 1 noise
Stereo	no	no	no	STE (1989)
Controller ports				
Joystick	no	yes	yes	yes
Mouse	yes	no	yes	yes

[1] later variants feature advanced CPUs like the MC 68030, clocked at 16 or 25 MHz for example
[2] from 1989
[3] Kickstart on disk, later incorporated in ROM (256 K, later 512 K)
[4] 1, 2 or 4 MB in the Atari Mega ST (from 1989)
[5] as well as further RAM for graphics, sprites, etc.
[6] Windows since 1985, but hardly usable on '80s PCs
[7] most variants came with two internal disk drives
[8] graphics card, e.g. monochrome Hercules; specs refer to EGA
[9] Blitter and Shifter in Atari Mega-ST (from 1989)
[10] Interlace: 320 x 512
[11] Interlace resolution
[12] coprocessor which takes care of I/O and of sound generation
[13] since 1988, Soundblaster cards with programmable FM synthesis and digi channel
[14] AY-3-8910 variant
[15] 32-bit RISC, ~ 4 MIPS

Commodore Amiga	Apple II gs	Acorn Archimedes	Sharp X68000	Fujitsu FM Towns
1985	**1986**	**1987**	**1987**	**1989**
MC 68000 [1]	65C816	ARM2 [15]	MC 68000 [1]	Intel 80386DX
7.2 MHz	2.5 MHz	8 MHz	10 MHz	16 MHz
AmigaDOS	ProDOS	RISC OS	Human68K	TownsOS
Workbench	GS/DOS	WIMP	SXWindow [2]	yes
256 K - 1 M	256 K	512 K	1 - 4 M [5]	1 M, 2 M [5]
9 M	8 M	512 K,1M	2 M	8 M
512 K [3]	128 K	4 M	128 K + 768 K	unknown
3.5" disk	5.25", 3.5" disk	3.5" disk	5.25" disk [7]	3.5" disk [7]
880 K	143 K, 800 K	800 K, 640 K	360 K	1.44 M
CDTV and CD32 only	no	no	no	always
A2000 (1987)	1986	A540 (1990)	ACE (1988)	1H und 2H (1989)
Agnus & Denise	VGC (6847)	VIDC	Cynthia et.al.	unknown
320x256/32 [10]	320x200/16	640x256/256	256x256	320x240/32.768
640x512/16 [11]	640x200/4	640x512/16	768x512/16	640x480/256
4.096	4.096	4.096	65.536	16.770.000
8	no	1 (Cursor)	128	1.024
Commodore	Ensoniq	ARM	Yamaha	Yamaha
Paula	5503 DOC	in VIDC	YM2151, MSM6258	YM3438, RF5C68
yes	yes	no	YM3012	YM6063
4 digital (8-Bit)	15 digital (16-Bit)	8 or 16 digital	8 FM, ADPCM	6 FM, 8 PCM (8-Bit)
yes	optional	yes	yes	yes
2	yes	no (on A3010 only)	2	yes
yes	yes	yes	yes	yes

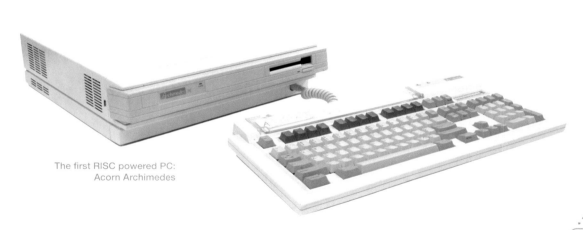

The first RISC powered PC:
Acorn Archimedes

Manufacturer Type	Philips CDi	NEC PC-Engine Duo	Commodore CD 32	Atari Jaguar
Year	**1991**	**1991**	**1993**	**1994**
CPU				
Type	MC 68070	HuC6280	MC 68EC020	MC 68000
Architecture	16-Bit CISC	8-Bit CISC	32-Bit CISC	16-Bit CISC
Clock speed	15 MHz	3.6 MHz, 7.16 MHz	14.3 MHz	13.3 MHz
Benchmarks				3.5 MIPS
Grafics chips	MCD 212	VDC (HuC6270)	AGA [1], Akiko accelerator	Tom [2]
Sound chip	MCD 221	–	Paula	Jerry [6]
Other processors	–	–	–	64-Bit-RISC-Blitter [9]
Memory (in Byte)				
Main RAM	1 M	8 K	2 M	2 M
Video RAM	–	64 K	–	–
Sound RAM	–	64 K	–	–
CD buffer	–	256 K	unknown	–
Back-up	8 K	2 K [12]	1 K	on every cartridge
RAM expansion	1.5 M [13]	2 M [14]	no	no
ROM	512 K	256 K	1 M	–
Graphics				
Resolution	384x280	256x224	320x200	variable
Resolution	768x560	512x262	1280x400 [16]	680x450
Colour depth	up to 24-Bit	8-Bit	up to 24-Bit	up to 24-Bit
Colour palette	16.7 Million	512	16.7 Million	16.7 Million
Sprites	no	64 (16x16)	yes	yes
Sound				
Channels	unknown	6 PCM, ADPCM	4 digital	variable
CD				
Speed	singlespeed	singlespeed	doublespeed	doublespeed [17]
Other formats				
CD-Audio	yes	yes	yes	yes [17]
Photo-CD	yes	no	yes[18]	no
CD+G	yes	yes	yes	yes [17]
Video-CD (MPEG1)	yes [19]	no	yes [19]	no
Other media	no	HuCard	CDTV	Cartridge
Ports				
Controller ports	1 and 1 infrared	1	2	2
Hardware link	no	no	no	no [20]
AV port				
SVideo/RGB out	yes/yes [21]	no/no [22]	yes/no [23]	yes/yes
Seperate audio out	2 Cinch, phone jack [25]	phone jack [25]	2 Cinch, phone jack [25]	2 Cinch

[1] Advanced Graphics Architecture: contains e.g. the Alice chip with Blitter and Copper
[2] contains two 32-bit GPUs (26.6 MHz, 26.6MIPs), 64-bit Object Processor and DRAM controller
[3] two 32-bit video processors clocked at 25 MHz each
[4] Video Display Processors, both 32-bit
[5] benchmark for the Geometry Transfer Engine: 66 MIPS

[6] 32-bit DSP with 26.6 MIPS, 26.6 MHz
[7] clocked at 25 MHz
[8] Yamaha FH1: DSP chip with 22 MHz; 68EC000: 11 MHz, 1.5 MIPS
[9] integrated inside the `Tom´ coprocessor
[10] 20 MHz, 20 MIPS
[11] MDEC (`Data Decompression Engine´) with 80 MIPS

Panasonic 3DO	NEC PC-FX	Sega Saturn	Sony PlayStation	Nintendo Virtual Boy
1994	1994	1994	1994	1994
ARM 60	NEC V810	two Hitachi SH2	LSI/MIPS R3000A	NEC V810
32-Bit RISC	32-Bit RISC	32-Bit RISC	32-Bit RISC	32-Bit RISC
12.5 MHz	21.5 MHz	28.6 MHz each	33.8 MHz	20 MHz
10~20 MIPS	18 MIPS	25 MIPS each	33 MIPS	18 MIPS
two Cel Engines [3]	unknown	VDP1, VDP2 [4]	GPU, GTE [5]	–
16-Bit-DSP [7]	unknown	SCSP [8], 68EC000	CPU, DSP	–
Math coprozessor	MJPEG decoder	Hitachi SH1 [10]	MJPEG decoder [11]	–
2 M	2 M	2 M	2 M	1 M
1 M	1.25 M	1.5 M	1 M	512 K
–	–	512 K	512 K	–
–	256 K	512 K	32 K	–
32 K	32 K [12]	42 K [12]	external only	on every cartridge
no	no	4 M [15]	no	no
256 K	unknown	512 K	512 K	unknown
320x240	unknown	320x224	256x240	384x224
640x480	640x480	704x480	640x480 [16]	384x224
16- or 24-Bit	up to 24-Bit	up to 24-Bit	4-Bit to 24-Bit	–
16.7 Million	16.7 Million	16.7 Million	16.7 Million	4 Shades of red
„Cels"	unknown	nearly unlimited	nearly unlimited	unknown
12 PCM	2 ADPCM, 6 digital	32 PCM and FM	24 ADPCM	5 + 1 digital
doublespeed	doublespeed	doublespeed	doublespeed	–
yes	yes	yes	yes	no
yes	yes	yes [18]	no	no
yes	yes	yes	no	no
yes [19]	no	yes [19]	no	no
no	no	Electronic Book [18]	no	Cartridge
1	2	2	2	1
no	no	yes	yes	no [20]
yes/no	yes/no	yes/yes	yes/yes [24]	–
2 Cinch	2 Cinch	no	2 Cinch [24]	Phone jack [25]

[12] externally expandable
[13] via DV Cart
[14] via Arcade Card
[15] via Ram Cart
[16] Interlaced
[17] with add-on CD-ROM drive
[18] with optional software
[19] with optional DV or Movie Card

[20] theoretically possible, but add-ons or cables were not available or not supported
[21] depending on model or series, either RGB or SVideo out
[22] RGB modification possible
[23] in France, RGB-Scart as standard (peritél)
[24] early models with seperate Cinch and SVideo out
[25] miniature phone jack

64-Bit and DVD consoles

Manufacturer Type	Bandai Pippin	Nintendo Nintendo 64	Sega Dreamcast
Year	1996	1996	1998
CPU			
Type	Apple, Motorola PowerPC 603	NEC, SGI MIPS R4300i	Hitachi SH-4
Clock speed	66 MHz	93,75 MHz	200 MHz
Level1 cache [2]	8 K (i), 8 K (d)	16 K (i), 8 K (d)	8 K (i), 16 K (d)
Level2 cache	no	no	no
Benchmarks	about 62 MIPS	more than 100 MIPS	340 MIPS, 1,4 GFLOPS
Graphics processor			
Manufacturer	–	SGI/Nintendo	Videologic/NEC
Type	–	RCP (SPDP)	PowerVR2
Clock speed	–	62,5 MHz	100 MHz
Memory (in Byte)			
Total memory	6 M [4]	4,5 M [5]	26 M
Main RAM	5 M	4,5 M	16 M
Type	unknown	RambusDRAM	SD-RAM
Clock speed	33 MHz, 40 MHz	62,5 MHz	100 MHz
Bandwidth	unknown	562,5 MB/s	800 MB/s
Video RAM	1 M	– [7]	8 M
Texture compression	no	no	no
Sound RAM	–	– [7]	2 M
Graphics			
Resolution	640x480	320x240 - 640x480 [10]	640x480 [10]
Pixel (including alpha channel et.al.)	8-Bit	32-Bit	32-Bit
Pixel/sec	unknown	0.02 G/s	0.2 G/s
Sound			
Channels	16-Bit-Stereo, 44 MHz	ADPCM [11]	64 ADPCM
Surround formats	no	Dolby Surround	Dolby Surround
Processor	Prime Time II IC, DFAC II IC	in SPDP	Yamaha AICA [14]
Storage medium	4x CD-ROM	ROM-Modul	12x GD-ROM
Capacity	0.6 G	up to 64 M	1.2 G
Transfer	0.6 MB/s	more than 10 MB/s	1.8 MB/s
Connections			
Controller ports	2 (4 via ADB)	4	4
Memory card ports	no [17]	1 (in joypad)	2 (in joypad)
Harddisk	optional, external	no	no
Net link	serial Geo Port	–	Serial Link
Other ports	Expansion port (X-PCI)	Expansion port	–
Modem	standard, external	no	standard
DVD movie	no	no	no
AV ports			
AV out	MiniDIN, Cinch	MultiAV 12pin	AVOut 16pin
Special AV ports	VGA, Stereo-Cinch	–	–
Video out			
Component (RGB)	no	no	yes
SVideo (Y/C)	yes	yes	yes
Video (CVBAS)	yes [18]	yes	yes [18]
Component (YUV)	no	no	no
VGA (RGB)	yes	no	yes [20]
Digital (D-Terminal)	no	no	no
Weight	3.5 kg	880 g [21]	1.5 kg

The GBA Player was released at the end of 2002 and made the Gamecube compatible with all Game Boy cartridges. It is connected to the parallel Highspeed Port on the underside of the Gamecube.

Sony PlayStation2	Microsoft Xbox	Nintendo Gamecube
2000	2001	2001
...oshiba, Sony	Intel	IBM
...motion Engine	PentiumIII/Celeron	Gekko [1]
...95 MHz	733 MHz	485 MHz
...6 K (i), 8 K (d), 16K scratch pad	16 K (d), 16 K (i)	32 K (d), 32 K (i)
...o	128 K	256 K
...50 MIPS, 6,2 GFLOPS	2 GFLOPS	1.125 MIPS, 13 GFLOPS
...ony	nVidia	NEC/ATI
...raphics Synthesizer	XGPU [3]	Flipper
...47 MHz	233 MHz	162 Mhz
...6 M	64 M	40 M
...2 M	64 M	24 M
...ambusDRAM	DDR-SDRAM	Mosys 1T-SRAM
...00 MHz	200 MHz	81 MHz
...,2 GB/s [6]	6,4 GB/s	2,6 GB/s
...M	– [7]	3,12 M [8]
...o	6 : 1	6 : 1
...M	– [7]	A-Memory: 16 MB DRAM
...40x480 - 1280x1024	640x480 - 1920x1080	640x480
...4-Bit	32-Bit	24-Bit + 24-Bit Z buffer
...2 G/s (1 texture)	3.7 G/s (2 textures)	unknown
...8+ ADPCM	256 [12]	64 ADPCM
...olby Surround, Dolby Digital [13], DTS	Dolby Digital 5.1 (AC 3), DTS	Dolby Pro Logic II
...PU [15]	APU (nVidia MCP)	in Flipper [9]
...x DVD-ROM	4x DVD-ROM	Mini-DVD (CAV)
...7 G	9.4 G	1.5 G
... MB/s	2.5 to 6.25 MB/s	2.0 to 3.2 MB/s [16]
	4	4
	2 (in joypad) [17]	2
...ptional, external	internal (10 GB)	no
...irewire or 10/100 Ethernet [22]	10/100 Ethernet	10/100 Ethernet (optional)
...x USB	–	2x serial, 1x parallel
...ptional	no	optional
...tandard	optional	no
...MultiAV 12pin	AVOut 12 pin	MultiAV 24pin
...Digital Audio (optical)	DigitalAV Out	–
...es	Europe only	yes
...es	yes	yes
...es [18]	yes	yes
...es	yes [19]	yes [19]
...o	no	no
...o	yes [19]	no
....4 kg	3.86 kg	1.4 kg [21]

[1] based on PowerPC 750CXe
[2] (i) = instruction cache, (d) = data cache
[3] based on GeForce3
[4] memory expandable with 2, 4 and 8 MB
[5] memory expandable to 8 MB, as a result higher resolution possible
[6] Graphics Synthesizer accesses embedded DRAM at 48 GB/s
[7] Unified Memory Architecture (UMA): No dedicated memory for graphics or sound
[8] embedded in the Flipper: Access to Frame Buffer at 7.8 GB/s and to texture cache at 10.4 GB/s
[9] Macronix 16-Bit DSP
[10] Interlace; hardware reduces flickering
[11] Each channel takes up 1% coprocessor rendering time. Most game soundtracks use 16 to 24 channels
[12] Including 64 3D channels
[13] 5.1 surround sound partially during intros and cut-scenes, not during game
[14] DSP on ARM7 RISC Core
[15] in conjunction with Emotion Engine 48+ ADPCM channels
[16] but lower access times than normal sized DVD-ROMs
[17] Memory Cards not required due to hard-drive
[18] AV cable (Cinch) was standard
[19] progressive scan possible
[20] via optional VGA box
[21] plus external power supply
[22] iLink was dropped after first series. From 2001, ethernet was an option, 2004 it was made standard

Manufacturer Type	Milton Bradley Microvision	Atari Lynx	Nintendo Game Boy	Sega Game Gear	Nintendo Game Boy C
Year	1979	1989	1989	1990	1996
CPU					
Type	Intel 8021 [1]	65sc02 [2]	Sharp Z80	Z80A	Sharp Z80
Architecture	4-Bit	8-Bit	8-Bit	8-Bit	8-Bit
Clockspeed	100 kHz	4.0 MHz	4.2 MHz	3.6 MHz	4.2 MHz, 8.4
Coprocessor	VDP (Hughes)	Suzy [3]			
Memory					
RAM (in Byte)	16 [4]	64 K	8 K	8 K	8 K
as well as	–	8 K VRAM	8 K	16 K VRAM	16 K VRAM
Game cart size (Mbit)	0.002	1 to 4	0.25 to 4	1 to 8	0.25 to 8
Graphics					
Resolution	16x16	160x102	160x144	146x160	144x160
Colours (palette)	–	16 (4,096)	4 shades of grey	32 (4,096)	56 (32,000)
Sprites	–	no limitation	40	64	40
Effects	–	Scaling, distortion, scrolling	scrolling	scrolling	scrolling
Sound channels	1 beeper	4 PSG	4 FM	3 PSG + 1 noise	4 FM
Networking					
Game link	–	Cable [6]	Cable, infrared	Cable	Cable, infrare
Link to other hardware	–	–	SuperNES, N64	–	SNES, N64, N
Controls					
Directional control	Paddle	Control pad	Control pad	Control pad	Control pad
Fire buttons	variable [4]	2 x 2	2	2	2
Other buttons	variable [4]	Option1 + Option2 Restart + Flip [10]	Start + Select	Start	Start + Select
Brightness/ Contrast	yes	yes	no [11]	yes	no
Headphone jack	no	yes	yes	yes	yes
Case					
WxLxH (in mm)	90x240x30	203x134x50	148x89x32	210x113x38	78x133,5x27,
Weight (with battery)	350 g (without battery)	440g (540g)	220g (300g)	380g (500g)	138g (188g)
Screen					
Diagonal		3.4 Inch	2.5 Inch	3.2 Inch	
Size (WxL)	3.6x3.6 cm	3.25"x1.88"		6.6x4.9 cm	
Specials		Flip-Screen			
Specific add-ons			Printer, camera	TV Tuner Pack	Mobile Adapte (Japan only)
Other functions	none	none	none	none	none

[1] ... or TMS-1000. CPU always on game cartridge, not in base unit
[2] integrated in 16-Bit, 16 MHz `Mickey´
[3] 16-Bit, 16 MHz, Blitter, geometry engine and math coprocessor
[4] on game cartridge, not in the base unit
[5] first Neo Geo Pocket: 8 shades of grey

[6] 62,500 baud
[7] 19,200 baud
[8] first Wonderswan: 9,600 baud.
   Wonderswan Color: 38,400 baud

This Game.Com Pocket is shown with the unreleased port of Metal Gear Solid on screen.

Tiger Game.Com Color	SNK Neo Geo Pocket, Neo Geo Pocket Color	Bandai Wonderswan, Wonderswan Color	Nintendo Game Boy Advance	Gamepark GP32
1997	1998, 1999	2003	2001	2002
Sharp	TLCS-900H	V30MZ	ARM7 variant	ARM9 variant
8-Bit	16-Bit	16-Bit	32-Bit RISC	32-Bit RISC
unknown	6.144 MHz	3.072 MHz	16.7 MHz	up to 133 MHz
	Z80, 3.072 MHz		Graphics	
unknown	12 K	64 K [9]	32 K	8 M
–	4 K (in Z80), 16 K display	16 Kbit Eeprom [9]	96 KByte VRAM, 256K WRAM, 16 K sound	–
up to 16	up to 16	up to 8, up to 32	up to 256	up to 256
160x200	152x160	144x224	240x160	320x240
4 shades of grey	146 (4,096) [5]	241 (4,049) [9]	512 (32,768)	65,536
unknown	64	128	4,096	not hardware implemented
unknown	scrolling	Transparency, scrolling	Alpha blending, scrolling, distortation, rotation	Alpha blending, scrolling
1 FM, 1 PCM	3 PSG + 1 noise	3 + 1 noise	32 + 4 PCM	9 FM
Cable	Cable [7]	Cable [8]	Cable [13]	2,4 GHz RF
–	Dreamcast	Mobile, PC, PlayStation	Gamecube	Mobile, PC
Control pad	360° stick	2 x 4 buttons	Control pad	Control pad
4	2	2	2	2
Menu + Pause + Sound	Start + Option	Start + Sound	Start + Select + 2 shoulder buttons	Start + Select + 2 shoulder buttons
yes	no	no	no	no
yes	yes	via adapter	yes	yes
190x110x25	122x74x24 130x80x30,5	121x74,3x17,5x24,3	144,5x82x24,5	147x88x34
300g (380g)	130g,125g (145g)	95g (110g)	140g (180g)	163g (200g)
3.5 Inch	2.6 Inch	2.8 Inch [12]	2.9 Inch	3.5 Inch
6.5 x 5.5 cm	4.5x4.8 cm	6x3.8 cm	4.08x6.12 cm	7.2x5.3 cm
Touch screen		Flip screen		
Modem	Wireless Adapter	Wonderborg, Wonderwitch u.a.	Wireless Adapter	
PDA, calendar, calculator	PDA, alarm, calendar, horoscope	none	none	MP3 player

[9] in Wonderswan Color. First series held 16 K RAM,
1 Kbit Eeprom and displayed eight shades of grey.
[10] light switch on Lynx II
[11] light switch on Game Boy Light
[12] first Wonderswan: 2.49 inch
[13] wireless connection since 2004

Manufacturer Type	Nokia N-Gage	NTT DoCoMo [1) 900i (iAppli)	Nintendo DS	Sony PSP-1000	Tiger Gizmondo
Year	2003	2004	2004	2004	2005 [2)
CPU					
Clock speed	104 MHz	app. 200 MHz [3)	33 MHz, 67 MHz	up to 333 MHz	400 MHz
Processor (core)	ARM9	ARM9	ARM9	MIPS4000	ARM9
Coprocessor	unknown	yes	ARM7 (33 MHz)	unknown	Nvidia GoForce
Memory (in Byte)					
Main	3,4 M	400 K embedded	4 M	32 M	see below
as well as	none	unknown	~1 M embedded VRAM	4 M embedded DRAM	~1 M embedded VRAM (SRAM)
Media	Card (MMC)	Card (miniSD), or Memory Stick	Card (compact), Game Boy cartridge	UMD disc, Memory Stick	Card (SD)
Game size (in Byte)	256 M	0.8 M	unknown	1800 M	1000 M
Graphics and sound					
Display	2.2" TFT	2.2" TFT	3" TFT	4.3" TFT	2.8" TFT
Resolution	176x208	240x320	256x192	480x272	320x240
Colours	4096	262,144	262,144	16 Million	unknown
Secondary display	no	1" OLED	3" TFT [4)	no	no
Stereo channels	yes	64 PCM [5)	16 ADPCM	flexible [6)	unknown
AV formats	MP3 [7)	MP3, MPEG4, Flash, Quicktime	only via external add-ons	MP3, MPEG4, ATRAC3	MP3, MPEG4
Interfaces					
USB	yes	yes	no	yes (USB 2.0)	yes
Wireless LAN	 Bluetooth	WLAN oder Bluetooth	spezielles WLAN, IEEE 802.11	 IEEE 802.11	 Bluetooth
Multiplayer	up to 8 players	no	up to 16 players	up to 16 players	yes
Mobile phone	GSM, GPRS	GPRS, UMTS	no	no	GSM, GPRS
Infrared	no	IrDa	no	IrDa	no
Headphone jack/TV out	yes/no	yes/some models	yes/no	yes/no	yes/no
Other functions					
Microphon	no	yes	yes	no	no
Camera	no	Photo and movie	no	no	Photo
Controls					
Directional control	Control pad	Control pad	Touchscreen, control pad	Control pad (analogue)	Control pad
Fire buttons	2	no	4	4	4
Other buttons	9 function keys, 9 alphanumerical	12 numerical et.al.	Start + Select, 2 shoulder buttons	Start + Select, 2 shoulder buttons	Home, 2 shoulder buttons et.al.
Dimensions					
WxLxH (mm)	134x70x20 [8)	50x104x26	148,7x84,7x29	170x74x23	unknown
Weight	106 g (137 g) [9)	115 g to 136 g	275 g	270 g	unknown

[1) DoCoMo mobile phones manufactured by NEC (N900i), Sharp (SH), Panasonic (P), Fuji (F), Sony (SO) et.al.
[2) Gizmondo was not released at deadline
[3) ARM9 based Application CPU is for example a Texas Instruments OMAP 1610 or an Xscale chip by Intel.
   Hitachi builds another solution for mobile phones: SH-Mobile, M32R
[4) Touchscreen
[5) ... or 50 FM and wavetable channels (for example in N900i)
[6) 7.1 and 3D sound possible
[7) Only the first N-Gage series had a radio, a Real media player and a MP3 player, not the QD
[8) N-Gage QD: 118 x 68 x 22 mm
[9) N-Gage QD: 143 g (with battery)

Computer and video game technology:
Notes and explanations on Bits and Bytes.

The Bit

… is the core measurement of the digital world. A Bit is the smallest storage unit and may have a value of either 1 (true, on…) or 0 (false, off…). In the field of electronics, these two values or statuses are realised as different levels of voltage, charge or other mutually exclusive states. When describing hardware, the Bit is for example used as a unit for:

Processor power: If the architecture of a chip is defined in Bit, it shows the amount of data that can be passed through or handled by the chip in one cycle. The system of naming micros or consoles in conventional steps of 8, 16 or 32-Bit is only vague and ignores other hardware components and sometimes even capabilities of the CPU. Thus, Amiga and Mega Drive are generally seen as 16-Bit machines although both utilize a 32-Bit processor.

Bit	represents
1	2 steps (on or off)
2	4 steps
3	8 steps
4	16 steps
5	32 steps
8	256 steps
10	1,024 steps
12	4,096 steps
16	65,536 steps
24	16,777,216 steps

Table 2: Conversion of Bit sizes into possible steps, for example for colour depth: The left row shows the number of reserved Bits per pixel (bpp), the right row shows the maximum numbers of colours that can be displayed.

	Register size	Bus width
Traditional 8-Bit processors		
MOS 6502	8	8
Motorola 6809	8/16	8
Zilog Z80	8/16	8
Traditional 16-Bit processors		
Intel 8088	16	8
Intel 8086, 80286	16	16
32-Bit processor		
Motorola 680x0	32	16/32
enhanced 32-Bit processors (RISC)		
MIPS R3000, ARM6x	32	32

Table I shows the internal and external Bit width, the register sizes and bus width of commonly used CPUs. There are data and address registers (often with differing Bit sizes); some CPUs use multiple purpose registers.

Data bus width: The Bit figure represents the amount of data that can be transferred by a bus (internal or external) at the same time. The bus width and clock frequency relates directly to the data transfer rate. This data rate (also used for data cables, modems & Co.) is measured in Byte/s and Bit/s.

Power of sound and graphics hardware: Both the sound and colour range of games hardware is often measured in Bit. `24-Bit graphics´ means that the hardware

is capable of displaying more than 16 million colours, corresponding to a photo-realistic spectrum (called True Color). Similarly, an early sound chip like the frequently used AY-3-8910 and its variants modulates its sound frequencies in 12-Bit (4,096 different pitches).

The Byte

… consists of 8 Bits and is used to measure RAM and ROM memory size, storage space of media, size of software or games.

	Abbreviation	$\approx$	$=$	
1 Byte				8 Bit
1 Kilobyte	1 K	10^3	2^{10}	1,024 Byte
1 Megabyte	1 M	10^6	2^{20}	1,048,576 Byte
1 Gigabyte	1 G	10^9	2^{30}	1,073,741,824 Byte

Table 3: Byte is the unit for information size. Strictly speaking, the units used alongside our abbreviations (left rows) are powers of 2 (4, 8, 16…). The easier conversion to powers of ten (1 K Byte = 1,000 Bytes, middle row) is also widely used, but contains a margin of error of about 5%.

Bit	128 K	256 K	512 K	1 M	2 M	8 M	64 M
Byte	16 K	32 K	64 K	128 K	256 K	1 M	8 M

Table 4: Conversion of memory sizes of Nintendo and Sega cartridges in Byte. Before the mid '90s, Japanese manufacturers and western licensees measured game size not in Byte but in Bit. The game Street Fighter 2 for SuperNES for instance was prominently advertised as a `16 Meg´ cart but contained only 2 MByte.

Hardware index

[1] A = Add-on. Runs only in combination with the base machine.
C = Computer with keyboard and (ports to) re-writable media.
G = Game console. No keyboard, no re-writable media.
M = Multimedia console. Compatible with other media
T = Tabletop. Stationary game machine with built-in monitor.
TC = Tabletop computer. Built-in monitor and keyboard.
H = Handheld game or multimedia machine with built-in display.
L = Laptop. Portable computer with integrated keyboard and display
DIY = Computer sold as a kit
etc = Audio and video equipment, non-programmable hardware & Co.

Bold numbers point to a photography of hardware

Games index

Games index

Bold numbers point to game screenshots

Bibliography

Books

USA: **Zap!** Scott Cohen, McGraw-Hill, 1984, **Electronic Games**, W. Buchsbaum & R. Mauro, McGraw-Hill, 1979, **Hackers**, Steven Levy, Penguin, 1984, **Software People**, Douglas Carlston, Simon & Schuster, 1985, **Virtual Reality**, Howard Rheingold, Summit Books/Simon & Schuster, 1991, **Game Over**, David Sheff, Vintage Books, 1994, **Digital Press Guide**, Joe Santulli et. al., Digital Press, 2002, **Masters of Doom**, David Kushner, Random House, 2003

Japan: **Video Game Perfect Catalog**, Tokumashoten, 1991, **Computer Game**, Koji Ichikawa, Nikkei Infotech, 1993, **Yokoi Gumpei's Game Pavilion**, Makino Takefumi, Aspect, 1997, **TV Game Game 1**) and 2), H.Mizusaki, 1997, **100 Computer**, S. Saito and T. Funada, Ascii, 1998, **The Emulators**, Shuwa System, 1998, **Revolutionaries at Sony**, Reiji Asakura, 2000 (US edition by McGraw-Hill), **Sega Consumer History** and **Sega Arcade History**, Famitsu DC/Enterbrain, 2002, **All About SNK**, Studio Bent Stuff, 2000, **Family Computer 1983 - 1994**, Kengo Ishiguro et.al, Ohta Publishing, 2003 catalog to the exhibition at the Tokyo Metropolitan)

UK: **Trigger Happy**, Steven Poole, Fourth Estate, 2000, **Digerati Glitterati**, Christopher Langdon & David Manners, Wiley and Sons, 2001

Germany: **Electronic Plastic**, Jaro Gielens, Die Gestalten, 2000, **Gameplan 2: Joysticks**, Winnie Forster & Stephan Freundorfer, Gameplan, 2003

Magazines

(volumes used are stated in brackets)

USA: Electronic Games (1981 - 1984), Computer Gaming World (1982 - 1990), Journal of Computer Game Design (1987 - 1993), Mondo 2000 (1991 - 1993), Wired (1993 - 1996), Next Generation (1995 - 1997)

UK: Your Computer (1982 - 1985), Popular Computing Weekly (1983 - 1987), Computer & Video Games (1984 - 1986), Crash (1984 - 1988), The One (1988 - 1991), Retro Gamer (2004)

Germany: Tele Match (1983 - 1984), Happy Computer (1986), Power Play (1988 - 1992), Man!ac (1994 - 1999)

Japan: Login und eLogin (1991 - 1996), Famicom Tsushin and special publications of Famitsu (1990 - 2004), Mega Drive Fan (1993), Game Labor (2000 - 2004)

Documents and supplements

Tekla Perry, Paul Wallich: **Design case history: Atari Video Computer System** in IEEE Spectrum, March 1983
Jack Connick: **...And Then There Was Apple** in Call-A.P.P.L.E., Oct 1986
Jason Brooks et.al.: **Playstation**: An exclusive supplement with Edge 58, 1997
Steven Collins: **Game Graphics during the 8-bit Computer Era** in ACM SIGGRAPH CG Quarterly, 2/1998
Anon: **Playstation** in Level 100, September 1999
Anon: **Nintendo Entertainment System Documentation** by Y0SHi on http://nesdev.parodius.com, not dated
Wataru Suzuki: **Unofficial PCEngine FAQ**, 2002
John Decuir: **Atari 2600 Program Development**, not dated
Anon: **What was Japan for Commodore?**, M. Tomczyk Interview on www.vorc.org, 2003
John Bayko: **Great Microprocessors of the Past and Present** (V 13.4.0), 2003

Internet sites

www.icdia.org (Jorg Kennis),
www.icwhen.com (Donald A. Thomas),
www.homecomputer.de (Kerstin und Stefan Walgenbach),
www.groener-online.de (Johannes Gröner),
www.machine-room.org (Alexios Chouchoulas),
www.heise.de
www.anandtech.com
www.tu-chemnitz.de/phil/hypertexte/gamesound (Jörg Weske)
www.digital-palm.com/88lib/library/frame1.htm
http://lair.thomsonistes.org

Picture credits

Apple Computer Deutschland: 20, 22
Computer Spiele Museum: 98
Cybermedia GmbH: 111, 151
IBM Deutschland GmbH: 99
Microsoft Corp.: 190
Nintendo of Europe GmbH: 130, 142
Sony CE Deutschland GmbH: 159, 161, 181, 182
Uwe Just: 78
Stefan Walgenbach: 42, 65
Jaro Gielens: 53

Imprint

Design & production: Wolfgang Müller
Photography: Christian Boehm and Joe Schloz
Translation & localisation: Rafael Dyll and David McCarthy
Additional research & support: Oliver Ehrle, Dieter König, Frank Salomon and Silvestre Zabala

Published in Jan. 2005 by
Winnie Forster
Gameplan
Diessener Str. 30
86919 Utting
Germany

www.game-machines.co.uk
www.gameplan-books.co.uk

© Winnie Forster/Gameplan

ISBN: 3-00-015359-4

Printed by Caruna Druck GmbH & Co. KG